Today's Top Stationery Artists 2

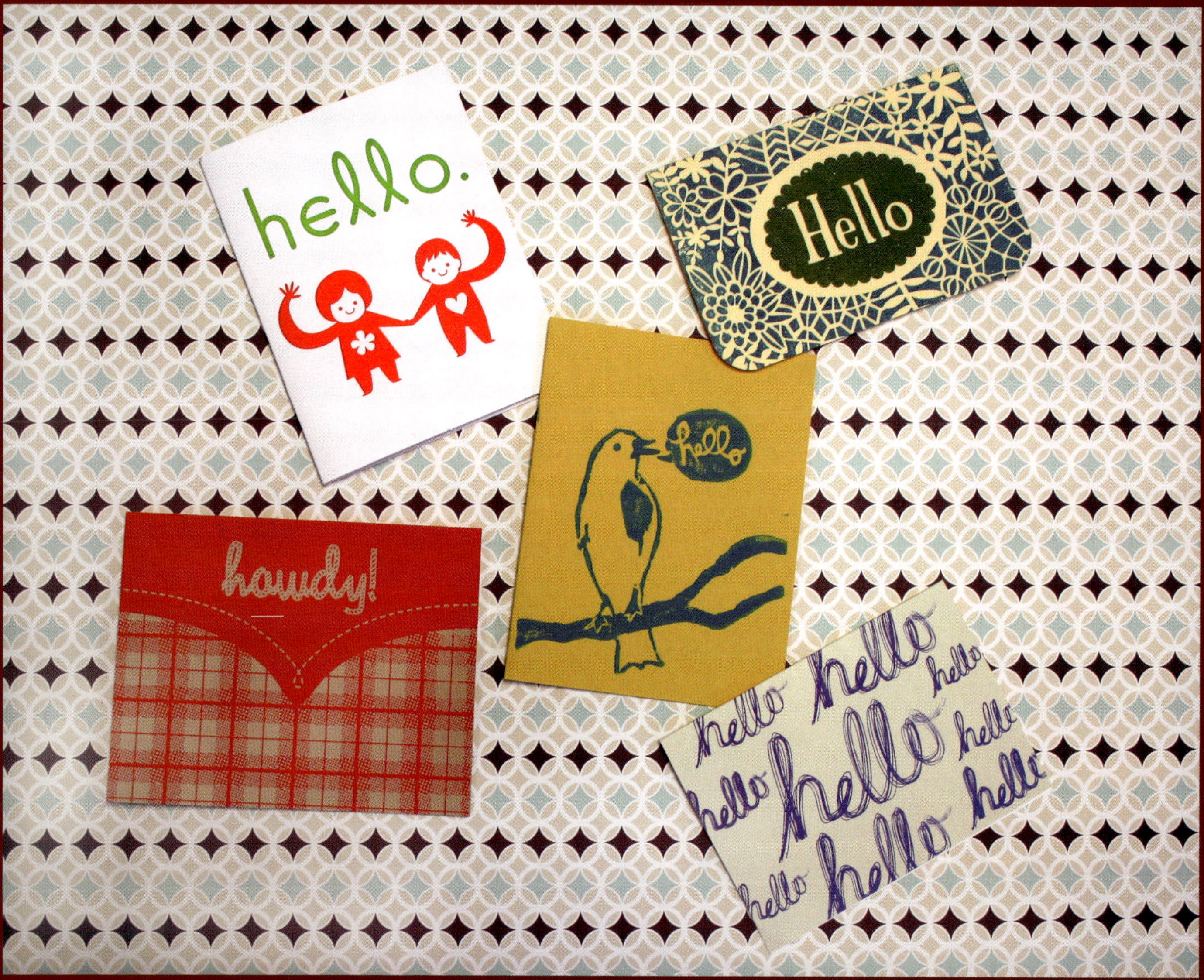

Greeting cards by (clockwise) Fugu Fugu Press, Morris & Essex, Ghost Academy, Susy Jack Contemporary Paper, LLC, and Two Trick Pony. Wrapping paper by Whimsy Press. *Photograph by Wendy Hicks.*

Today's Top Stationery Artists 2

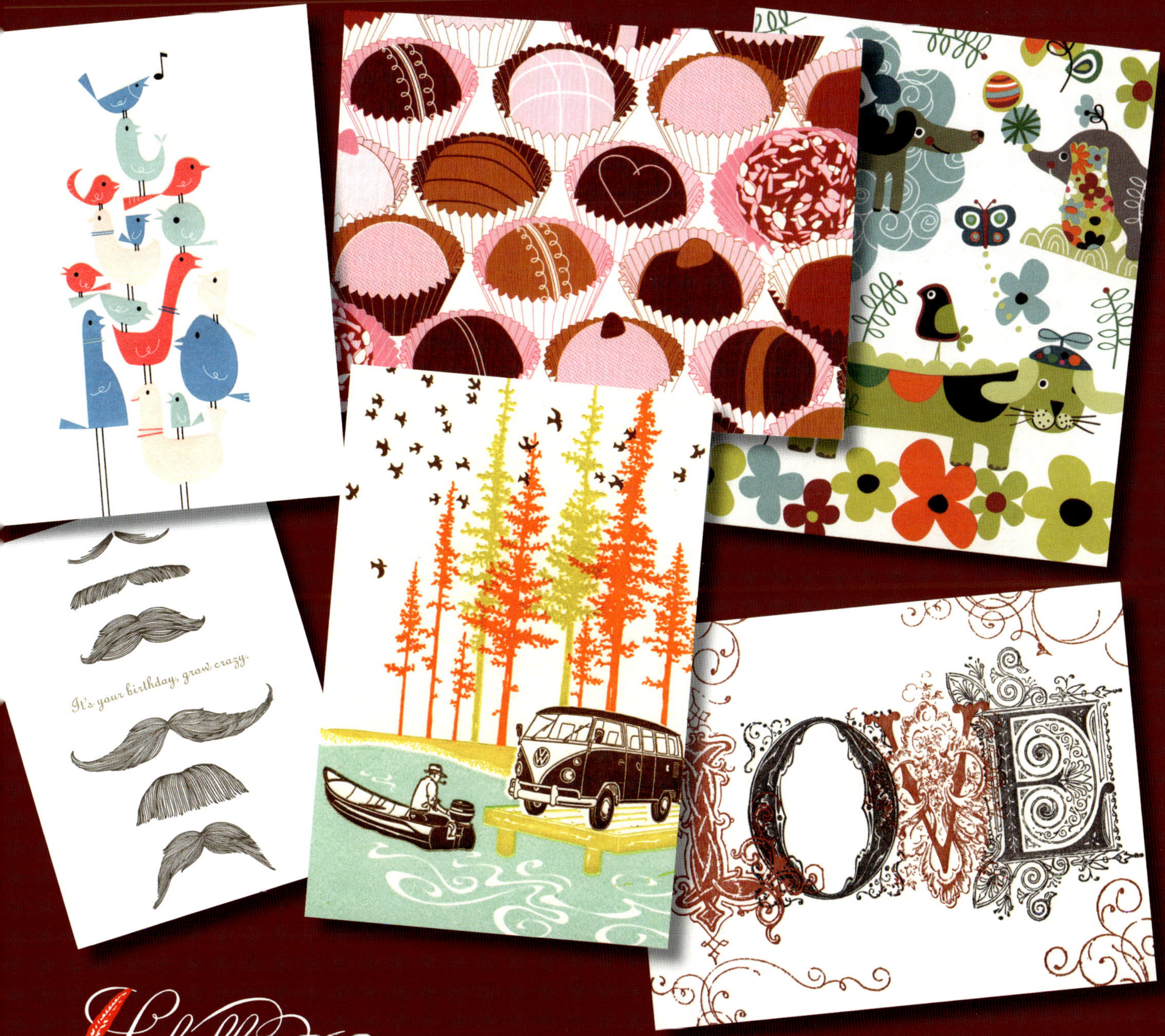

Schiffer Publishing Ltd®

4880 Lower Valley Road Atglen, Pennsylvania 19310

Tori Higa

Other Schiffer Books By The Author:
Today's Top Stationery Artists. ISBN: 9780764328329. $24.95

Library of Congress Control Number: 2011921110

Designed by Bruce Waters
Type set in Zurich BT

ISBN: 978-0-7643-3737-6
Printed in China

Schiffer Books are available at special discounts for bulk purchases for sales promotions or premiums. Special editions, including personalized covers, corporate imprints, and excerpts can be created in large quantities for special needs. For more information contact the publisher:

Published by Schiffer Publishing Ltd.
4880 Lower Valley Road
Atglen, PA 19310
Phone: (610) 593-1777; Fax: (610) 593-2002
E-mail: Info@schifferbooks.com

For the largest selection of fine reference books on this and related subjects, please visit our website at **www. schifferbooks.com**
We are always looking for people to write books on new and related subjects. If you have an idea for a book please contact us at the above address.

This book may be purchased from the publisher.
Include $5.00 for shipping.
Please try your bookstore first.
You may write for a free catalog.

In Europe, Schiffer books are distributed by
Bushwood Books
6 Marksbury Ave.
Kew Gardens
Surrey TW9 4JF England
Phone: 44 (0) 20 8392 8585; Fax: 44 (0) 20 8392 9876
E-mail: info@bushwoodbooks.co.uk
Website: www.bushwoodbooks.co.uk

Dedication

For my Mom, who gave me an appreciation for style, design, and written correspondence, and for my Dad who gave me encouragement and inspiration to follow my creative dreams.

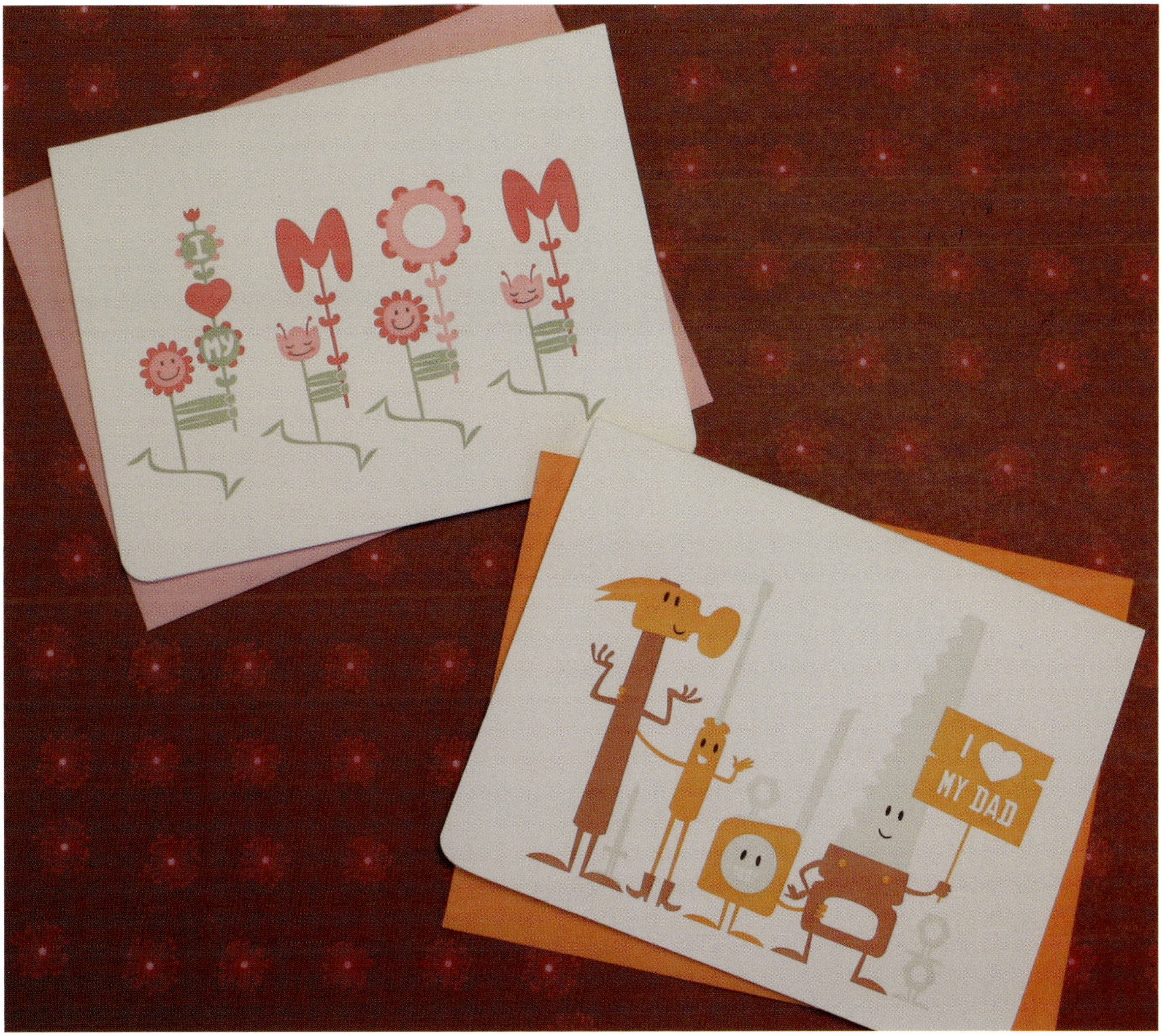

Greeting cards by Maginating. Wrapping paper by Whimsy Press.
Photograph by Wendy Hicks.

Contents

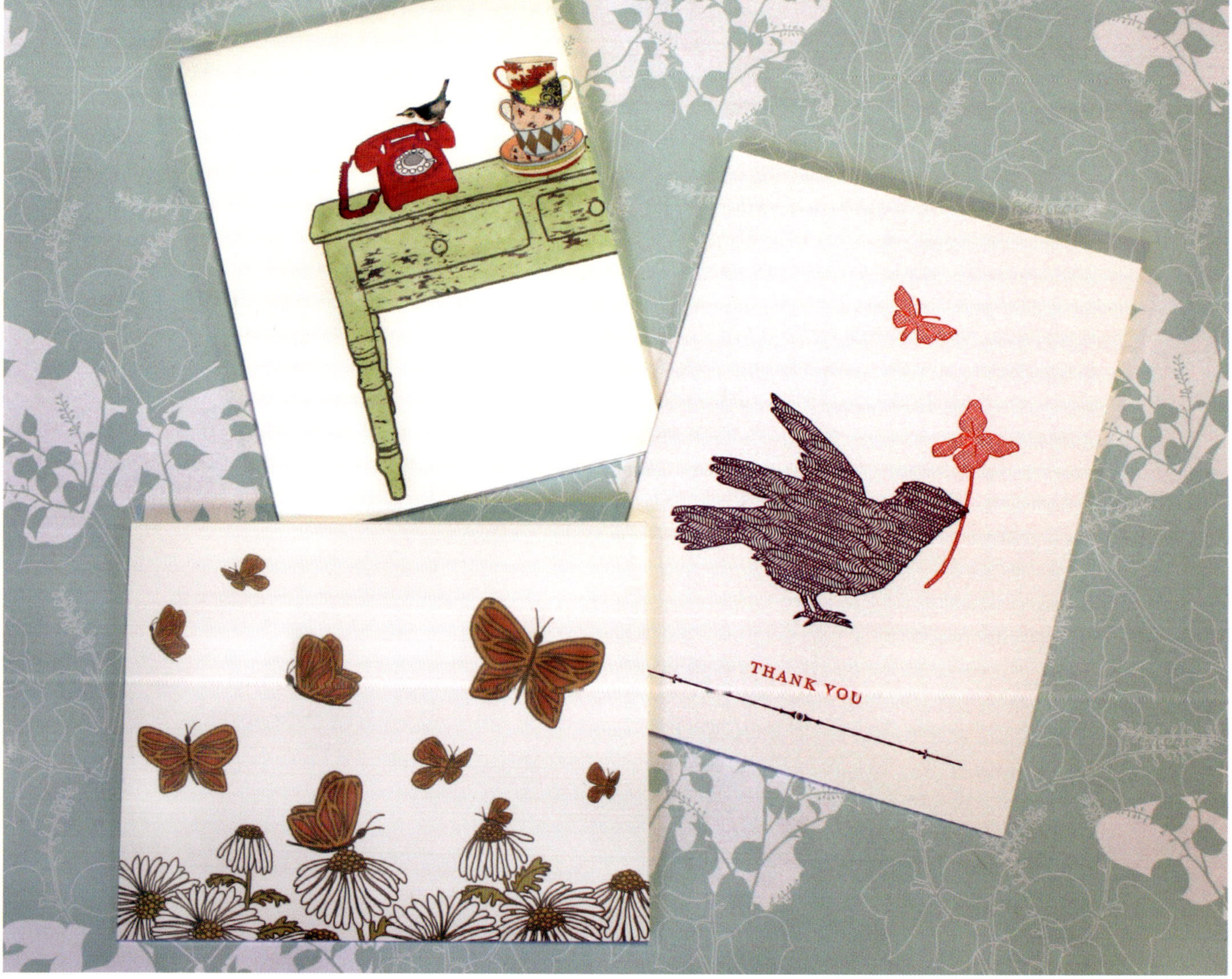

Greeting cards by (clockwise) Screech Owl Design, Sesame Letterpress, and Kate & Birdie Paper Co. Wrapping paper by Whimsy Press. *Photograph by Wendy Hicks.*

Introduction

I was both thrilled and honored to be asked to write *Today's Top Stationery Artists 2*, a follow up book to *Today's Top Stationery Artists*. I absolutely love stationery and it is always so inspiring to get the opportunity to collaborate with the best of the best stationery designers and learn a little bit more about what makes them tick. Since the first book came out in 2008, the stationery industry has experienced a great number of changes such as the rise of the Internet, a tough economy for retail sales, and an increase of online stores such as Etsy.com.

The most notable change has been the use of the power of the Internet. No one knew what online social networking was back in 2007 when I was working on the first book. Facebook and Twitter seem to have happened overnight; and now, in order to keep up with customers, having a Facebook and/or Twitter account is a must for any stationery artist. Because online shopping has increased, stationery artists have had to adapt in order to stay relevant. Many stationery artists who wholesale work to retail stores also design for online stores with customizable capabilities and low prices like *Cardstore, Tiny Prints, Minted, Kodak Gallery,* or *Shutterfly*.

Another change that stationers have had to deal with since the first book was published is tough economic times. Because the retail industry has been hit so hard by the economy and many stores have closed up shop, stationery artists have been starting pop up stores (temporary retail stores that "pop up" for a short amount of time), participating in local art and craft shows, or focusing on their own personal online stores. These options offer a low overhead cost with potential for a greater profit margin than strictly selling their work in wholesale outlets.

Etsy (an online community to buy and sell handmade items) has also been a great resource for a number of stationery artists. Now when designers want to launch a company, they can simply open an Etsy shop, get noticed by a few blogs, and they are in business. Many of these designers are just as talented and valid to the industry as designers who have led the way in the past by strictly selling their work to wholesalers through trade shows and regional sales reps. In fact, many buyers discover new talent for their stores through Etsy and blogs.

Although the world of retail is changing because of the rise of the Internet, an increase in online shopping, and consumers needing to tighten their purse strings, top stationery artists are willing to make the necessary changes along with the times in order to continue to thrive in their business. There are some things, however, that thankfully haven't changed for these artists. The most successful designers are always the most unique and true to themselves—they are trendsetters and not trend followers. The bottom line is that the most talented stationery artists will continue to thrive in this ever-changing environment.

I also noticed many similarities among the artist's various personal backgrounds. One thing I have learned from compiling two books about stationery design is that the artists involved are just as sweet, witty, friendly, clever, and creative as their card designs suggest. I have found that stationery artists are generally optimistic and just simply nice people. *Why wouldn't they be?* They get to do something they love for a living and help others send happy thoughts and sweet sentiments on a very tangible piece of miniature art that they have created. *What is there to be grumpy about?* Mollie Green of *La Familia Green* says it best, "You buy a card, write a note, and send it out into the world. I never know how many people will experience—hold, use, enjoy—my work." What a great feeling for an artist!

Another common thread is that so many of the stationers brought up having memories from childhood of either designing stationery or setting up a pretend shop. Penny Richards Eversole of *Pinkerton Design* reminisces, "You know those free cards you get in the mail—designed by some charity organization as a fundraiser? I used to try to sell those to my parents when I was little ... along with my own creations, of course." And Jennifer Tatham of *Night Owl Paper Goods* remarks, "I do believe that my love for all things *Hello Kitty*—including paper goods, pencils, erasers, stickers, and the like, led me exactly to where I am today. At a young age, my mom would take me to a small local print shop to purchase recycled scrap paper note pads. When we'd get back home, I'd then draw on each page and make my own personalized stationery." I find it very interesting that so many of the successful stationery artists today were *playing* stationery artists when they were little. It's just another reminder to try to turn work into play so that it's no longer work. The top stationery artists in this book have done just that.

I hope that as you flip through the pages of this book you find the inspiration to play for a living instead of work, soak up all of the innovative designs from some of the top stationery artists in the business, and rekindle your love for good old fashioned handwritten correspondence in this fast paced, ever-changing technological age in which we live.

Artist Studios

8mm Ideas

When did you become a stationery artist?

Starting back in 1999, my sister and I owned a shop in NYC called French General and I used to sell one-of-a-kind cards. The first set I ever made and sold were all vintage gum wrappers, so strange and tactile. I made the business "official" when I showed at the New York Stationery Show in May of 2004. It was hard to make the leap from one-of-a-kind to a larger production card line, but we do it all in-house and that makes it a more down-home process for me.

How did you come up with such a unique concept for your company?

8mm Ideas was born out of my love for the weird and wonderful and the vintage collections that inhabit those categories. Over the years, I've gathered ephemera and vintage books and found photos that eventually became part of the extensive collection I work from today. I send cards for every single event possible, so it was a natural choice of artistry.

You show your work in art galleries as well. Do you mostly consider yourself a fine artist or a stationery designer?

I mostly consider myself the youngest of five kids, coming from a really creative family, lucky enough to have this amazing mom and dad. I suppose, if I had to choose, I'd say I'm a designer because I see most things through the prism of a color palette or as a collection to be curated.

Can you tell us a little bit more about your art?

Born from the mini-art-card-pieces, I also create much larger artwork that I call "historical fiction." I have such an extensive collection of ephemera from the 1800s to the 1950s, I decided to start mixing them to tell a story of an invented past. It's usually filled with romance, or unrequited love, or a quirky obsession: I come up with an entire back-story for each piece as I'm creating it. Often, when I'm showing the work and telling the story behind it, people get so caught up in this larger-than-life-experience they forget that it's not real and wonder how I ever "found" this person and this piece! Then I happily start over again...

What is your favorite part of your studio space that you couldn't live without?

The stuff, the stuff, the stuff! What I'm surrounded by is what I can't live without (hotel keys, photos, books, medical paraphernalia, alphabet cards, postcards, on and on). It's not just one thing. At the same time, while I love certain items, I count nothing as precious because I have to let it go. When I'm making a new piece, I might need to use that exact thing I love so much ... So, it's not just one item, but the continuous revolving, never-ending world of items (some might call junk) that come through my world and keep me going.

How do you enjoy spending your free time? Do you have any hobbies?

Writing has always been a hobby: I love having the time to write for my blog, *Little House in the Clouds*. Photography has always been a big hobby, as well: Shooting photos of beautiful homes for my other blog, *First Girl at the Party*, helps fulfill that on a public level. When I'm not in my studio, I have an old bike that I like to tool around town on and am often caught in the act of thrifting and finding estate sales and flea markets—complete obsessions! I also come from a very tight family and consider my siblings and my parents, along with my husband, my very best friends. When we can, we all go home for a month and just hang out with each other. And, I love to read. Love it! If I could lay around all day and read ... well, I probably would!

How much time do you devote to social networking, etc., for your business?

I really like personal contact. I like mail. I like the phone. It's actually a great thing when I get to meet or speak with a customer who has otherwise only ordered from me via the website. I like to send cards, postcards, and new product whenever I can. It's fun to find new shops where the cards become a great match.

Do you have any little known facts about yourself that you would like to share?

I used to be part of a sketch comedy group in NYC called The Flying Queens, which led me into doing stand-up: Biggest rush in the world!

I was never much of a dog or cat person, but we recently rescued a beautiful mutt we named Stella and now I'm a covered-in-hair-don't-mind-picking-up-poop-my-dog-goes-everywhere-I-go-she's-more-than-a-dog kind of person. It's WEIRD.

I buy cards more than anything else.

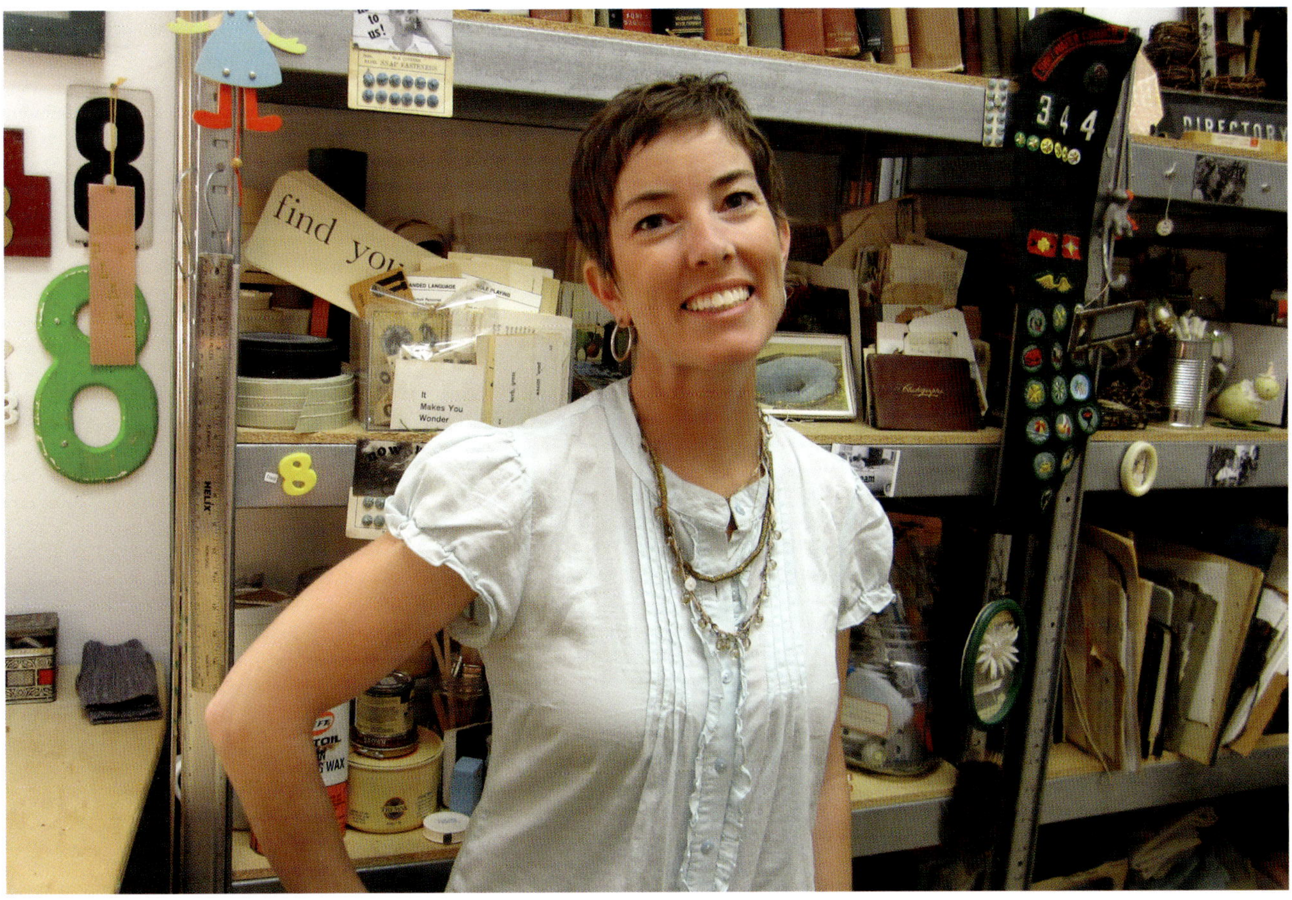

Molly Meng of 8mm Ideas in her studio. *Courtesy of Molly Meng.*

Amy Smyth Made It

What do you think of first—the greeting or the artwork?

Greeting. It is a strange mix of torture and reward.

What is your art background?

BFA in Illustration. I was a freelance editorial illustrator for four years and was published in editorial, trade, and children's magazines.

What is your business background?

Really, really love business and wish I had double majored in college. After a previous failed business, (in between this business and the illustration career) I took a thirteen-week business plan course. This sounds dramatic, but it changed my life. I had some business sense, but this course put all the pieces together. The plan I wrote after that class, I have followed since launching Amy Smyth Made It in May 2006.

You have licensed your work to some great companies and have sold your self-published cards all over the country in a relatively short amount of time from when you first started your business. What is the secret to your success?

You flatter! The secret to my success is all of the following working together: the support, advice, and guidance of my family (specifically my husband, parents, brother, and his wife), the ability to adapt to feedback and what the market is telling me, a tenacious attitude, and a healthy fear of returning to a job in a cubicle.

What is your typical workday like?

There is no typical workday, which I really enjoy. But things that happen almost every day are: order entry, order fulfillment, some form of marketing (planning, strategy, mailings, etc.) design, ideas, emailing, and money collecting. I work about a nine to twelve hour day, but it is in a comfortable and flexible environment, so it is long and hard work, but pleasant.

Where do you draw the most inspiration?

The ridiculousness of pop culture, the irony of life, psychology, interactions with my family and husband ... My current best seller is: (front) Happy Birthday to a man of few words (inside) from a woman of many, many words. Didn't have to go far for inspiration on that one ...

What is your favorite part of your job?

Freedom. No boss, no set schedule, and no commute.

Have you always wanted to be a stationery artist?

No, just wanted to be my own boss.

How has the social networking craze played a part in your business?

I have a Facebook fan page which has 16 fans (three are actual fans, others are all family members), a blog with 0 comments, and a twitter account with 96 followers. As you can see, I have absolutely no grasp on social media. But I refuse to give up! I believe there is tremendous marketing potential and marketing data to be found.

What is next for your company?

Licensing. I just completed a program with LIMA (Licensing Industry Merchandisers' Association), which has given me the skills to participate in the Licensing Expo this June.

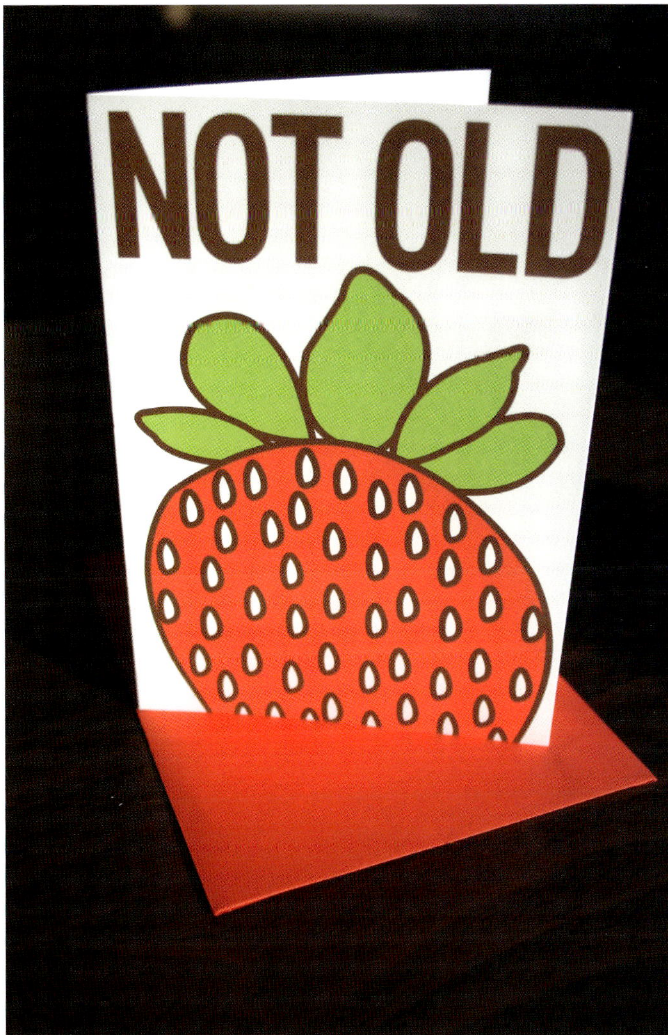

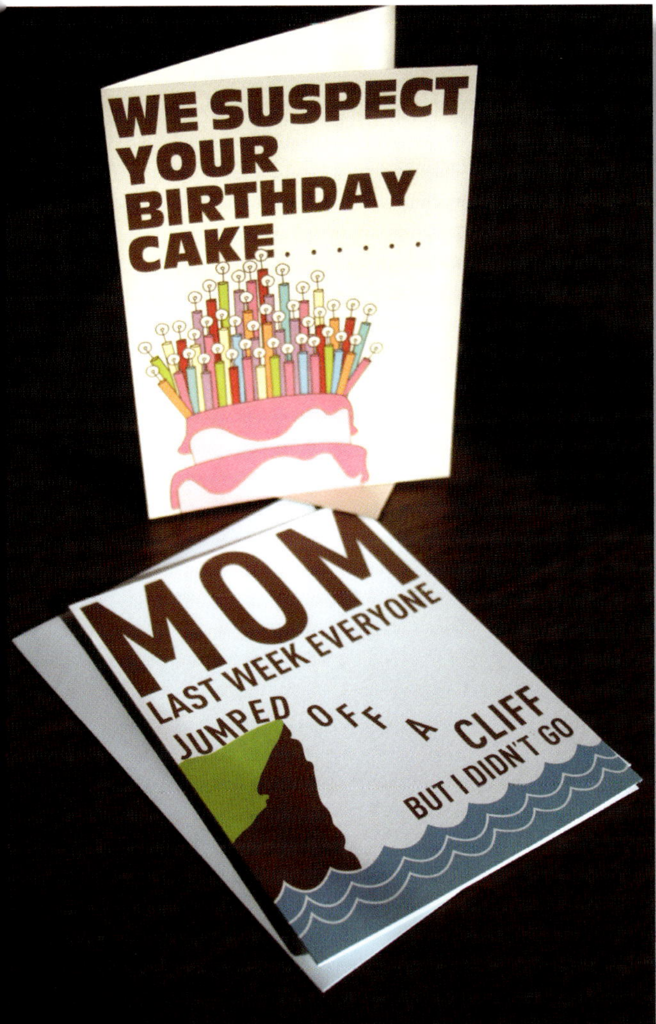

Greeting cards by Amy Smyth Made it.
Photographs by Wendy Hicks.

What inspires you the most?

Graffiti in old books, printing that's just a little off register, paper that has yellowed, halftones, gummed storage labels, the clank of an old typewriter, stitches, mechanical pencils, succulent plants, albino animals, moss, foxes in the backyard, the rattling of the tree tops on a windy day, my talented friends and family.

How did you come up with the name "Art School Girl" for your company?

While I was attending The School of the Art Institute of Chicago I just loved the creative-anything-goes style of all the "art school girls." It was when I caught a glimpse of myself in a mirrored building on my way to class that I realized I was one of them. I bought the URL in 1999 with the intention of making an online gallery of my work and the work of my friends that never came to fruition. So when I started making cards and books in 2004 it was just natural to keep that business name.

How large is your vintage material collection and how often do you add to it?

It is big, too big. I have been collecting for twelve years now. Recently I decided to consign a large portion of my library at one of my favorite shops in Chicago. I am always collecting and sourcing new materials. In fact, I just got back from a church rummage sale this morning (those are my favorite).

You sell your work to some really great online stores as well as brick and mortars. Which came first for you and does one seem to help the other?

I launched my company when I was working as an in house designer for the stationery store Greer, in Chicago. Owner, Chandra Greer, was my first customer. She was very supportive of my work. I love shopping local whenever possible, brick and mortar shops are so inspiring and add so much character to their neighborhoods. I also love the virtual community my online stores have. My hat's off to the owner of every independent shop I sell or shop at for being a visionary and building community.

Do you hand-make everything yourself or do you have help?

I hand-make most designs with the help of my trusty interns. Some pieces are produced by skilled printers and then finished and packaged in the studio. There are so many talented hands that make each and every Art School Girl product. I think people would be surprised if they knew how much human power went into each little card.

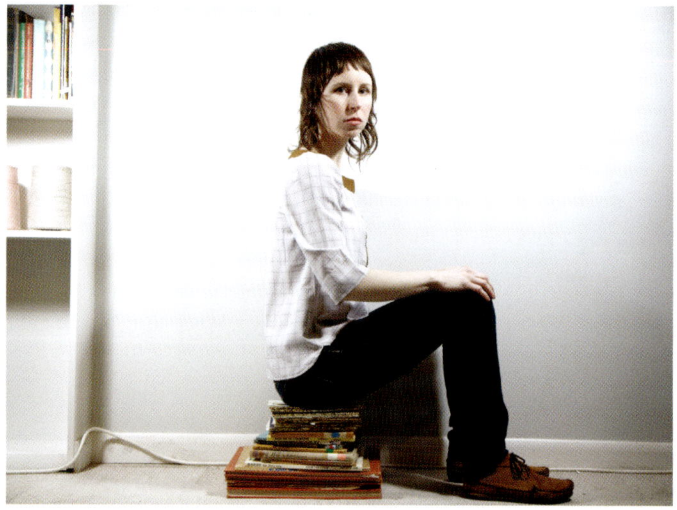

Amy Rowan of Art School Girl and images of her work. *Portrait Photograph by Kyle LaMere.*

What are you most proud of in regard to your company?

The press I've gotten is really encouraging—from *Lucky Magazine* to *The Chicago Tribune*. Being represented in some of the best boutiques in the country is a huge honor.

What is your typical work day like?

I generally work 9-6 but will often do some handwork at night while relaxing. When I have an intern in the studio we take a long lunch and walk to a nearby cafe for some fuel.

For an aspiring stationery artist, do you recommend researching the industry or just jumping in with both feet? What worked for you?

I think with anything you want to master you need to immerse yourself in it first. Find a mentor or get an internship. I interned with Snow and Graham right out of college and worked in a stationery store before launching my own line.

What is the most rewarding aspect of being a stationery artist for you?

I get great fulfillment knowing that my products encourage personal correspondence. Nothing can take the place of a handwritten letter; I feel a responsibility to keep written correspondence alive and well. I love that a card I made will likely brighten someone's day.

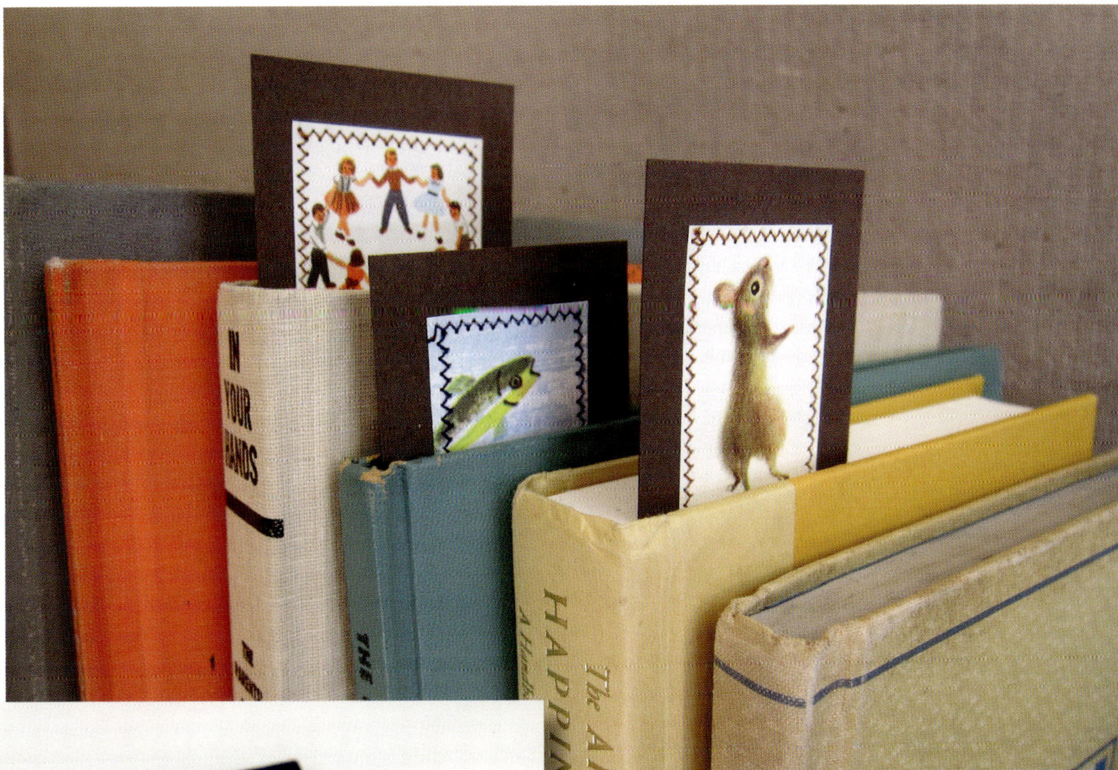
IN YOUR HANDS

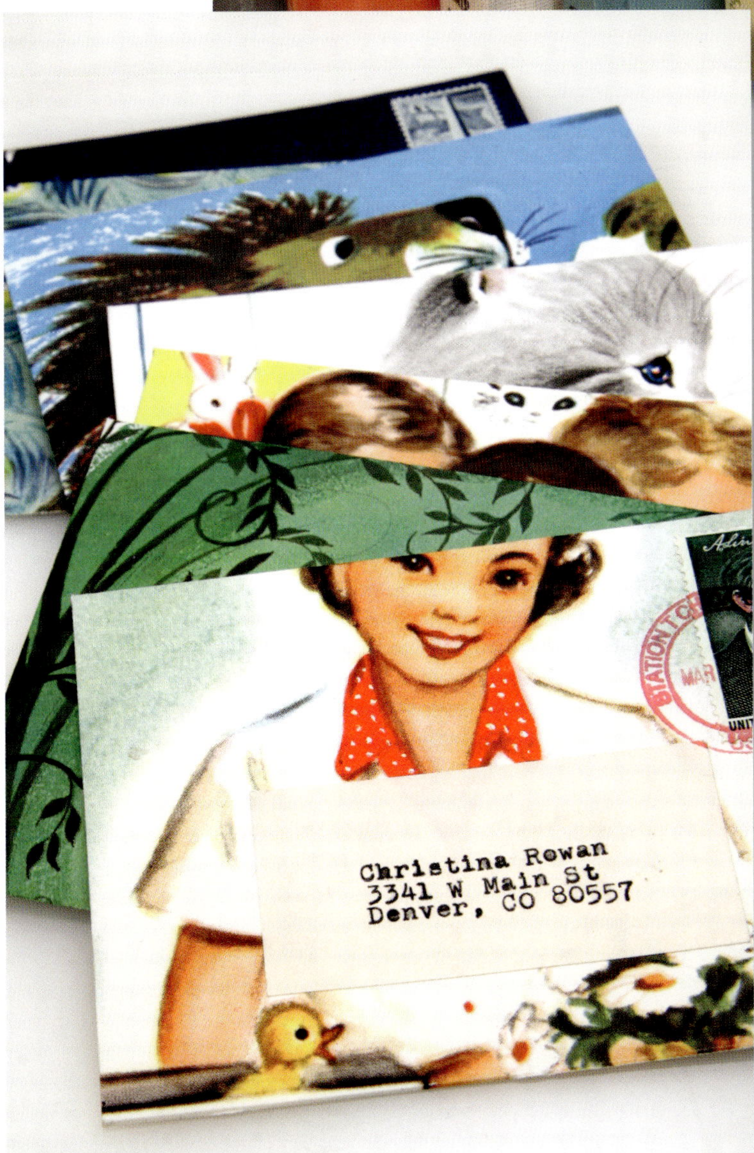
Christina Rowan
3341 W Main St
Denver, CO 80557

Cheree Berry

How did your corporate background at Kate Spade equip you to run your own successful stationery company?

My experience at Kate Spade was the key component of why I'm doing what I'm doing now!! I loved my job at Kate Spade and I loved it even more when they partnered with Crane & Co. to develop the Kate Spade stationery line. I feel so lucky to have learned about the wedding invitation business from the expert team at Crane & Co.

How did you break away from the comfort of a corporate job as an art director to starting your own business? Did you work on your own company part time at first or did you just take the plunge and work on your business full time from the beginning?

Outside of my day job at Kate Spade, I devoted my spare time to designing wedding invitations for friends and friends of friends and friends of friends of friends. After four incredible years at Kate Spade, I was ready to move back home to St. Louis to start my own stationery business. I thought I had all the key components to starting my own business—drive, energy, and talent —so I just dove right in.

What inspires you most for your line?

I am inspired by legendary graphic designers such as Paul Rand, Cipe Pineles and Tibor Kalman as well as current stationery greats such as Rifle Paper Company and Mr. Boddington's Studio. I find inspiration on eBay and blogs such as dailydropcap.com and pentagram.com ... in Peter Callahan's mini bites ... in Kate Spade's constant charm and wit ... in vintage Valentine's cards... in my niece's drawings ... in Tom's charitable mission ... in cocktail names ... in tile formations ... in Veer fonts ... etc. And if you open your eyes wide enough, you can find inspiration in the unlikeliest places.

Do you meet most of your wedding clients in person or do you mainly work via email or phone?

We don't always have the opportunity to meet our clients. Since our company is based in St. Louis and the majority of our clients are not in the Midwest, we do a lot of phone calls and emails. We are sending packages out most days, as we want our potential clients to see our work in person before committing to working with us. It's so much better to see the product in person! My business partner and I spend a lot time commuting back in forth to NYC where the majority of our clients reside. If we don't meet them at some point during their wedding engagement, we usually have a second chance once the baby announcements come around.

What is the best part about being a self employed artist?

The best part is controlling the thermostat in the office! Aside from that, the best part is working with an amazing group of girls, a fabulous roster of clients, and a blank canvas.

What has been the biggest learning experience you have had since starting your own business?

Quality control! A few years ago, one of my clients called to tell me that the patterned envelope liner had rubbed off onto the back of her invitation. Eek! So, to avoid things like this, we are constantly mailing invitations to the office to see how they present themselves in the mail.

If you weren't a stationery designer, what would you do for a living?

I'd own a winery!

What is a typical work day for you like?

There is no such thing as a typical day at CBP. Surprises always pop up but I love the mystery of each day (as long as coffee is involved).

Do you have any advice you would like to share with aspiring custom wedding stationery designers?

Bring a lot of energy to the table!! Enjoy the client interaction and be prepared to make friends! Find the individual and personal flair in your clients. Create a recognizable design style for your product. Take risks!

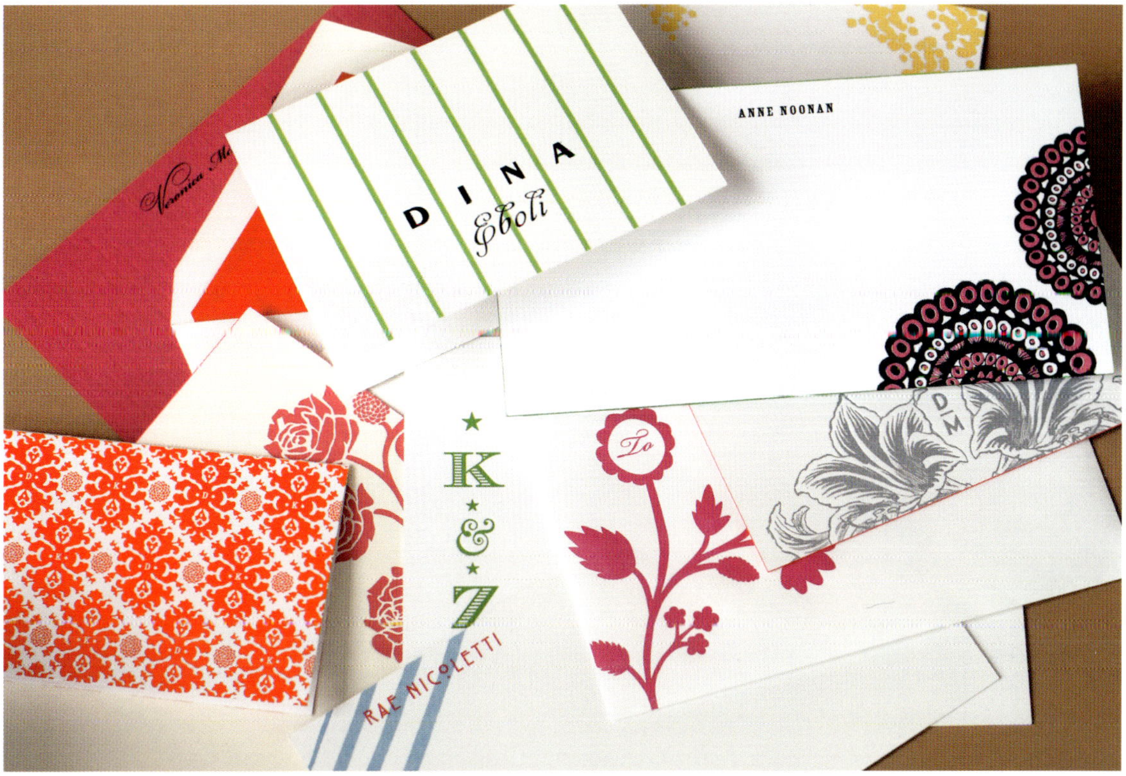

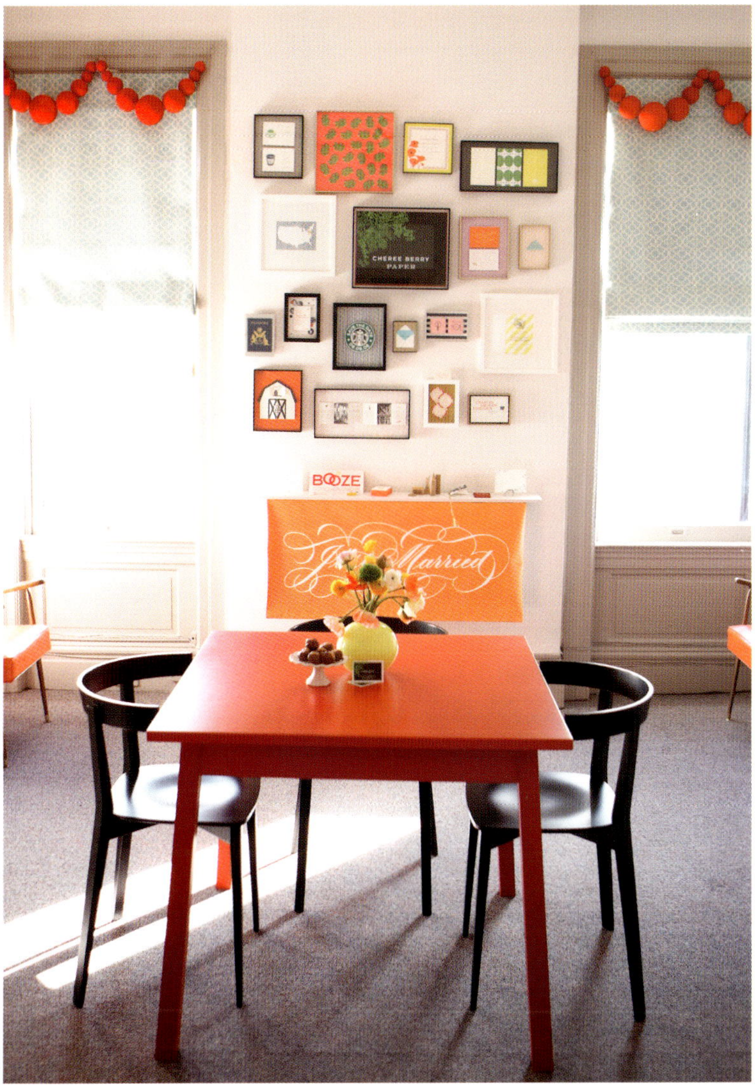

Cheree Berry Paper. *Photograph by Susan Jackson.*
Cheree Berry Paper studio. *Photograph by Scott Clark Photography.*

Delphine

What is the meaning behind the name of your company?

Delphine is my maternal grandmother. She is in her 80s and lives with us. She helps out nearly every day in the studio, packaging cards, wrapping wedding orders, and making lots of espresso.

You have a great corporate image. Is corporate branding something you have always deemed important to your business from the very beginning?

Thanks so much! I think corporate branding is one of the most important keys to a successful business (besides offering a crazy good product that people want to buy).

Where do you go to find inspiration?

Nature is inspiring, movies are inspiring, my family is inspiring. Books, artwork, travel ... even mundane details like the way a sugar packet looks is inspiring to me. Where don't I find inspiration? It's all around me. I even design in my dreams. Sometimes I wish I could turn it off.

How important is it to your company to offer other services such as custom graphic design work?

I love working with other entrepreneurs, so I don't see myself ever giving up custom graphic design work. It's some of the most creative work I do; I really enjoy the challenge of designing a brand.

You manage so many different things in your business so well (illustration, graphic design, licensing, online sales, and custom wedding invites to name just a few). Which aspect takes up the most time and do you have a lot of help? Which aspect do you enjoy the most?

Thanks for the love! Keeping up with the business of running a business (emails, phone calls, paperwork) takes up most of our time at the studio. I do have a lot of help. My husband John Arquette is our COO: he does all the books, manages the website, tweaks the code, handles the wholesale side of our business, manages the warehouse, and supervises all the packing and shipping and receiving and ordering of materials. Bobbi Jo Duley is my right hand—she's a designer and helps with proofing, preparing files for the website, and designing new products. Besides John and Bobbi, we get a ton of help from family and friends, part-time helpers, and a bevy of interns. The thing I love the most about Delphine is the fact that every day is different. Some days I get to be super creative: styling photo shoots, designing new products, illustrating new cards; other days I get to map out a quarter's worth of ad budget, work out a new marketing strategy, or update the business plan; and other days I get to meet with real brides and grooms, design logos, and create brand strategies for clients and their businesses, or consult with other entrepreneurs. It's never boring, always creative, always challenging—I guess that's why I love what I do!

What is the best part of being a stationery artist?

I get to design things that make people happy! Most days I design wedding invitations: correspondence that spreads the message of joy and love. How amazing is that?

What is your typical day like?

I get up before the sun, make coffee, and review the day's projects. I'll answer a few emails, then help get my son ready for school. After dropping him off, I squeeze in a quick workout, then head back to the studio to answer more emails and return phone calls between bites of breakfast. I tend to be most creative in the morning, so that's when I plan appointments with new clients, work on logo or design jobs, and draw or shoot photographs. After lunch I review proofs, place orders with printers, and handle the other minutiae that comes with running a business. After my son comes home from school I hang out with him for snack time (more coffee for me) then head back to the studio for more emails, phone calls, and design work. After dinner ... more emails! They never end. This is also when I work on my blog, catch up with friends, read other blogs, and curl up with a magazine or a book.

You seem to balance work and home life very well. Any tips for other creative working moms?

I am totally spoiled—I live in a four-generation household (my parents and grandmother live with my husband, son, and me). So I have a lot of help everyday with managing the "home life." Everyone pitches in to help raise the little one, and I don't know what I would do without them. I would say my biggest tip is to accept help when it's offered. Don't be too proud or shy about it. If you're struggling to do the laundry every week, or don't have time to pick up groceries, and one of your friends or relatives offers to do it, just say thank you and accept the help.

What is the secret to your success?

Wow. That's a hard question. I don't think I can answer that one. I wish I knew the secret to success.

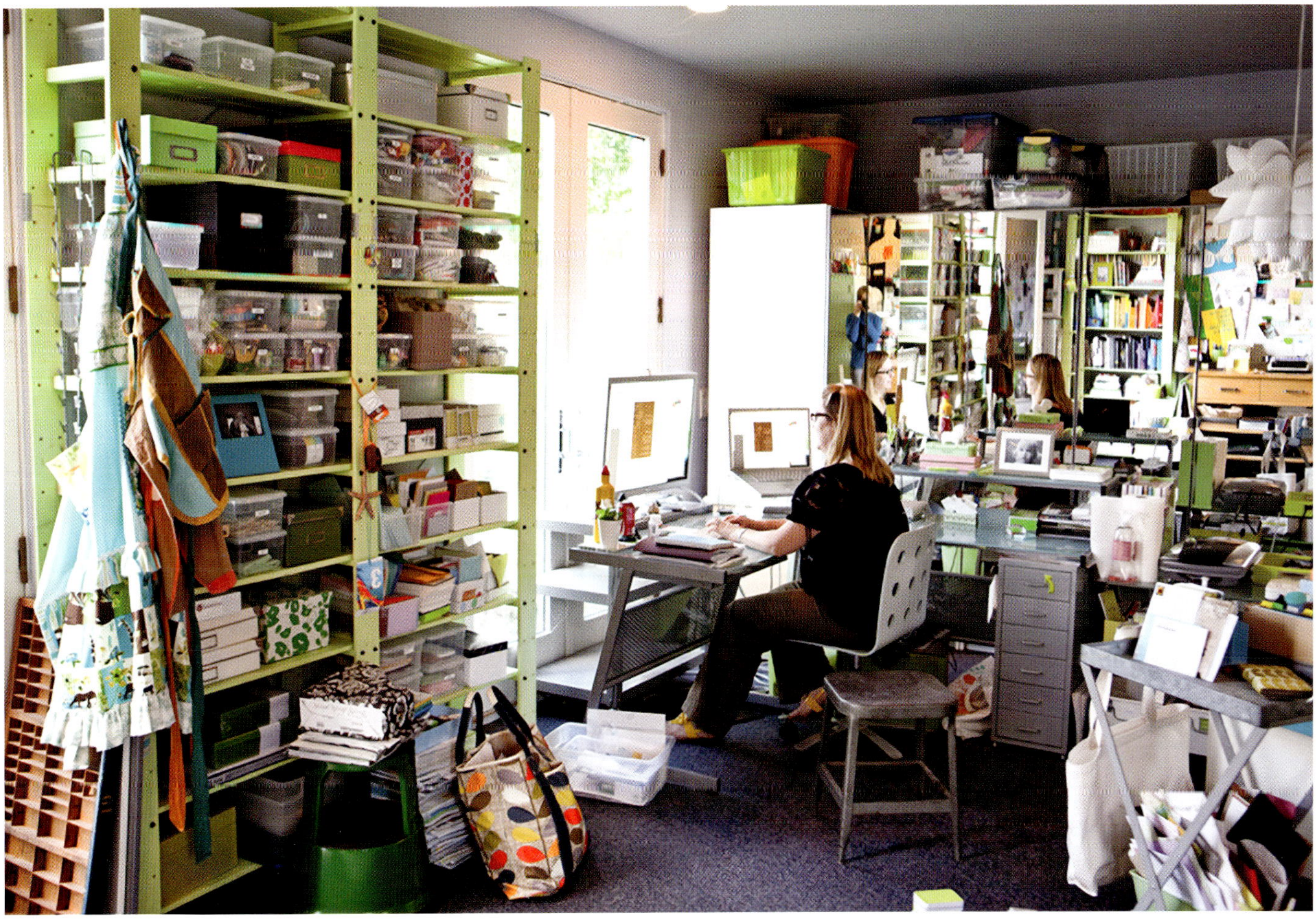

Erika Firm at work in the Delphine studio. *Photographs by Vallentyne Photography.*

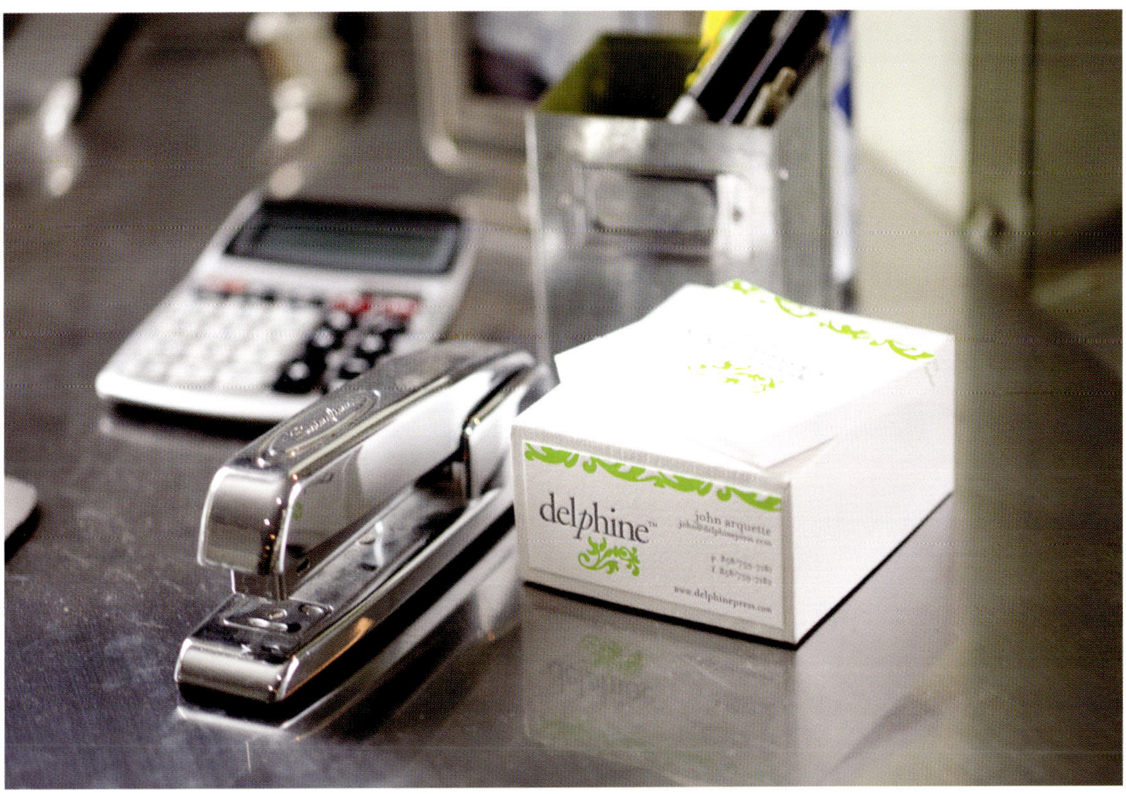

Dutch Door Press

How has it been as two friends working together?

It's been really great! It's so nice to have a partner in an endeavor like running a stationery company to bounce ideas off of each other and to just not be isolated as an artist working alone might be. We also have so much in common and have similar tastes and interests and that's made working together even more enjoyable.

How did you know that you were meant to work together?

We were work colleagues before starting Dutch Door Press, so we knew we worked really well together. We both learned letterpress printing independently of each other and we each had wanted to start a letterpress company of our own, so we decided that it would make sense to start one together!

Do you both have similar talents or do you balance each other out with different skills?

We have very complimentary talents. Mara's sense of the stationery industry, impeccable style, and taste has guided the direction of the Dutch Door Press look. She is also an expert letterpress printer and spends a large part of her time printing our beautiful cards. Anna is our talented designer/illustrator and brings our collaborative ideas to life and she also prints many of our custom projects.

Tell us about your studio. How does working in such a unique space play a roll in your inspiration, creativity, and just your day-to-day life?

We love our studio! Actually, we attribute much of our inspiration to our studio's entrance, which is a Dutch door! Our studio is a wonderful, light-filled space that has four distinct spaces for our work: a meeting/work room, a pressroom, an office, and a storage room. It's a space that seems as though it was designed specifically for us and it has a homey-feel and charm that make it a really nice place to work.

You have a very successful Etsy shop. How did you get the word out about your site?

When we first started, we did very little marketing. Then we started to do a few Etsy Showcases here and there, but then the bloggers started mentioning us more and more frequently and that's brought a lot of traffic to our shop. We now send out email newsletters once a month or so to promote certain products.

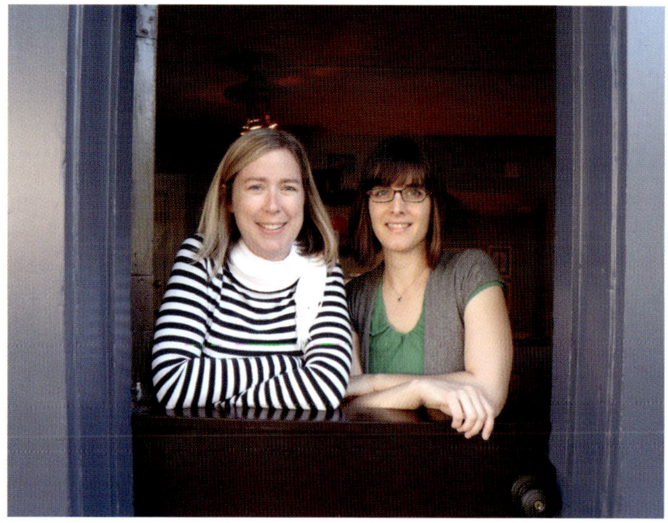

Dutch Door Press studio and founders Mara Murphy and Anna Branning. *Courtesy of Dutch Door Press.*

How much time do you devote to the custom side of your business?

About fifty percent of our time is devoted to custom at the moment. We are always working on new products so that might shift in the future.

What is the most surprising thing you have learned about the stationery industry?

We knew the stationery industry is competitive, but didn't realize exactly how competitive it is. We find that we have to constantly work on new products and keep our look fresh in order to stay relevant.

What is the best thing about your job?

We love that we've found a way to work in a creative environment while working for ourselves. We both have children so it's nice to have a flexible schedule.

If you could give one piece of advice to an aspiring stationery artist, what would you say?

Start with one card and then keep going!

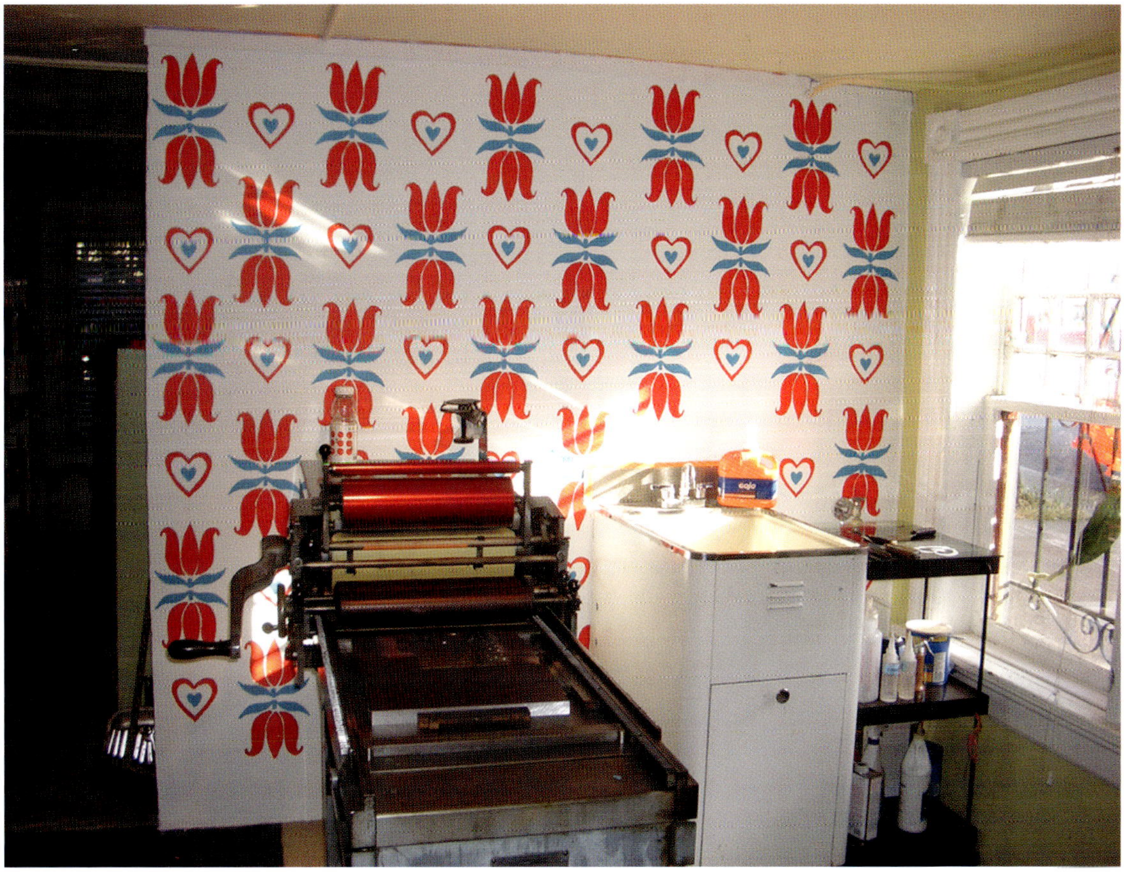

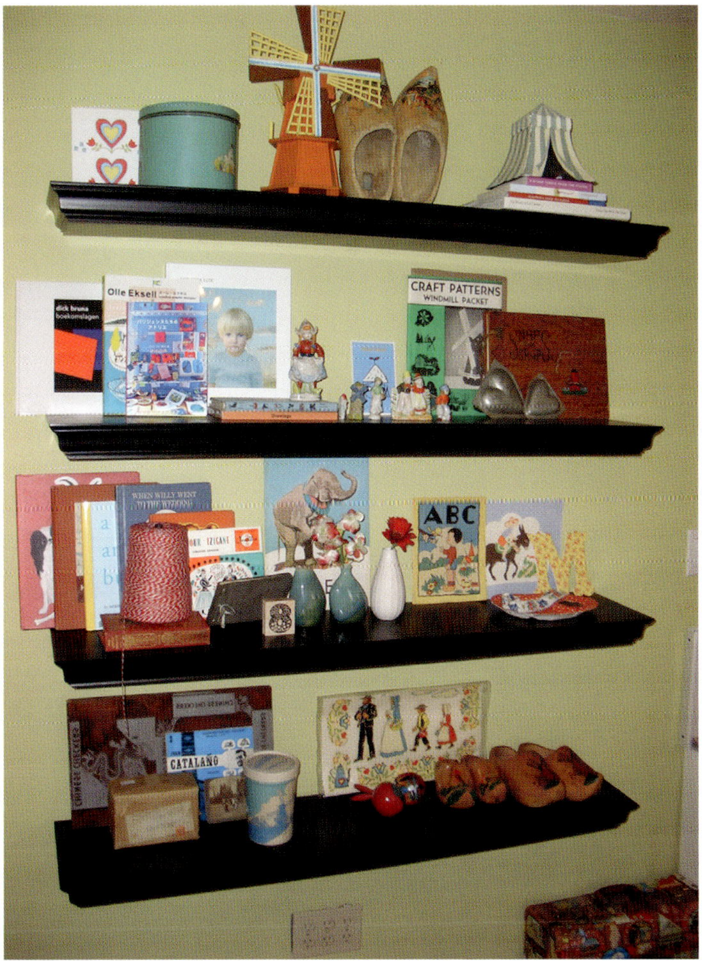

dick bruna
boekomslagen
Olle Eksell
CRAFT PATTERNS
WINDMILL PACKET
WHEN WILLY WENT
ABC
CATALANO

Ecojot

You work with one of the best art-licensing agents in the business, Lilla Rogers Studio. How has being such an in-demand artist enhanced your creativity for your own line of Ecojot products?

It forces me to create all the time. I go back and forth between commissioned work and Ecojot and one inspires the other.

Your stationery products have been sold in large chain stores as well as independent boutiques all over the world; what steps did you take early on in your business to get in front of the right buyers at the right time?

We do the gift show in New York twice a year plus the Stationery Show in May. These shows gave us great exposure to show off Ecojot when we first launched. Since then it has just grown but you can never do enough to promote your company. You have to work at it all the time, it's never ending.

What is the very first sale you ever made?

Ecojot was pre-sold to Indigo/Chapters Books and Music, which is a National Book Chain in Canada. They were the first to take a chance and hop on board. They have been great supporters ever since.

When did you know that you wanted to be a stationery artist?

It wasn't a conscious thought or event. I had been designing for our paper company Mirage, but when we were in the early planning stages of Ecojot in early 2007, it was like a new beginning. The product was new and fresh and so were the designs; it was like a rebirth as a designer for me, which I have been for more than twenty years. It gave my design career a kick-start and elevated it to another level and then I signed with LRS, so it's been *go, go, go* ever since. I work for Ecojot and Ecojot works for me. A win, win situation really ...

How important is managing your blog for your business?

Well, my Designerjots blog started off as a result of all of this. It has now sort of gone off on it's own. It takes a great deal of commitment and dedication to manage it and do it well. Sometimes I am just not inspired to update it, but know that my fans expect something, so that inspires me to create, which spurs on something else. So it's a work in progress, we should say.

What tips would you offer to other creative bloggers?

Your blog should be very focused and you should update often. I think people are interested in your creativity and that in turn inspires theirs.

Tell us about your studio. What sort of inspiration do you surround yourself with to help keep your creative juices flowing?

I have a gorgeous renovated studio/office at the back of my house. It has a sunny bay window with a window seat for power naps. The view in the summer is lovely with lots of trees and a dog park. Lots of light and color, lots of workspace, and precious elements for inspiration ... paintings by friends, photographs by siblings, cut outs, collages, and drawings by my daughter Lily are hung up on the walls.

What is the best advice you have ever received about business and/or design?

Never stop working, never stop creating, but always take a break to refresh and unwind, so you don't burn out.

What is the ideal creative workday for you?

To create a new design from a sketch or an idea that I had in my head and know that people are going to love it just like I do!

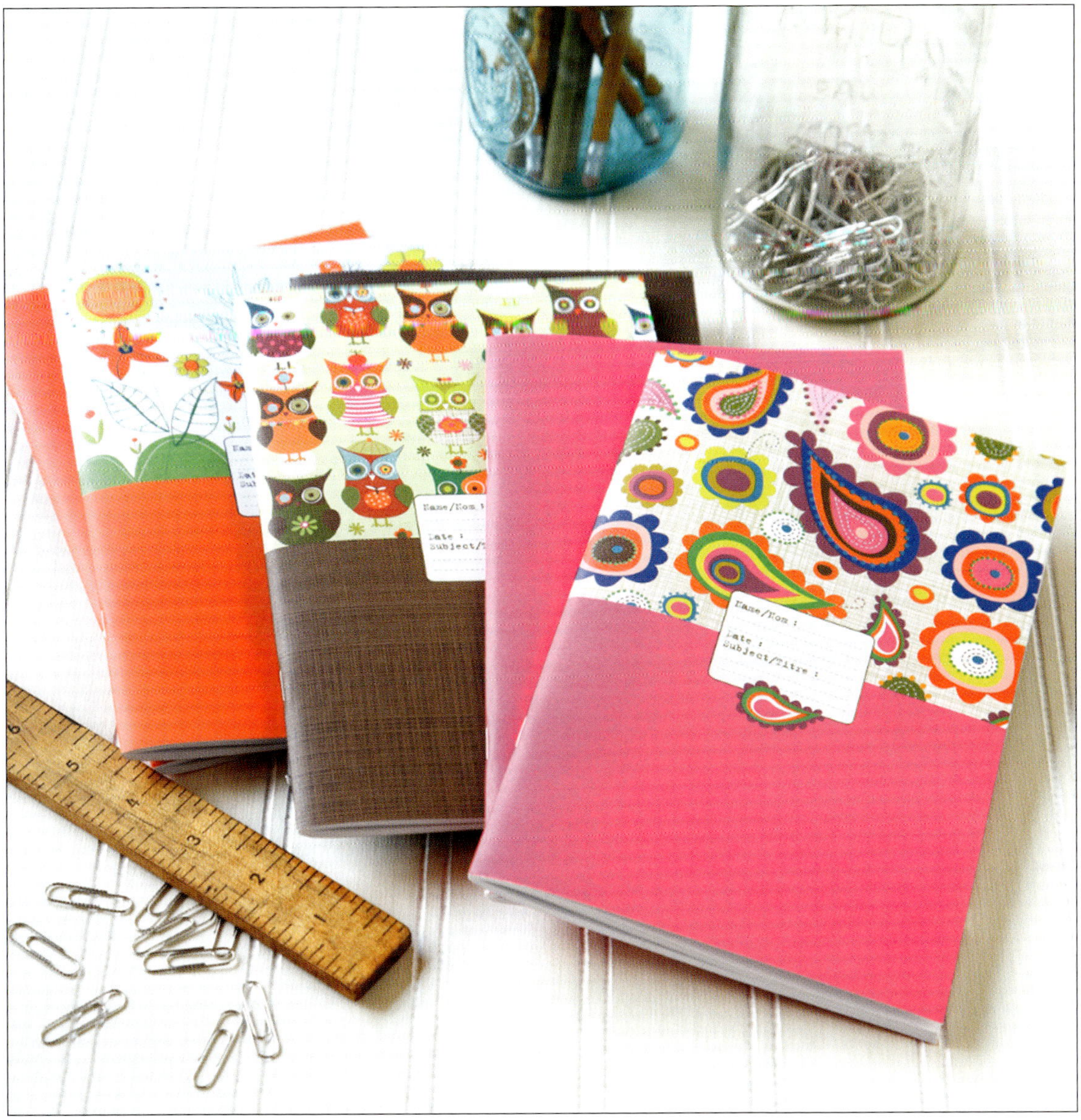

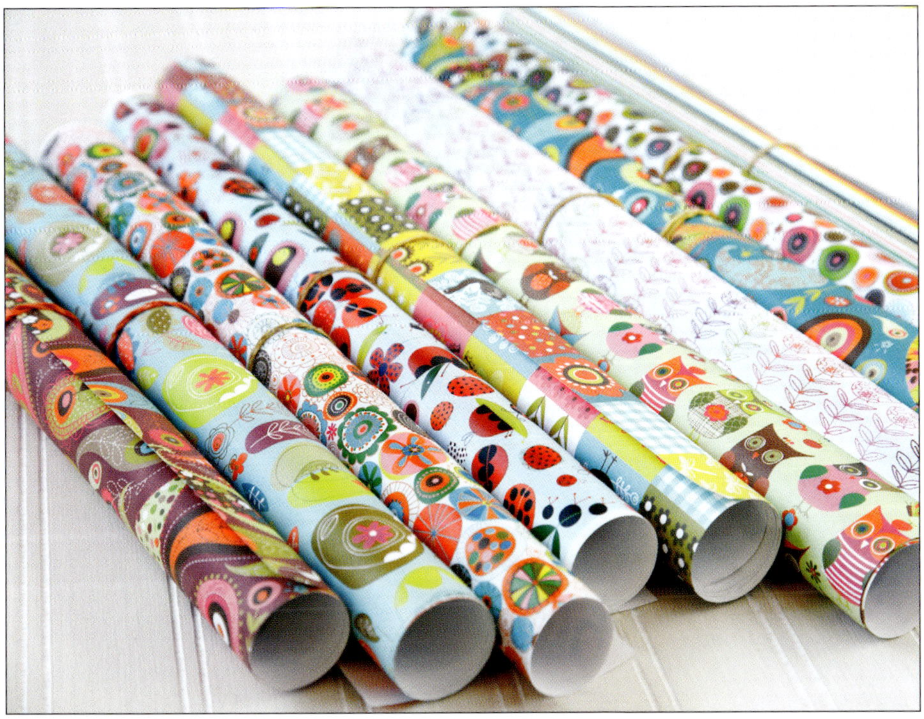

Ecojot notebooks and wrapping paper. *Photographs by Jodi Pudge.*

Fugu Fugu Press

How did you come up with the name for your company?

I am Japanese, and Ken and I both love the ocean, so we wanted our name to reflect those things. And we love that the blowfish (fugu means blowfish in Japanese) are a little slow and awkward at swimming, and pretty goofy looking, yet deathly poisonous!

What steps did you take to learn the art of letterpress?

I worked for another letterpress company for about two years and learned how to print on the Kluge and Chandler & Price presses there. When Ken and I bought our own presses, Davy, the man we purchased from, taught us how to print on the Heidelberg. It's kind of funny that I learned about letterpress way after college, since the school I went to has an amazing letterpress printing facility.

What were the first steps you took to get your stationery into stores?

We started by selling to a store owned by a friend of a friend. Then we started selling on Etsy, and a couple of other stores found us there and decided to carry us. After that, we got a booth at the National Stationery Show, and that's where we got a bunch of stores.

Tell us a little bit about your studio environment.

It's an old building with a brick wall on one side and a big metal door that opens wide on the other (it was a radiator repair shop back in the day). It has a high ceiling and a concrete floor, and we can be messy there without ruining anything. Ken has a beat up old piano there and practices there sometimes. We normally have our door and gate open to let the air flow through while we work there, and people walking by stop and watch us or talk to us often. We have either NPR or music on when we're printing, and sometimes we bring our pit-mix dog Morgan with us to keep us company.

How do you delegate tasks? Do you each have different talents and backgrounds, if so, what are they?

Ken is definitely better at printing (even though he learned way after I did), and also better at figuring out what's wrong with the presses. I do pretty much everything else—designing, packing, shipping, managing website, etc., and I still print as well. Ken still teaches piano five days a week, sometimes gigs playing the piano on top of that. I'm pretty much doing Fugu Fugu full time, unless I get a freelance illustration job.

What are the most important aspects of design that you think about when creating a new greeting card?

If it communicates instantly.

Where do you hope to see your business in the future?

We hope to keep growing, but would still like to be a little mom and pop. It would be cool if I can do more design work on different surfaces other than greeting cards. And Ken would like to teach less and print more.

What is the most hectic time of year for you work wise?

Before the National Stationery Show. We have a long list of things to do, and it keeps growing longer!!

What is the most important thing you have learned on your stationery design journey?

I think I'm still learning.

Do you have any tips for aspiring letterpress artists?

Can't think of any good ones, but I know we had tons of questions when we were starting our business! I guess to not be shy and ask other people how they did it. Everybody has their own way, and you'll find yours eventually.

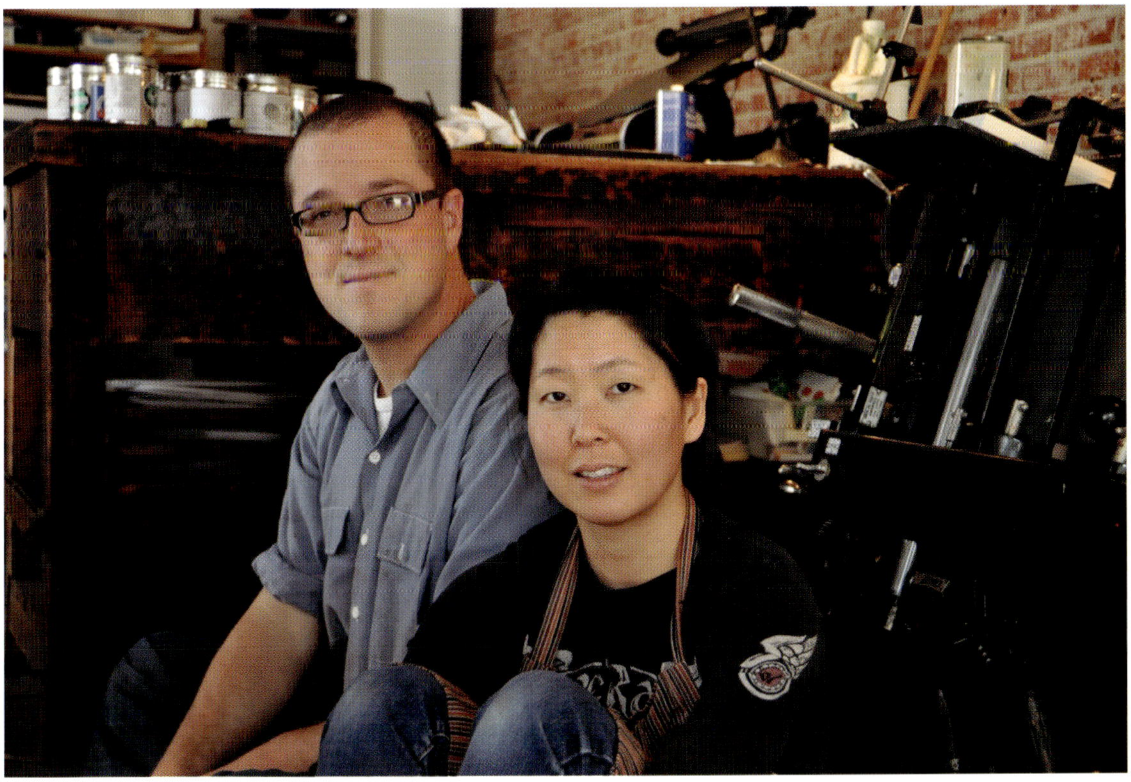

Ken and Shino Charlson in their Fugu Fugu Press studio. *Courtesy of Ken and Shino Charlson.*

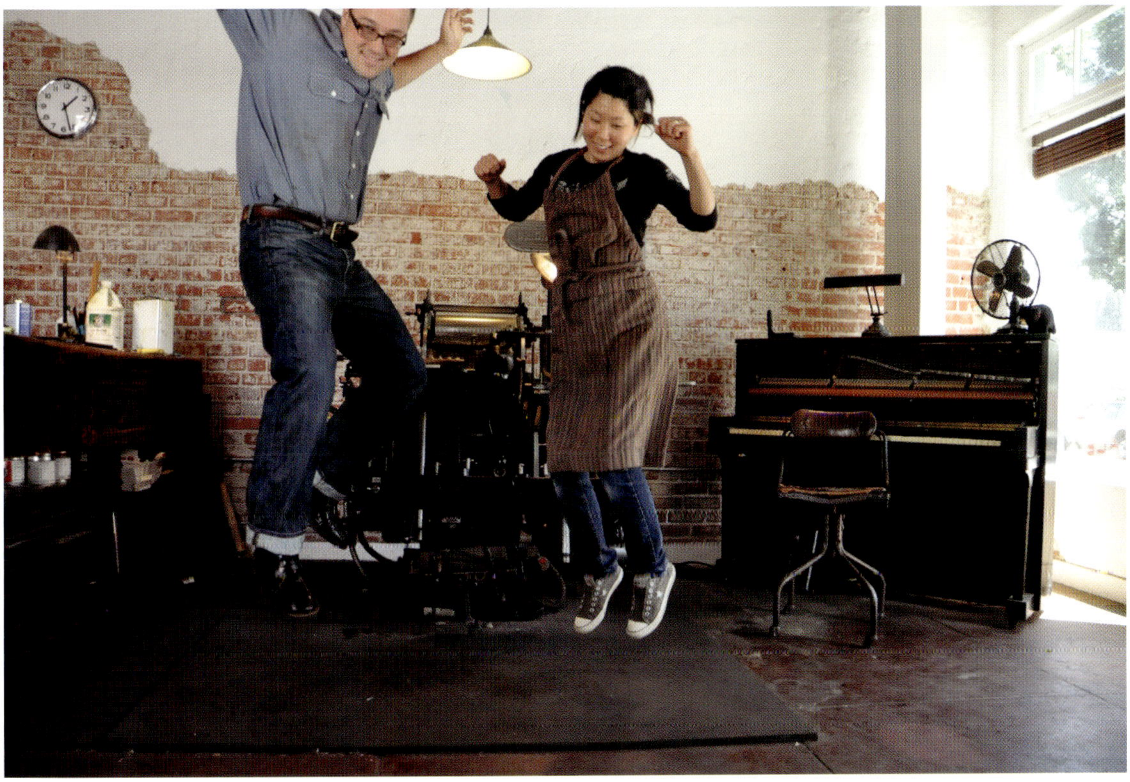

Ink + Wit

You license your artwork to several top greeting card companies (Great Arrow Graphics, Graphique de France, and Cardstore.com); how did you get your start in art licensing?

I was fortunate to hit it off with Great Arrow Graphics in 2005. I had submitted my designs to them and fit into the company's look, full of bold shapes and line art. The experience was really great and the cards became best sellers. You never know with licensing sometimes in terms of how long you may wait to be contacted by the company. They receive so many submissions and their design concepts and stories change so it is a timing thing quite often. I had submitted designs to Graphique de France and heard back two years after that they wanted to license my work. Cardstore.com and I met at the 2008 National Stationery Show. Trade shows are a great place to show your work and network. Cardstore.com invited me to be one of their artists and I happily accepted. That is also how Bella Figura came to be as well. Bella Figura and I have worked together for two years on wedding suites for their line. Overall licensing works two ways, you either submit your work or the companies will find you. It is a great experience to pitch your ideas and work with a team on creating a new product line.

What kind of advice do you have for artists who want to license their work to greeting card companies?

Create a lot of options for them to review. And, do not throw out the designs you think they may not like just because you are not sure. I had a few designs I was on the fence about but we actually tweaked them and made them work for both of us. Which is another key factor. Make work that you love and the company will love. It will ultimately represent you and them so it should have your voice in it. My work has evolved quite a bit since 2005, but when I look back on the designs I made for Great Arrow I still see INK+WIT in them.

You keep a beautiful blog. How much time do you devote to it each week?

I am so thankful the blog has made people happy and continues to inspire. Thank you! I thought when I started it I would post three times a week but now I try to post every day. I would estimate I spend two hours a day creating a post, images, and promoting the post through Twitter. If I am writing a longer article for the blog, it can take three to four hours as I dedicate half a day to research, writing, spell check, and editing.

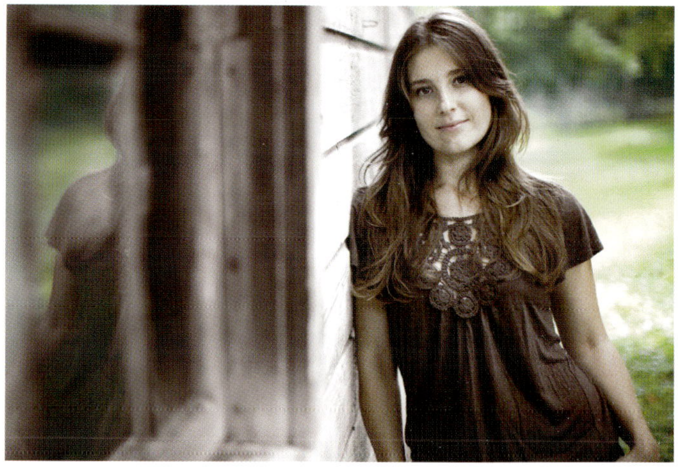

Tara Hogan of INK+WIT and her studio. *Portrait photograph by Grant Taylor Photography, studio photographs are courtesy of INK+WIT.*

You have a very diverse company. What keeps you the busiest: custom wedding designs, licensing, illustration, online sales, or your own line of cards?

It all blends together since I am illustrating and designing all round for custom wedding, the INK+WIT line, licensing calls, and brand IDs and websites. Retail ebbs and flows depending on the season. August through January are always busy months but post holiday retail slows down a bit and then picks back up in May.

What is the most important thing you have learned in the stationery industry?

Research, learn the history of illustration, design, and typography, go to your target market stores to see what is selling, and get to work. Stationery can be quite trendy now and to make a best seller that can stick around takes a lot of investigating as to what people find memorable and classic. It has always been my goal to create work that has a timeless feel and can sell a year from now. In addition, stationery has gone beyond actual paper, branching into wood, fibers, and digital online media. It is important not only to address the medium appropriate for your concept and style but also to experiment with different forms of expression.

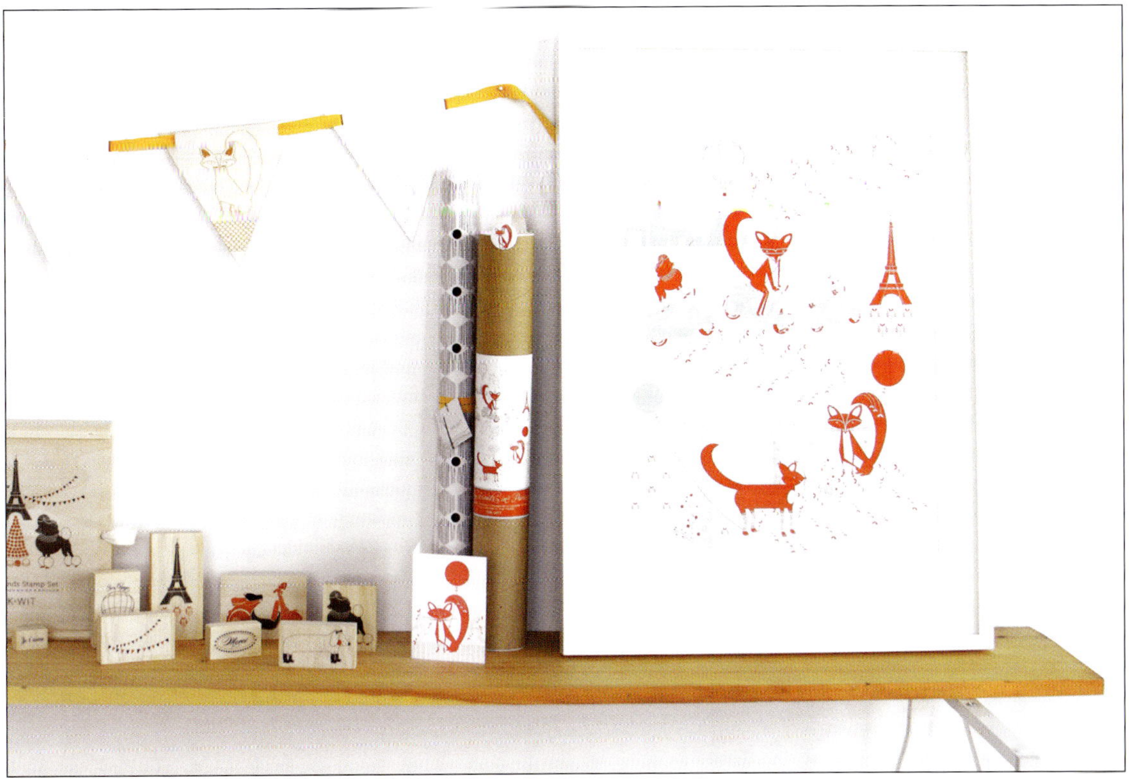

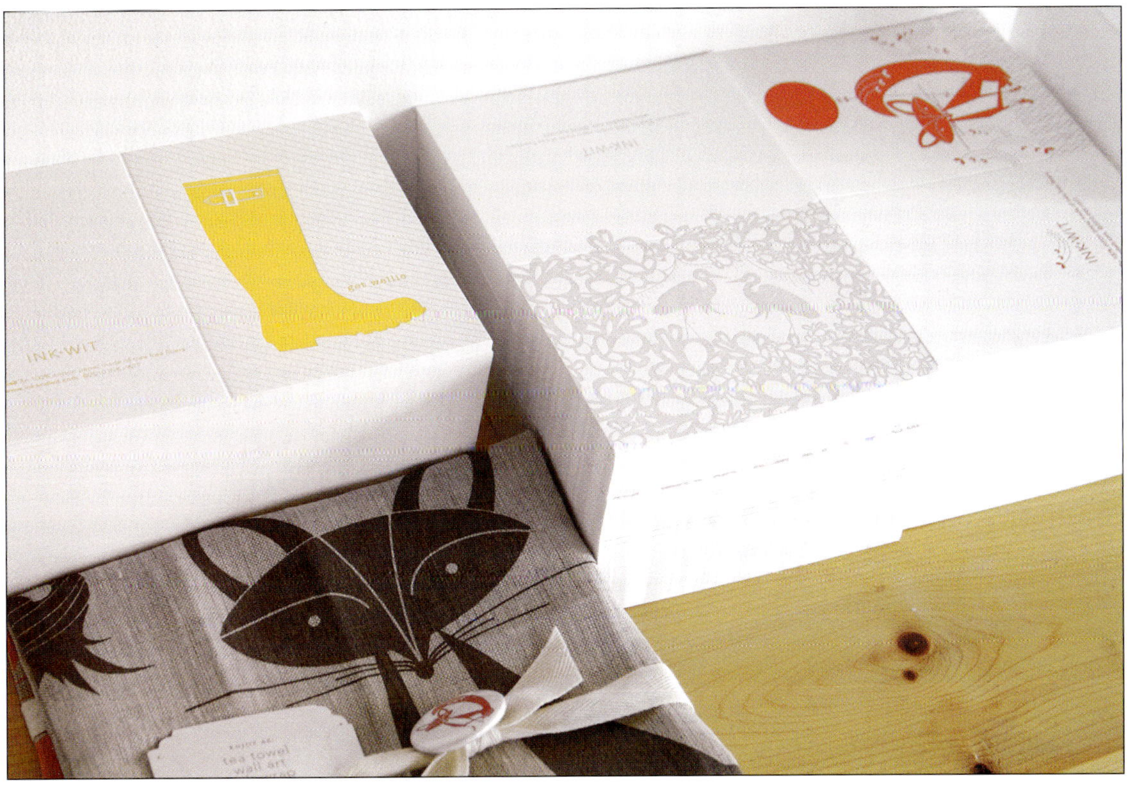

La Familia Green

What is the best part about making each individual greeting card by hand?

I feel like each card is a little work of art —each is special and unique and labored over. And I love hearing about someone sending or receiving one of my cards—I know that I designed, printed, collaged, and folded that very card.

What is the worst part about making each individual greeting card by hand?

The time that it takes for me to fill orders. Lots of pressure and sore wrists and late nights.

If you didn't have a stationery company, what would you do for a living?

I really love not having a boss! So I would probably still work independently—maybe as a painter or textile designer. I also love visual merchandising—which I dabbled in a bit years ago.

What is your all time favorite project or greeting card design to date?

I love the "You snooze, you win" card. I am a late sleeper. This card says a lot about me!

How did you first start selling your cards to stationery stores?

I worked for a great card store here in Chicago, and I started out by selling my cards there. Then I progressed to craft fairs, like Renegade. I was lucky to experience the buying side of the business while working in the store. That gave me the confidence and knowledge to approach other retailers.

How often do you release new work?

I release new work—both seasonal and everyday—for Valentines, spring holidays, and winter holidays. I also release a small collection in May.

How do you stay inspired?

I keep a notebook of potential ideas. So when it is time to release new cards, I have material to pull from. I suppose that I am just constantly looking for good card ideas.

What inspires you most?

My collections: Scandinavian ceramics, 1970s tennis manuals, Mexican textiles, Japanese packing tape, "floaty" pens, and international fashion magazines. I also love all animals. My husband Andrew and I have three rescue tabby cats and one rescue pit bull/pointer mix dog. I donate a portion of all sales to local animal charities.

What is the best business advice you have ever received?

Hire an accountant.

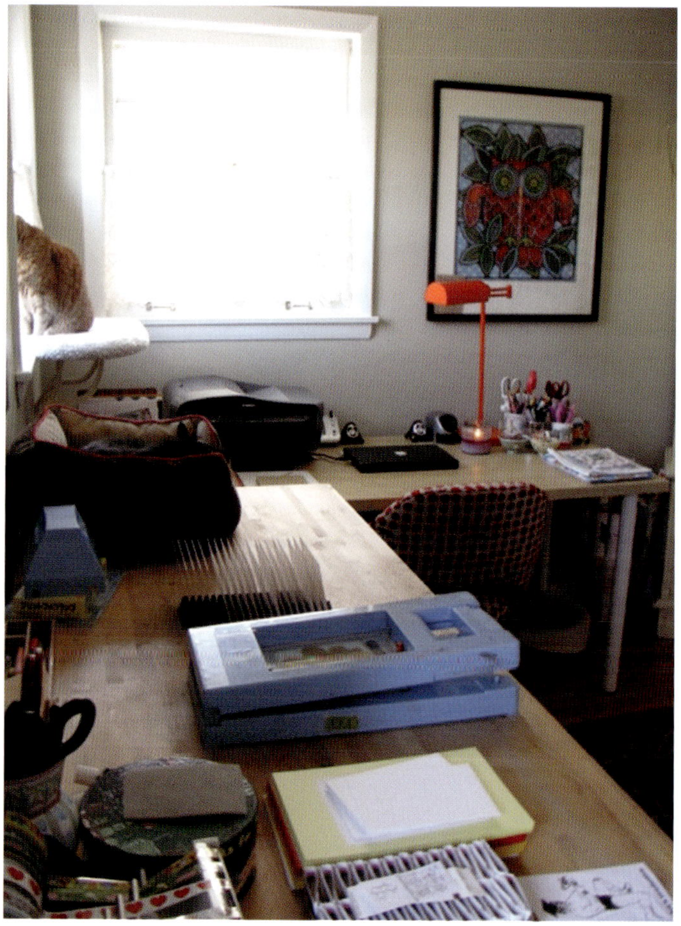

La Familia Green studio. *Courtesy of La Familia Green.*

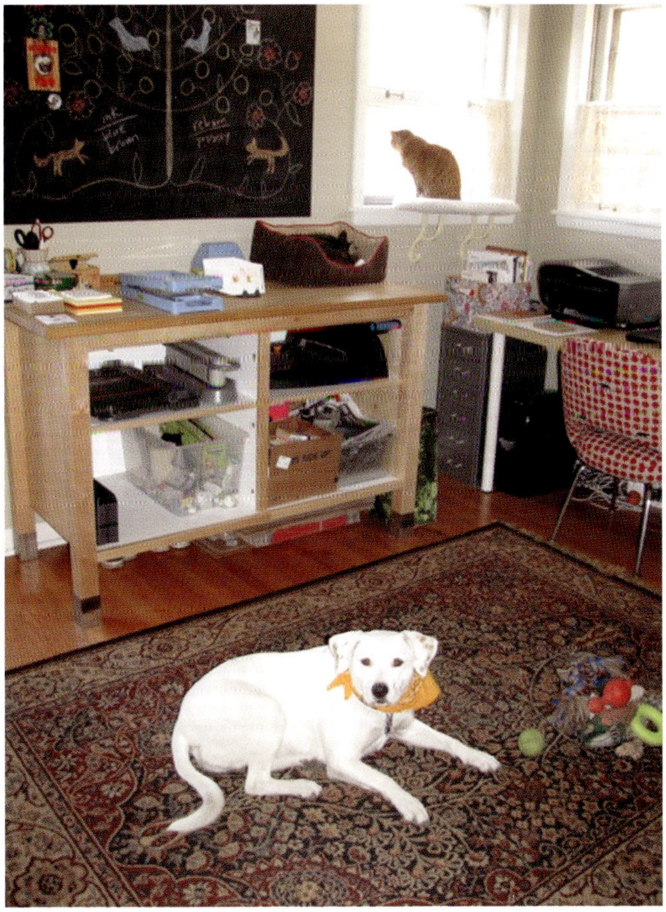

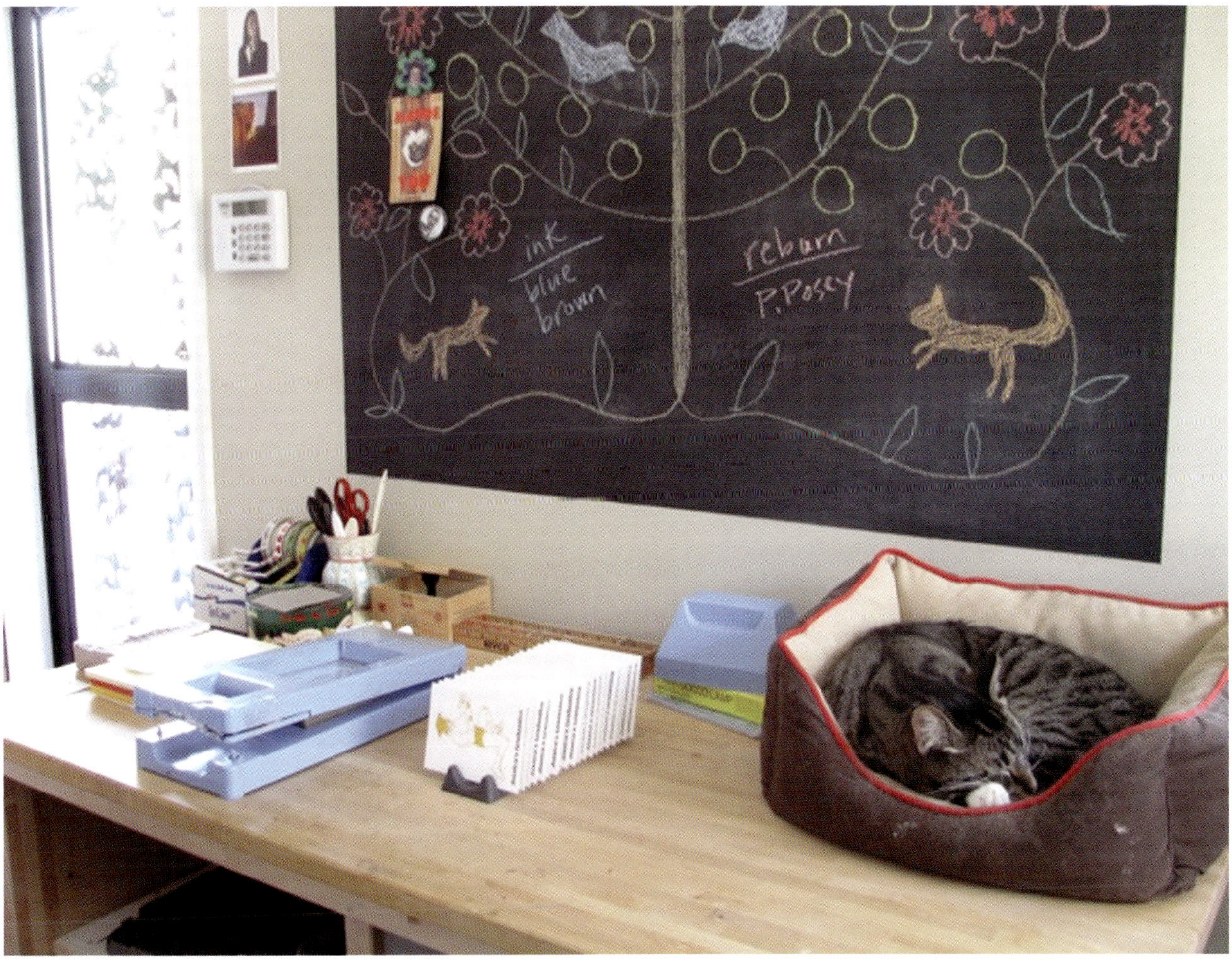
ink
blue
brown
reborn
P.Posey

Marzipan Inc. / Fin Roe

Do you find that offering multiple design styles has helped your business grow?

There were a couple reasons behind choosing to branch out into different design styles and product offerings. The first reason was purely selfish. While I love designing my Marzipan Inc. greeting card line, I felt a little limited. My design style, for those cards, is very specific and I felt like I had so many other ideas that I didn't have an outlet for. The second reason for offering another design style, and a whole other type of product to my business was definitely about building my business and helping it grow. I feel very strongly about not having all my eggs in one basket. By diversifying into several areas within the same industry, I'm able to take advantage of my current customer base as well as add a new customer base, which has helped to bring my products into places they had not been before.

How much time do you spend on social networking each day and has it paid off in sales or benefited your business in some way?

At times I feel that I spend way too much time on social networking. Then, something happens which leads to a door opening that would never have been placed in front of me before. It's times like these that reinforce my addiction; um ... I mean time spent on necessary social networking. So, although I'm not sure I can place a number on how much time I spend on social networking, I do believe it has paid off and benefited in contacts and sales. My one piece of advice would be not to expect it to happen overnight. It takes time to grow a network and to see results.

What is your ideal workday like?

We recently decided to forego childcare and keep our two young boys (ages 5 and 2.5) home with me during the day. This makes for a crazy, hectic workday. If I were able to have the perfect workday, it would go something like this: all-day childcare, a never-ending mug of Chai tea, a great play list on my iPod, and an all day design session in which ideas just pour straight from my brain onto the computer. How's that for super-unrealistic?

What is the most significant change in the industry since you started your business?

There are definitely a lot of changes that have happened in the industry since I started my business. One of the things that has greatly affected the industry is the Internet. Not that the Internet didn't exist when I started, but things have grown substantially. For example, things like Etsy have affected the industry in both a positive and negative way. While it's a great way for new and upcoming designers and artists to build their business for a very minimal cost, it has also brought out hoards of people who aren't necessarily interested in building businesses. These types of hobbyists tend to sell things for way less than someone who's trying to build a business can afford to do. This undercuts the market and puts an unrealistic price point out there, which business owners now need to try and "compete" with.

What is the best thing about your job?

The best thing about my job is that I'm my own boss. I've said it a million times .... I'd rather work 100 hours a week for myself doing something I love than 40 for someone else!

What are you most proud of in regard to the stationery companies you have created?

Beside my designs, which are each like my little babies, the thing I'd have to say I'm most proud of is simply sustaining my business and earning a living at what I love to do. I honestly can't think of anything I'd rather earn a living doing.

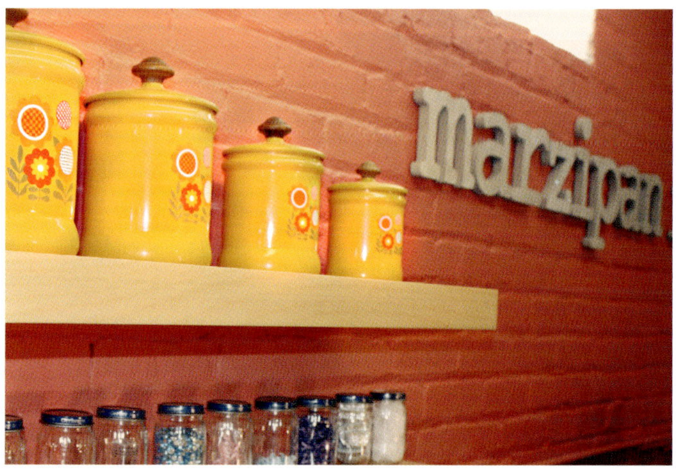

Marzipan Inc. studio, storage room, and kid's art area. *Courtesy of Lori Dunbar.*

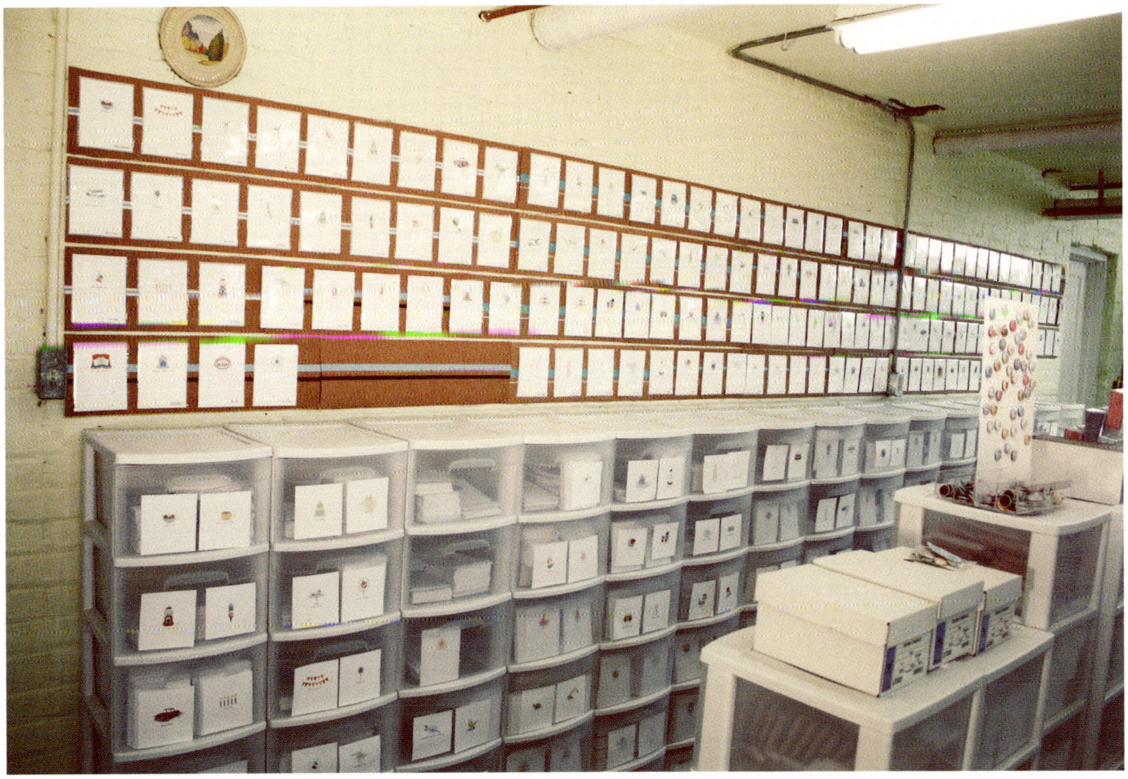

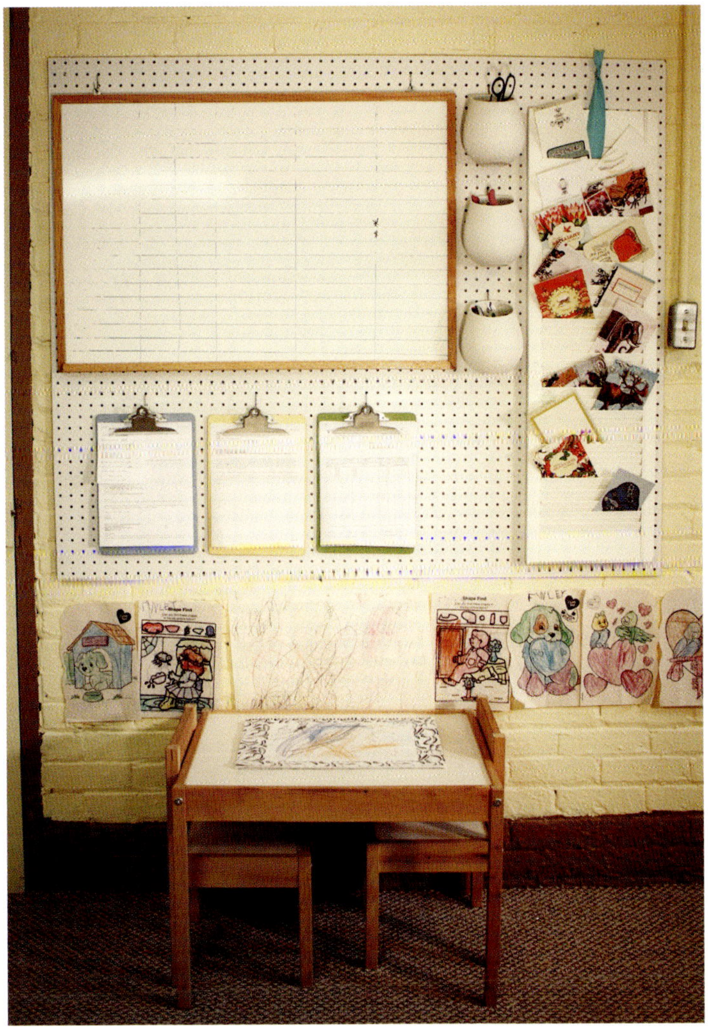

Night Owl Paper Goods

How did you decide on naming your company and branding it in such a creative and memorable way?

Honestly, we went through a few name changes. Being designers, we like to keep thinking about a project even after it's supposed to be complete. We finally truly settled on Night Owl Paper Goods when Alan called me up one day and said, "What about Night Owl Paper Goods?" I replied "What, really? I just bought an owl collection from an estate sale, so heck YES!" We were always going after a name that would be easy to say, reflect what we do, and have a logo that was easily recognizable and very friendly. Night Owl Paper Goods suited us perfectly since our business started in my basement, where we printed at nights after our full-time day jobs.

How did you come up with the idea of printing on wood?

Alan and I had the idea at about the same time. I was at an advertising agency working on a project for Habitat for Humanity and Alan was doing freelance design for an architect. Neither one of our projects came into fruition, but it did spur us on to create work for our night business.

Were buyers and customers immediately drawn to your work or was there a slight learning curve because your product is so fresh and unique?

Our product wasn't always fresh and unique. While working our day jobs, we had lots of total loser cards. Back when we had only two sales reps, one of them wanted to drop our line as it wasn't selling that well in her territory. Three things started to make reps, buyers, and customers notice our line. One, we added more texture (wood) into our line. Two, we started to create our signature "modern yet folksy" style. Three, we exhibited at our first National Stationery Show.

When did you know that you wanted to be a creative business owner?

Alan will say that he always knew. I'll say this; it wasn't until coming back from our first Stationery Show, that I totally knew we could do it full-time! We had such great feedback from that show that we knew we were destined to be our own bosses ... very soon.

What has been the biggest challenge in your job?

Alan and I say that the biggest challenge in our job is knowing when to hire, who to hire, and what position we're hiring for. Finding great people is very rewarding though. Being a "boss" is something new to us. That too can be a challenge.

You design a wide range of beautiful products, what is your favorite thing to design?

I love to draw furry, fuzzy critters. Alan loves to design graphic patterns. He'd make a great textile pattern designer! Once we have graphic designs, we love to see them cross over from cards to our journals and our jotters and our wall art & more!

What is the secret to your success?

Everyday we're thrilled to be working for ourselves! We work tremendously hard and love, love, love everything we do. We both live and breathe Night Owl Paper Goods! We're always inspired by nature and have a passion for combining textures and love all forms of wood and paper. We also make time to have a coffee break each afternoon to unwind, regroup, and reassess what we have going on.

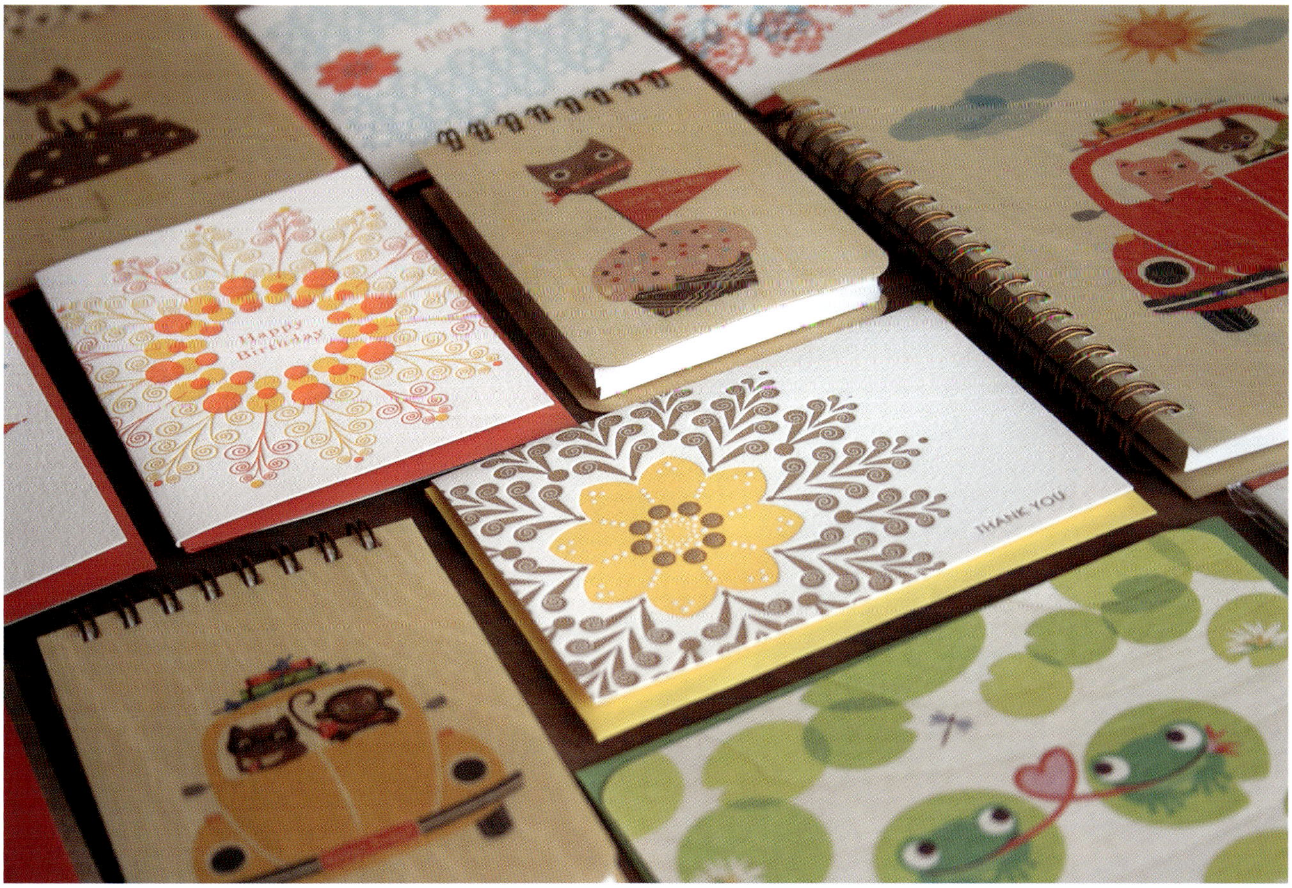

Night Owl Paper Goods products and co-owners Jennifer Tatham and Alan Henderson. *Courtesy of Night Owl Paper Goods.*

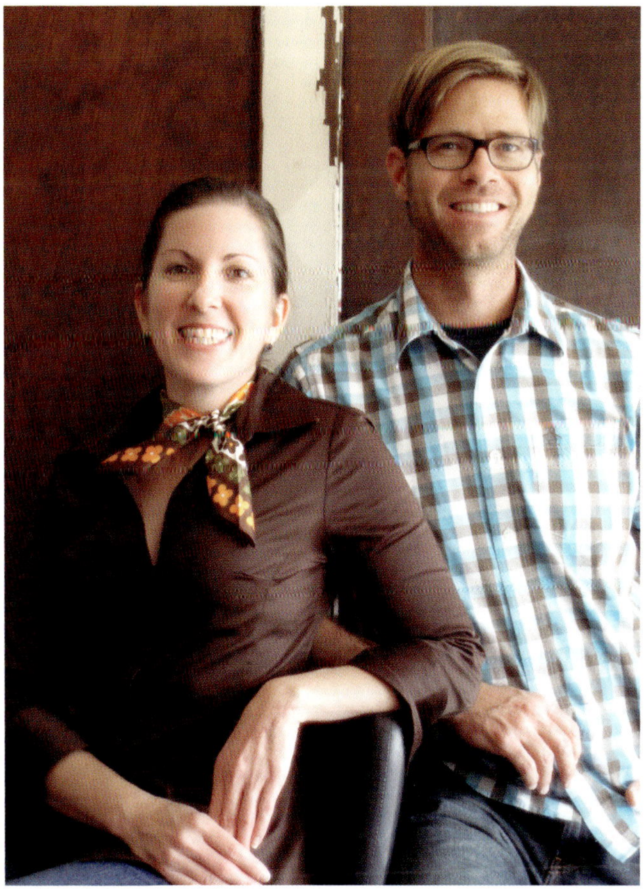

Rifle Paper Co.

What is your art and design background?

Growing up I focused on fine art (painting and drawing) but I attended college for graphic design. After graduating, I worked at a national magazine as an art director for a little over a year before going freelance. As a freelancer I worked as both a designer and illustrator and after a few years I began to focus on designing stationery products.

When did you know that you wanted to put your artwork onto stationery products?

A few close friends asked me to design their wedding invitations and I immediately fell in love. It was such a great medium to experiment with illustration and designing a whole package of paper goods. I started getting more and more wedding work and that led me to focus on designing stationery products.

What do you focus on most as a stationery artist—your custom wedding collection, personalized notes, or new product development?

For the past year or so I was focusing on custom wedding invitations, but I'm beginning to shift my attention to new product development. I love coming up with new ideas and seeing products through from the first sketch to final production.

What is your typical workday like?

Lately my workday is all day long. I've been working a lot the past year to get the business up and running. I typically put in about 12 to18 hours a day doing everything from illustrating custom work to overseeing production to managing aspects of the business (which usually means lots of emails).

Your work has been featured on many of the popular blogs; was that something that you aspired to or did it happen by chance?

It happened by chance when one or two blogs first featured one of my wedding invitations and coverage sort of spiraled from there. I feel very fortunate to have been embraced by the blogging community this past year. They've been so wonderful and supportive of our work and I would not be where I am today without them.

What are some of the pros and cons of being a husband and wife team?

At the end of the day I couldn't ask for anyone better to work with than my husband. The biggest con is that somtimes it's hard to separate work life from our personal lives and we can get lost in the business. The pro is that I have my best friend with me and our business partnership is rooted in something so deep. It's great to be able to be so honest and open with each other and have someone to bounce ideas off of and make decisions with. I'm not sure that it would work for everyone but I think one of the biggest keys for us is that we also complement each other in our skill sets as business partners.

What are some of your challenges and how do you overcome them?

My biggest challenge right now is balance. Because we're so new and in a period of growth I've been devoting everything I have to our business. I love it but it's also important to balance life and work so that you feel recharged and energized to create new things.

Tell us a little bit about your studio. What is the most inspiring thing in your studio?

We moved into our new studio a few months ago and I love the space. I think the location is the most inspiring thing about it. We're located in a quaint shopping district with brick streets and it's easy for me to take a walk to a park or a cafe. We're opening a retail space in the front of the studio so I'm also very excited about that and being in touch with people from the community.

Do you have any words of wisdom to artists who aspire to become stationery designers?

My advice is to not be afraid to take a risk and/or fail. I think a lot of people are intimidated to start a business but you really just have to take that first step and not be afraid of what might happen. I would also say that you should focus on having a unique voice and to ask yourself how your stationery line is different and unique.

What can we expect to see from you in the future?

I'm very excited about some upcoming projects. We're starting to branch out a little bit from strictly paper goods. For example, we're about to debut our new handcrafted wooden recipe card boxes. I'm also working on some personal projects that are an extension of the Rifle Paper Co. brand. I'm always open to new things and ideas so you never know what the future will hold! We just know that we're excited to be doing what we're doing and plan on sticking around for a while.

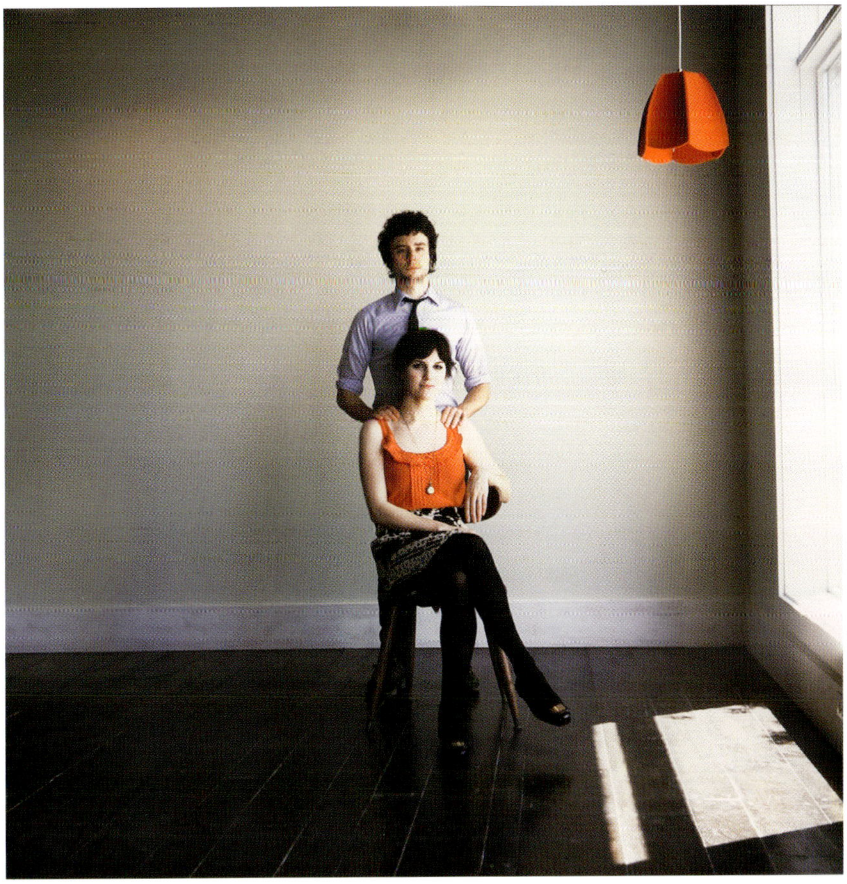

Nathan and Anna Bond in their Rifle Paper Co. studio. *Photographs by DuckDuck Collective.*

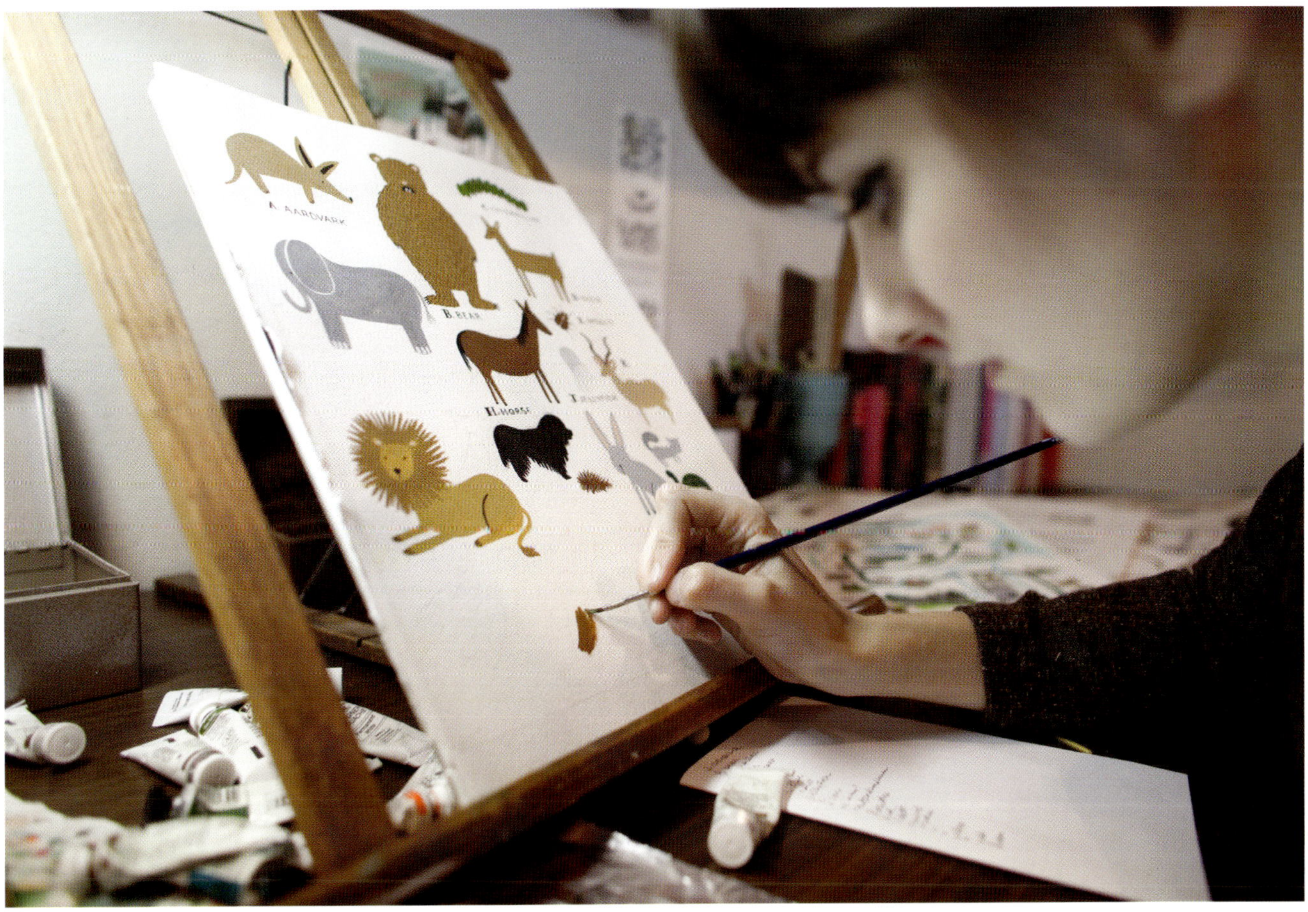

Sukie

You have such a wide range of products other than stationery; what is your favorite product to design?

I still love designing the notebook side of our range the most.

As parents of young twins, how do you manage to keep your family life and work life balanced?

Oscar and Jacob are two years old and we also have our daughter, Kitty, who is now five. We have an office and a studio in our home, so it can be somewhat noisy! In the day to day we have to keep the work side of the house quite separate but it works well for us as it gives us a lot flexibility. Also it means that we get to see the children a lot more than we would otherwise.

What kind of art background do you both have?

Julia and I both studied art at school, then did a year's foundation course followed by a BA in Illustration at Brighton University (where we first met!). After that, I went on to do even more studying at the Royal College of Art in London for two years. It was after graduating from there that we set up Sukie.

What inspires you most during the design process?

I love collecting old books on lots of different subjects. Children's books, nature study books, school books, and books on birds, plants, trees, flowers, planes, buildings, folk art, insects, etc. I also have a collection of old notebooks, from accounts books dating from 1840 to 1930s diaries to 1960s American stationery to modern Indian notebooks. I am also always inspired by printing processes; whether it's letterpress, lino, faxing, or rubber-stamping, I love the fact that an image I have created goes through a process and becomes something else.

How much time do you commit to design versus business?

At the moment I would say that 80% of our time is taken up with business. When I do get a chance to do some design it has to get squeezed into a couple of weeks here and there. That said, we are always discussing and having ideas for new ranges and products.

Tell us about your studio. How important is it to you to keep an inspirational workspace?

Our Office /studio is functional but I find it very necessary to be surrounded by inspiring stuff. So we have a mix of pictures, postcards, old maps, and posters on the walls and various random objects that find themselves on shelves.

You have a very successful line of paper goods with Chronicle Books and Nineteen Seventy Three, how did those partnerships start?

We have always loved what they do at Chronicle Books and we would always see and talk to them at trade shows such as the New York International Gift Fair. We were always a bit wary of how we could work together, seeing as we are both producing stationery products. After about three years of saying hi, we decided to give it a go and signed up to start with a small range for them that would not conflict with the products that we were producing. We haven't looked back since, as they are so enthusiastic, easy to work with, and do great stuff with our designs.

Nineteen Seventy Three approached us a couple of years ago to produce a range of wrapping paper for them. Cards and wrap are an area that we had not explored so when we saw their lovely range and knew that our style would fit in well. They also happen to live just up the road from us!

Do you have any advice for stationery artists who want to get started in licensing their work?

We started by making the books ourselves and by hand selling them to stores, this evolved into getting the books manufactured for us, as the bulk of our business is wholesale supply to stores. I think this gave us exposure to companies such as Chronicle Books who then had the confidence to start a relationship with us. So my advice would be to get your designs out into the world any way you can!

What is next on the horizon for Sukie?

A new range of children's textiles, a new range of notebooks, and some new home accessories. Also more projects for Chronicle Books and Nineteen Seventy Three.

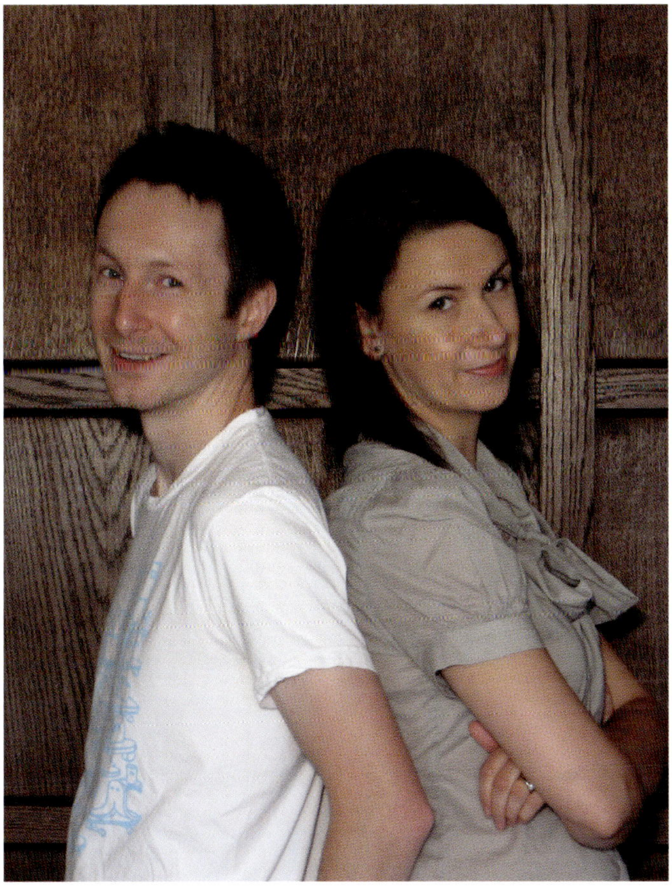

Darrell and Julia Gibbs in their Sukie studio.
Courtesy of Sukie.

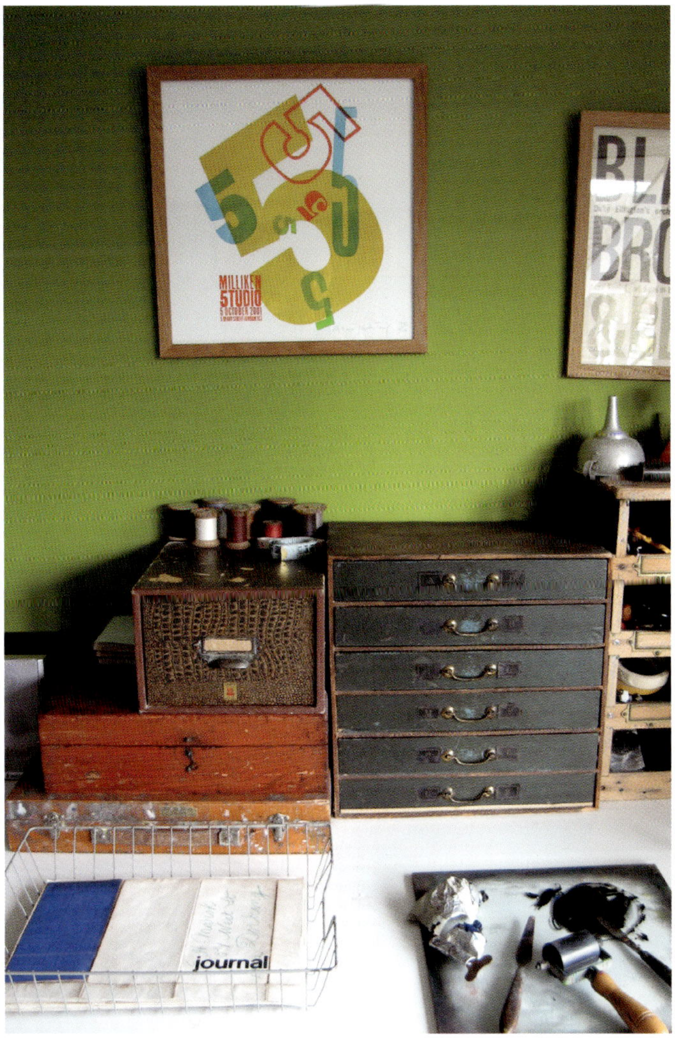

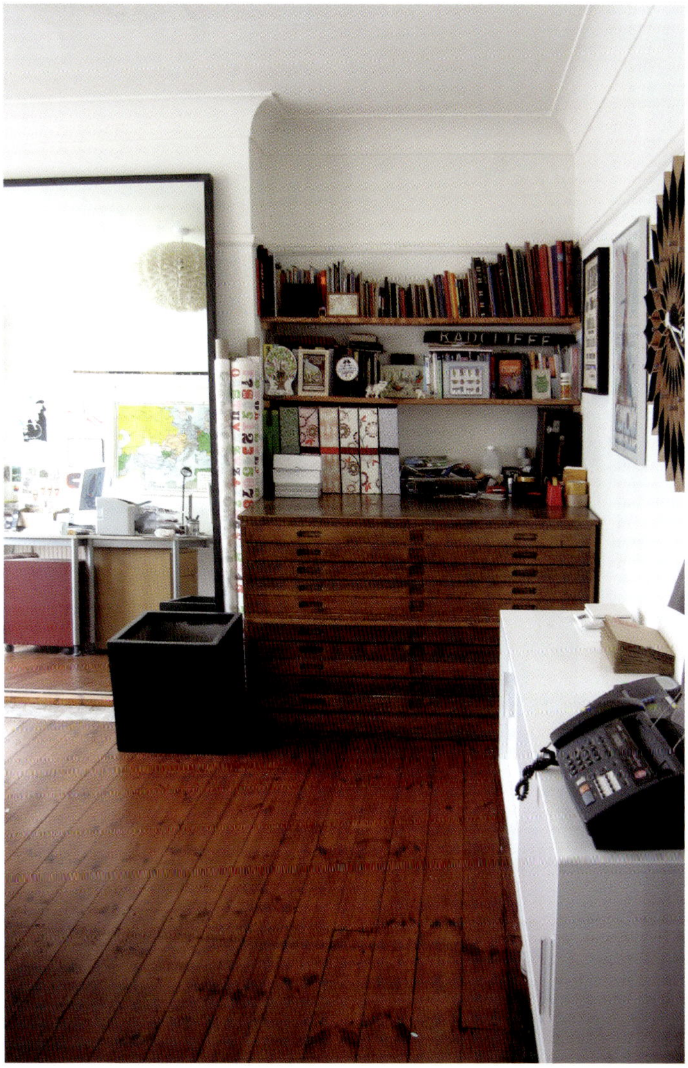

Whitney English

How did you get your start in the stationery industry?

I started working at a stationery store in 1994, stocking shelves, cleaning, and wrapping gifts. I worked there all the way through high school and college, eventually creating custom invitations for clients. After college, I decided to take the custom aspect of the business to a wholesale level.

How important are trade shows to your business?

Trade shows are vitally important to our business. As more of the retail world moves online, however, we're seeing a shift in trade shows heading towards the online world as well, resulting in more localized shows. The core principle of showing our products in a trade setting remains at the heart of our business, nevertheless.

How often do you launch a new collection?

We launch a line of products for summer every January. In May, we do two releases: a selection of fall and holiday products, as well as a collection of wedding and baby products.

How do you stay on top of the trends?

I'm constantly inspired by trends in fashion and home interiors. Not only do I constantly read magazines and design blogs, I attend design conferences across the nation.

What inspires you most?

My family is my most inspirational influence. Every Christmas, I design new products for all of them, and many of those go on to become some of our best sellers.

When did you know it was time to hire employees?

The best move I ever made was to hire a guru of a bookkeeper. I knew it was time to hire when I started spending more time processing orders and answering the phone than I did creating products.

How important has social networking been for your company?

Networking, in the physical sense and in the online sense, has been a key factor in propelling our company towards major success. The connections I have made in the industry over the years continue to encourage us and challenge us to be better.

What is the most important thing you have learned in all of the years of running your own company?

Running a business is nothing but constant reinvention of yourself and your ideas. To stay on top, you have to keep thinking up new ideas, and infusing the company with fresh vision and perspective. Additionally, hire people smarter than you are.

What advice would you give to an aspiring stationery artist?

Stationery is an easy market to get into, but that also makes it an easy market to fail in. In this day and age of desktop publishing, anyone can print note cards, but not everyone can make them unique and different. If you want the support of the industry, and to experience success driven by your designs, only dive in if you have something different to offer.

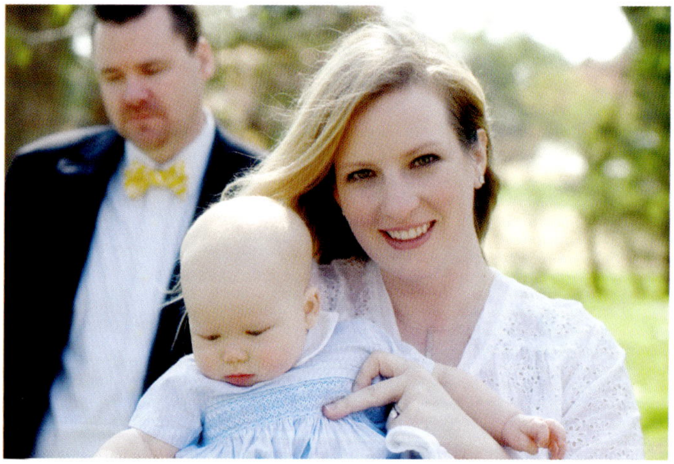

Whitney English Kolb, founder of Whitney English. *Courtesy of Whitney English Kolb.*

Yellow Bird Paper Greetings

When did you know you wanted to be a stationery artist?

I didn't—I fell into this role of stationery designer quite unintentionally. In retrospect it seems so "logical" that I would end up in the stationery business as at an early age I had a love for all things paper and collected wrapping paper, matchboxes, stickers, and paper shopping bags.

How has your background in fashion and marketing helped you run your own creative stationery business?

It is one thing to be creative and quite another to have a head for business. To be able to "marry" the two is the key to being successful. My background in the fashion industry was very corporate and taught the importance of a business plan, forecasting, assortment planning, sell throughs, etc.

What were the first steps you took get your stationery into stores?

Stores started calling me—from there I took on cold calling until the line was large enough to seek the help of sales reps. Now our fabulous reps take on that role.

You have an impressive number of designs in your collection (over 1000). How often do you launch new designs?

I launch a new collection every three months.

How do you stay inspired?

It sounds so cliché, but truly inspiration is everywhere I look.

What is a typical day like for you?

I am up at 5am with my youngest son—check emails—make breakfast / lunches for my three boys, get them out the door to school / daycare—dash to the office by 9am—my office time is far from "typical." I do anything and everything from designing, helping our shipper pack orders, customer service calls, press checks, and meeting with customers. You name it and it can happen for me in a workday. I then dash to pick up my children at 3pm. When my children are in bed at 8pm, I am back on the computer working remotely from home. I usually try and wrap up my workday by 11pm. When you are blessed to get to do what you love to do, it really is effortless and I am indeed blessed.

What is your favorite part about working for yourself?

Everyday I am so grateful that I get to do what I love to do ... I am humbled by the fact that people like what I do and buy my designs. It is so important in life to do what you love first and foremost—everything else will "fall into place."

What is the biggest change you have seen in the industry in the last five years?

Online businesses seems to be popping up everywhere.

What would you say is the mantra for your company?

Have fun—work hard—laugh lots!

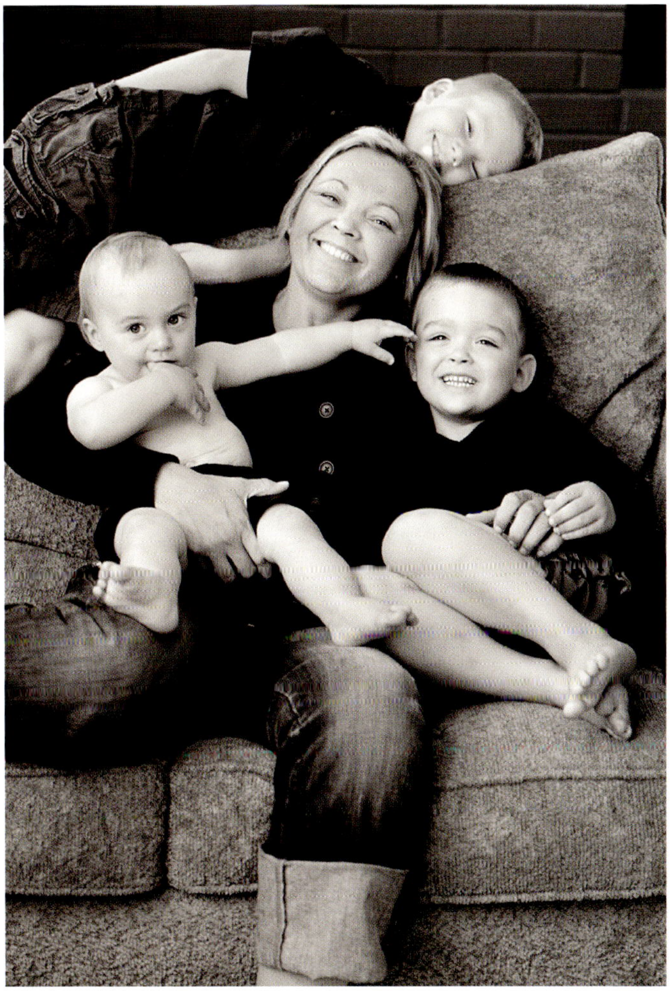

Charmaine Carlson of Yellowbird Paper Greetings with her kids. *Photograph by Shannon Eckstein.*

Gallery of Work

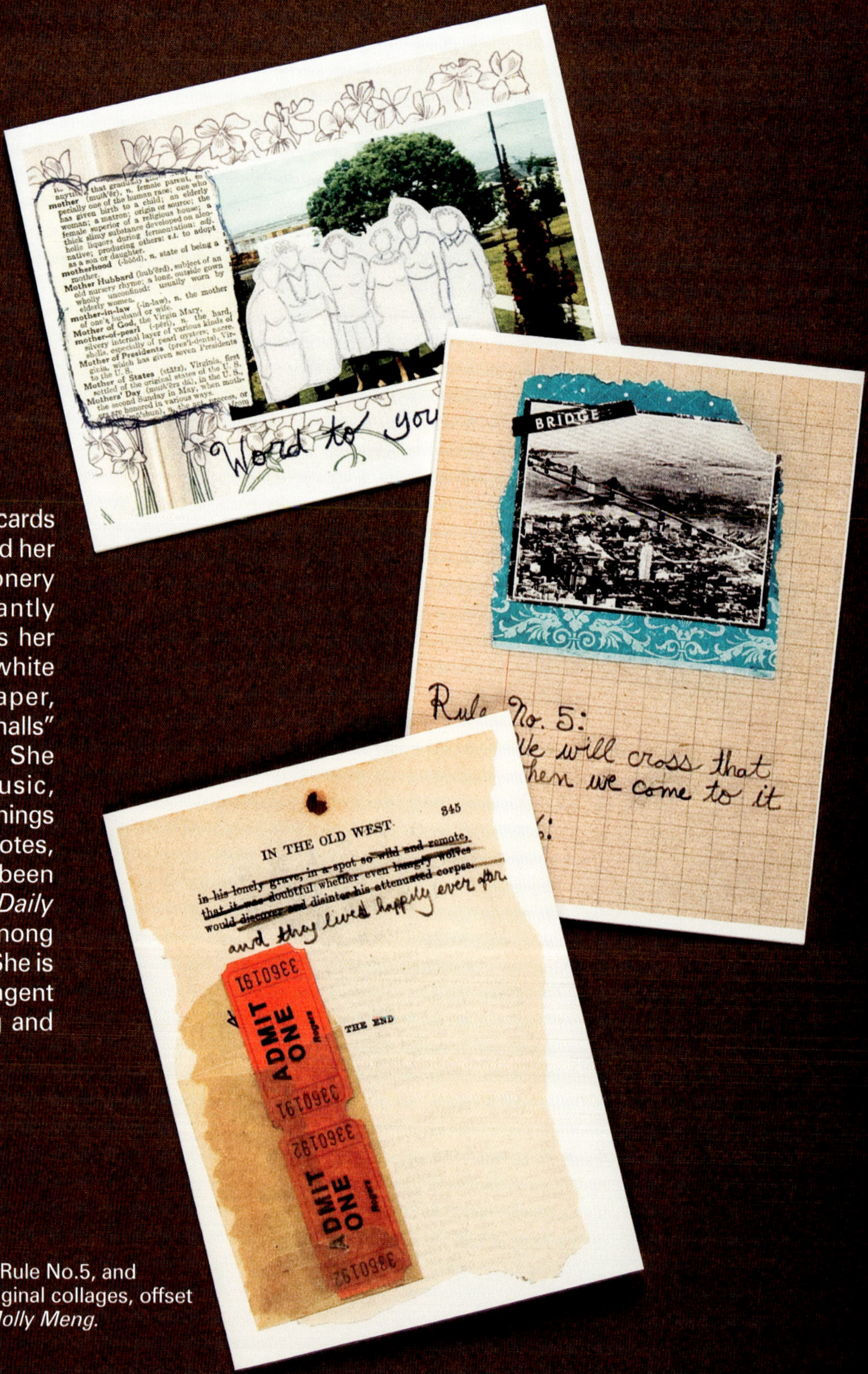

8mm Ideas

www.8mmideas.com

Molly Meng has been making cards since 1999, but officially launched her company at the National Stationery Show in 2004. She is constantly inspired by the past: the stories her elders tell her, the black and white photos she finds, vintage paper, textiles, children's books, and "smalls" (objects that fit in your hand). She is also highly inspired by music, dictionaries, all reference books, things she overhears, inspirational quotes, color, nature, and love. She has been profiled on *Apartment Therapy, Daily Candy,* and *Design*Sponge* (among other design-specific websites). She is currently working with a literary agent who would like to turn her blog and artwork into a book.

Word to Your Mother, Rule No.5, and Happily Ever After. Original collages, offset printed. *Courtesy of Molly Meng.*

Little Boy Rides, Merrily on Her Way, Bulldog, and Beat of a Different Drummer. Original collages, offset printed. *Courtesy of Molly Meng.*

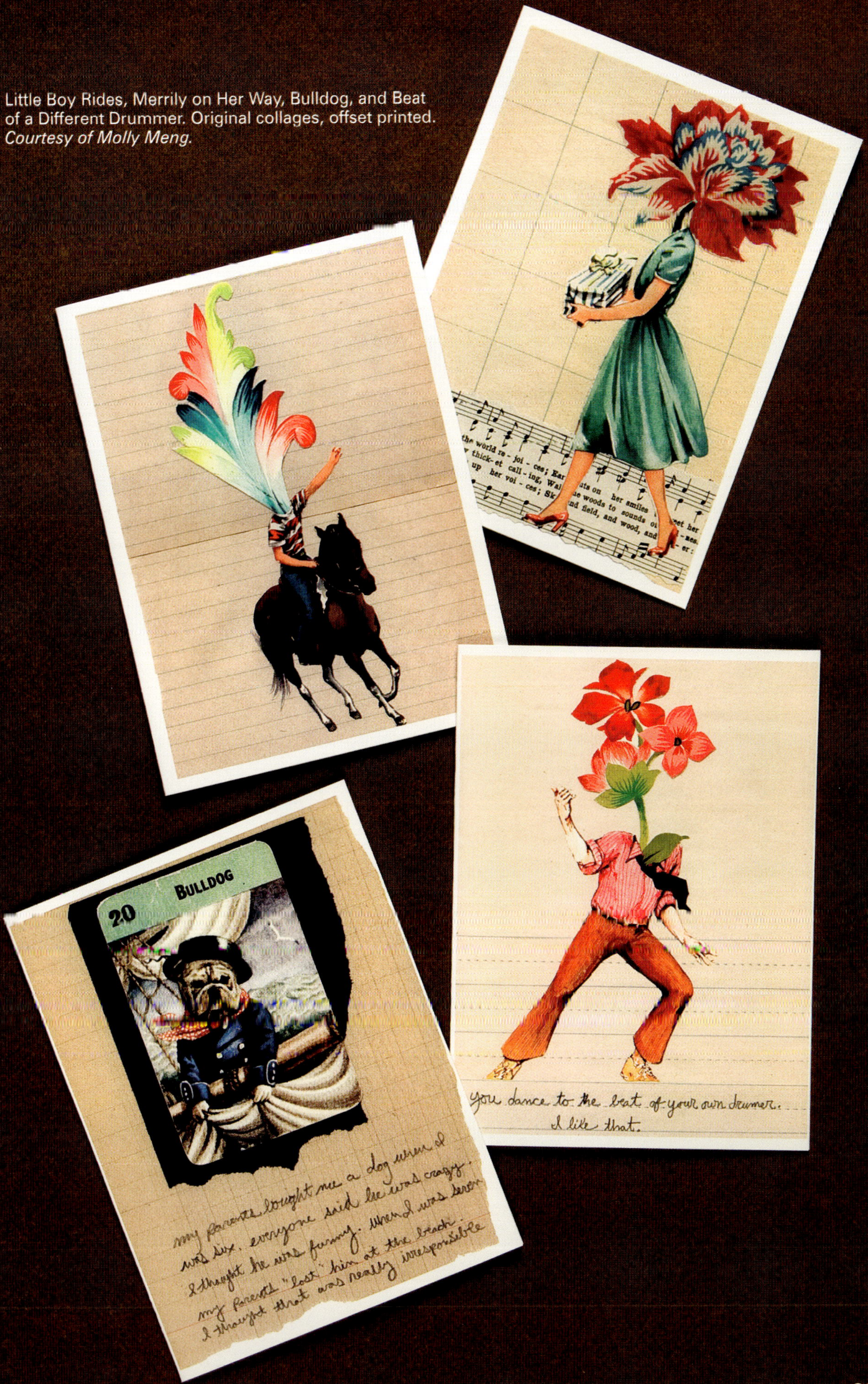

a. favorite design

www.afavoritedesign.com

Amber J. Favorite started creating cards as a hobby in 2003 and started creating under the name "a. favorite design" in 2005. She is a graphic designer turned letterpress artist and has always had a passion for design and typography which has fueled her desire to learn the art of letterpress printing and create a line of stationery. Her mission is to encourage long distance warm fuzzies through snail mail. Her inspirations include flea markets, sweet home Chicago, her muse Tom, amazing typography and carnivals, seeing live music, playing cards with friends, hunting for vintage treasures, watching the full moon rise over Lake Michigan, collecting pretty things, wearing Converse All-Stars and morning rubies, and playtime with the other love of her life, Smokey-doo (her 13 year-old Border Collie Lab mix shelter dog).

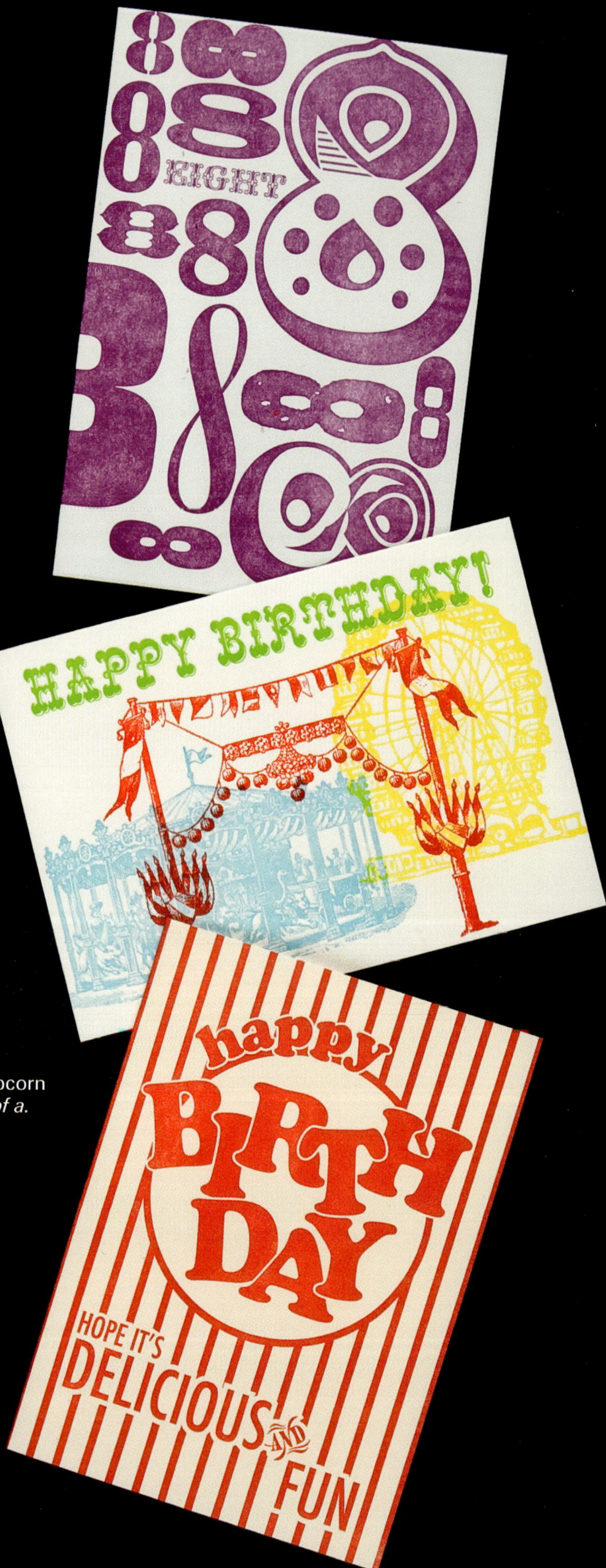

No. 8, Carnival Birthday, and Popcorn Birthday. Letterpress. *Courtesy of a. favorite design.*

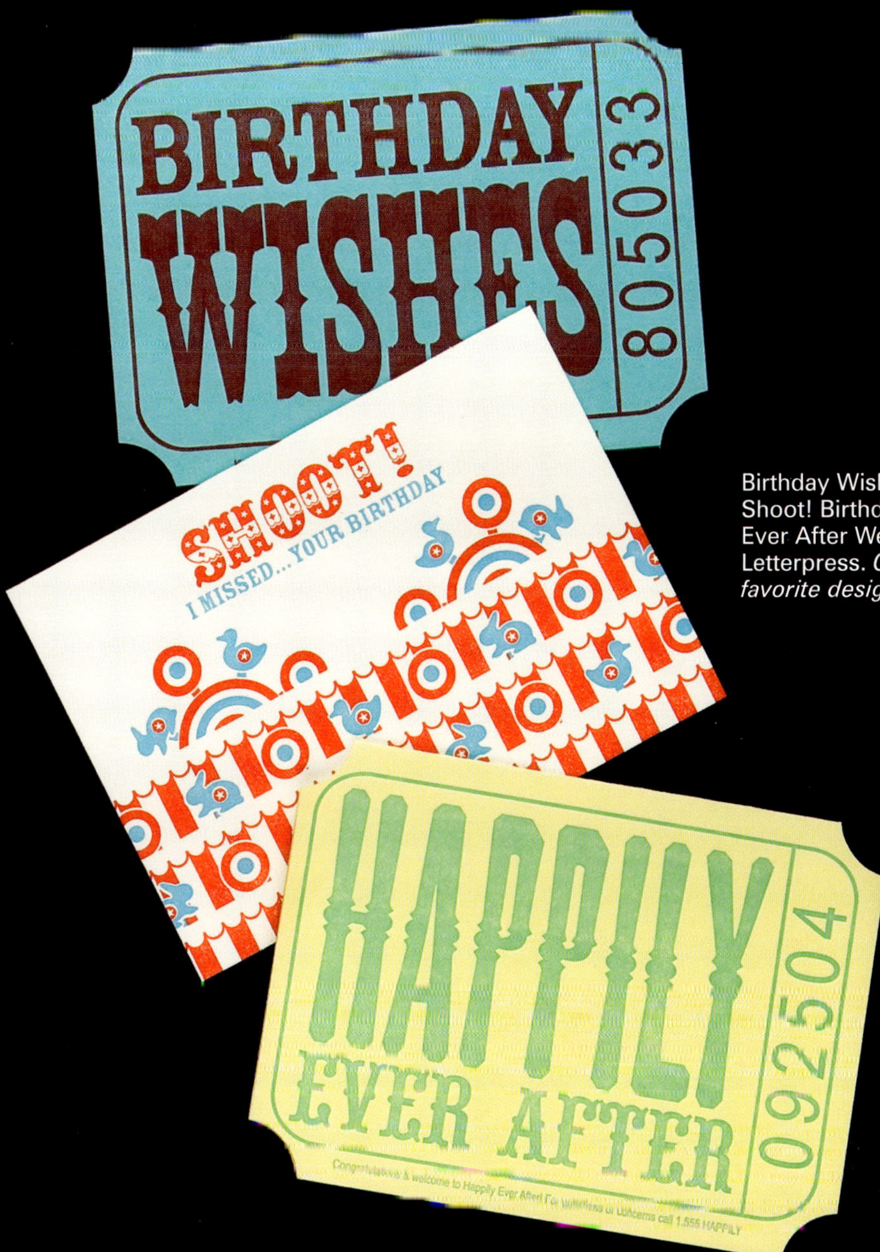

Birthday Wishes Ticket, Shoot! Birthday, and Happily Ever After Wedding Ticket. Letterpress. *Courtesy of a. favorite design.*

Amy Smyth Made It

www.amysmythmadeit.com

Amy Smyth launched her company at the National Stationery Show in May 2006. She has had a love of paper, color, and design for as long as she can remember. As a little girl she would be entertained for hours by looking through catalogs and feeling the paper. When Amy decided to start a stationery business based on her illustrations it was only natural that the products were going to have attitude; she is from Jersey, her family lives in Philly, and her husband is from Brooklyn. Amy also keeps busy by licensing her work. In 2007, her company partnered with Inkadinakdo to create a designer focused collection of clear and wooden stamps. In 2008, she partnered with Smilebox to create animated greeting cards for its online photo service and with Cardstore.com to provide customers with the opportunity to add photographs to her greeting card designs.

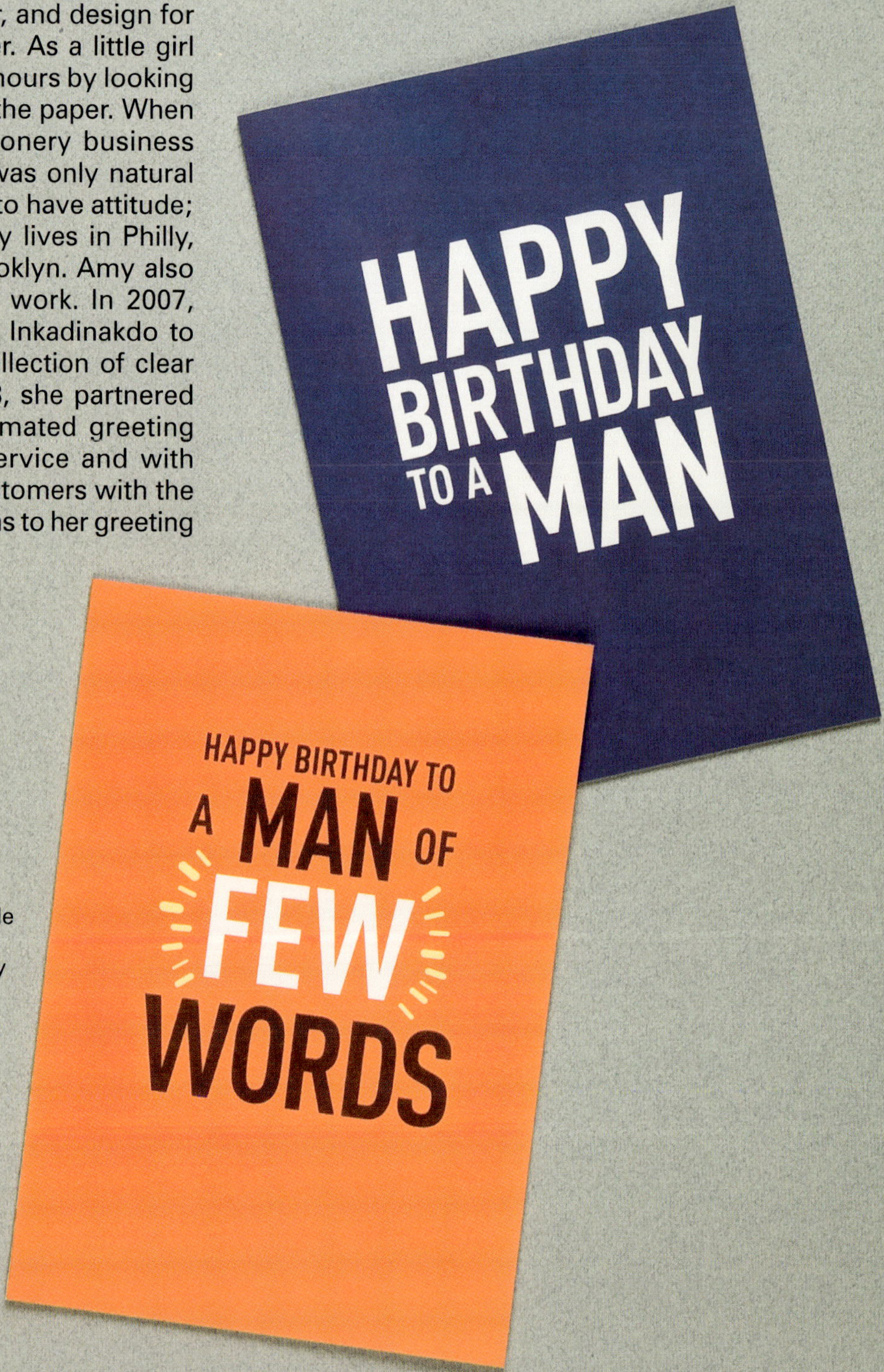

Happy Birthday to a Man (inside greeting: Who Has Good Taste in Women) and Happy Birthday to a Man of Few Words (inside greeting: From a Woman of Many, Many, Many Words). Printed with vegetable inks on 100% PCF paper. *Courtesy of Amy Smyth Made It.*

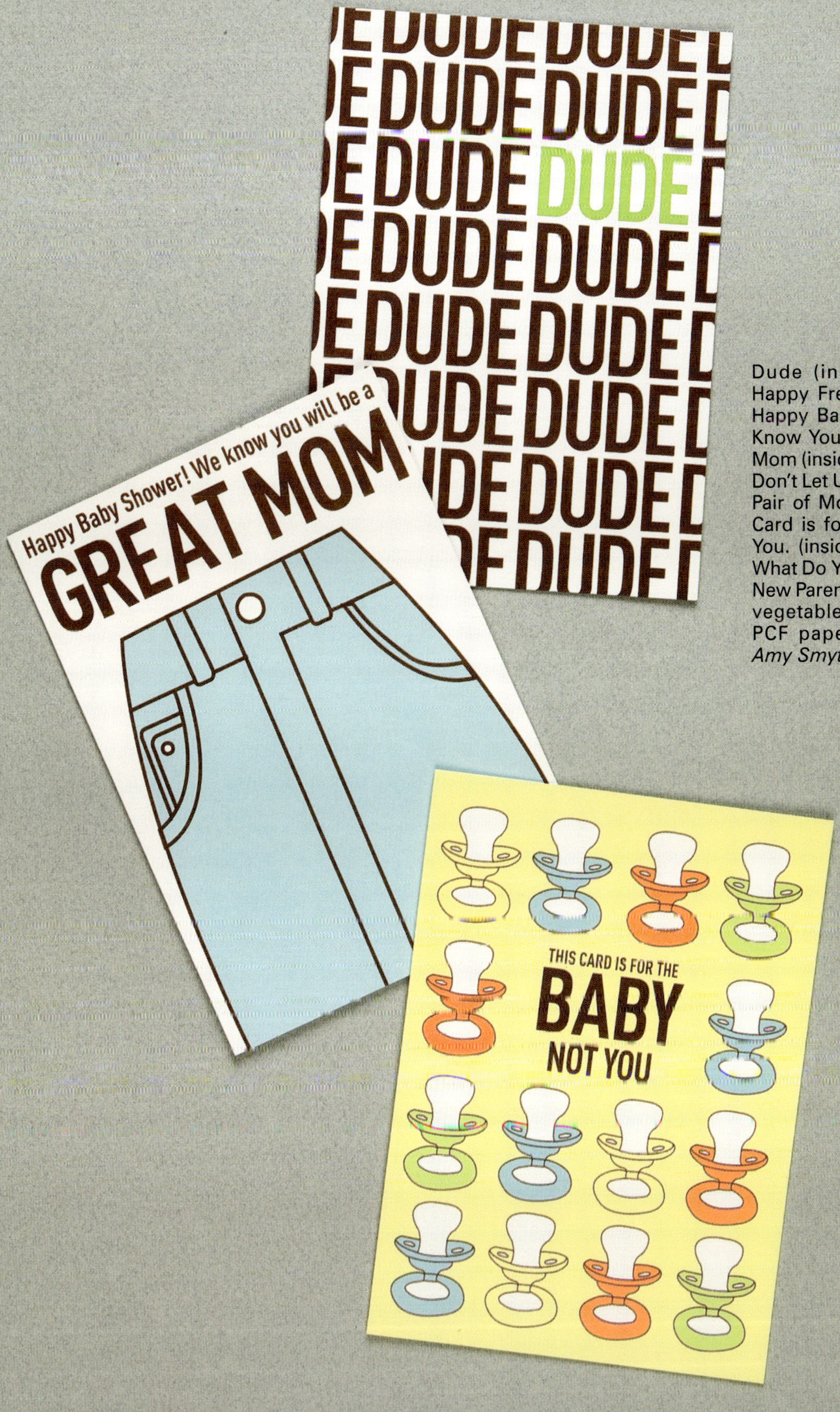

Dude (inside greeting: Happy Freakin' Birthday). Happy Baby Shower! We Know You Will Be a Great Mom (inside greeting: Just Don't Let Us Catch You in a Pair of Mom Jeans). This Card is for the Baby. Not You. (inside greeting: So, What Do You Think of Your New Parents?) Printed with vegetable inks on 100% PCF paper. *Courtesy of Amy Smyth Made It.*

Art School Girl

www.artschoolgirl.com

Amy Rowan became a stationer in September of 2004. She runs a small hands-on stationery company creating art and paper goods from vintage, recycled, and repurposed materials. Her aim is to design clever, limited edition stationery sets, books, art and greetings, with an eye to the past and a heart for modern personal communication. Her personal philosophy is to try to consume less, recycle more, and reuse wherever she can. In her work she tries to resuscitate surplus, discarded, and ordinary materials by repurposing them. She enjoys making old cast-offs desirable again as well as creating products that encourage personal correspondence and creative thinking.

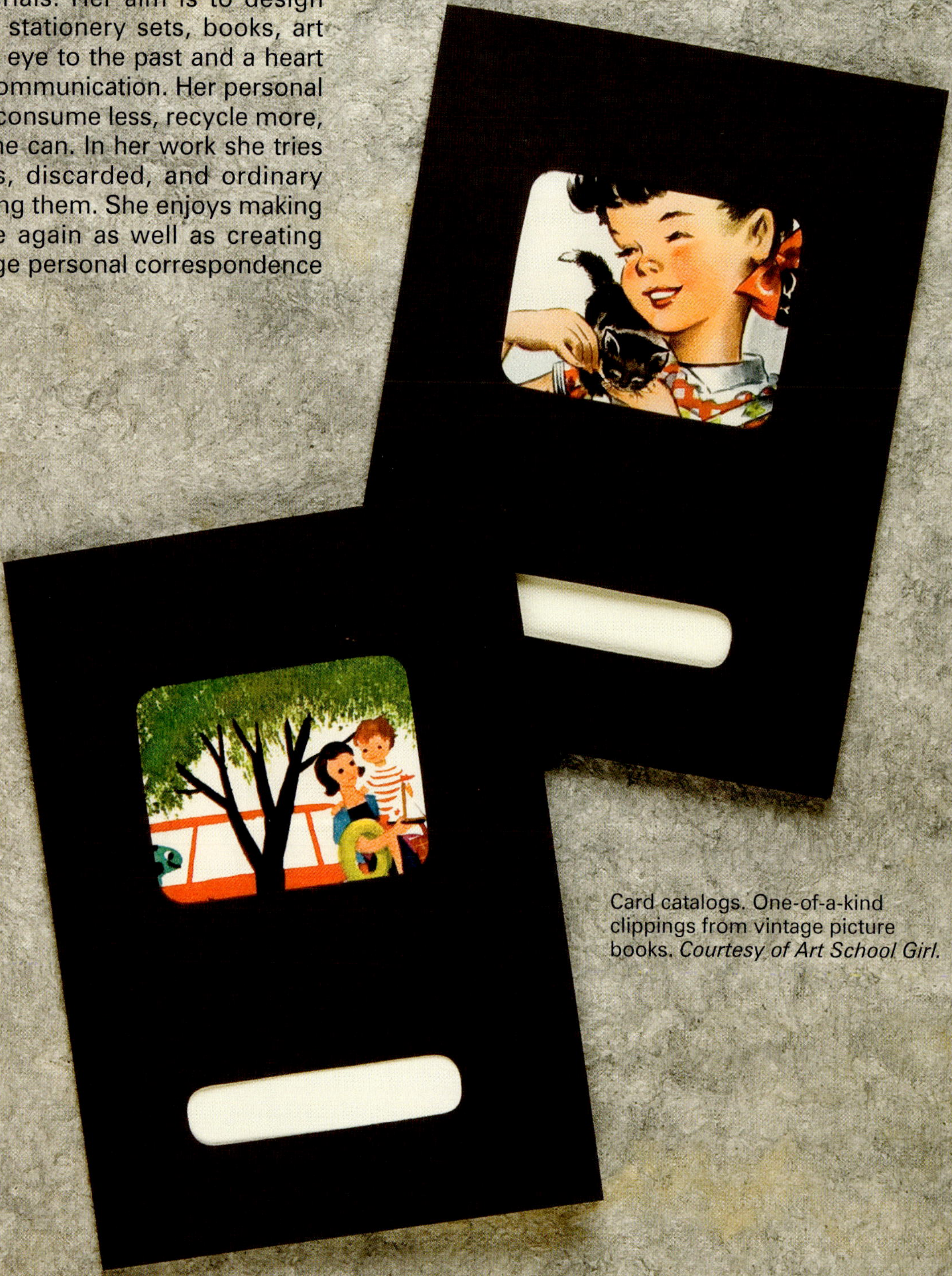

Card catalogs. One-of-a-kind clippings from vintage picture books. *Courtesy of Art School Girl.*

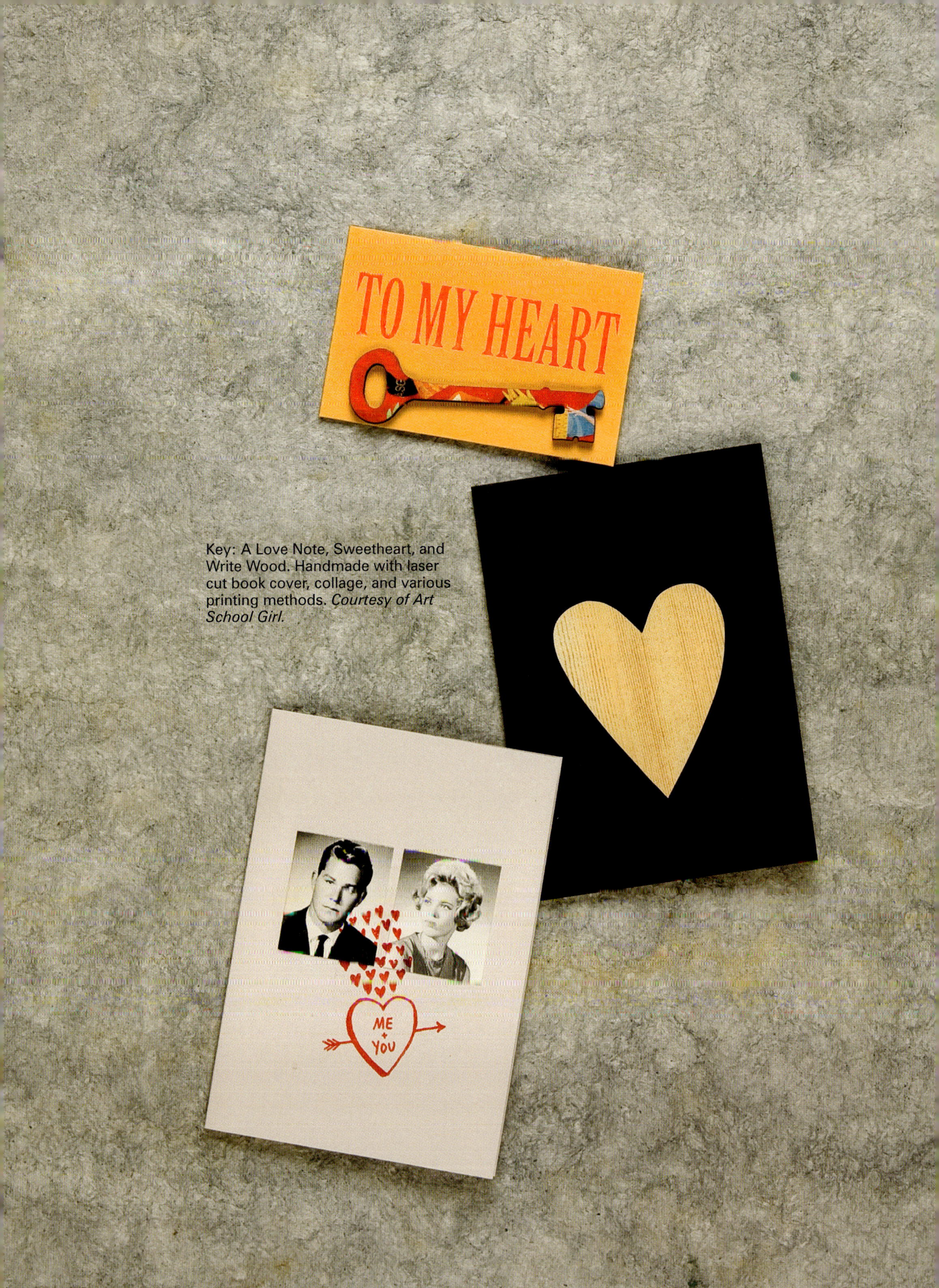

Key: A Love Note, Sweetheart, and Write Wood. Handmade with laser cut book cover, collage, and various printing methods. *Courtesy of Art School Girl.*

Blue Ribbon Design

www.blueribbondesign.com

Designer Kimberly Driessen started her stationery company, Blue Ribbon Design, in 2005. She is motivated by a lifelong love of decorative pattern and ornament and draws inspiration from a wide range of decorative arts including textiles, botanical prints, china patterns, and New York City's historic ironwork. Also, in addition to its beautiful architecture, New York's many museums, parks, and botanical gardens provide constant inspiration for new designs. The resulting designs are rich with references to the past, yet utterly modern in their simplicity, elegance, and exquisite craftsmanship. They have been featured in many publications including *Town & Country Weddings, Elegant Bride, Modern Bride, Lucky,* and *Vogue Australia.*

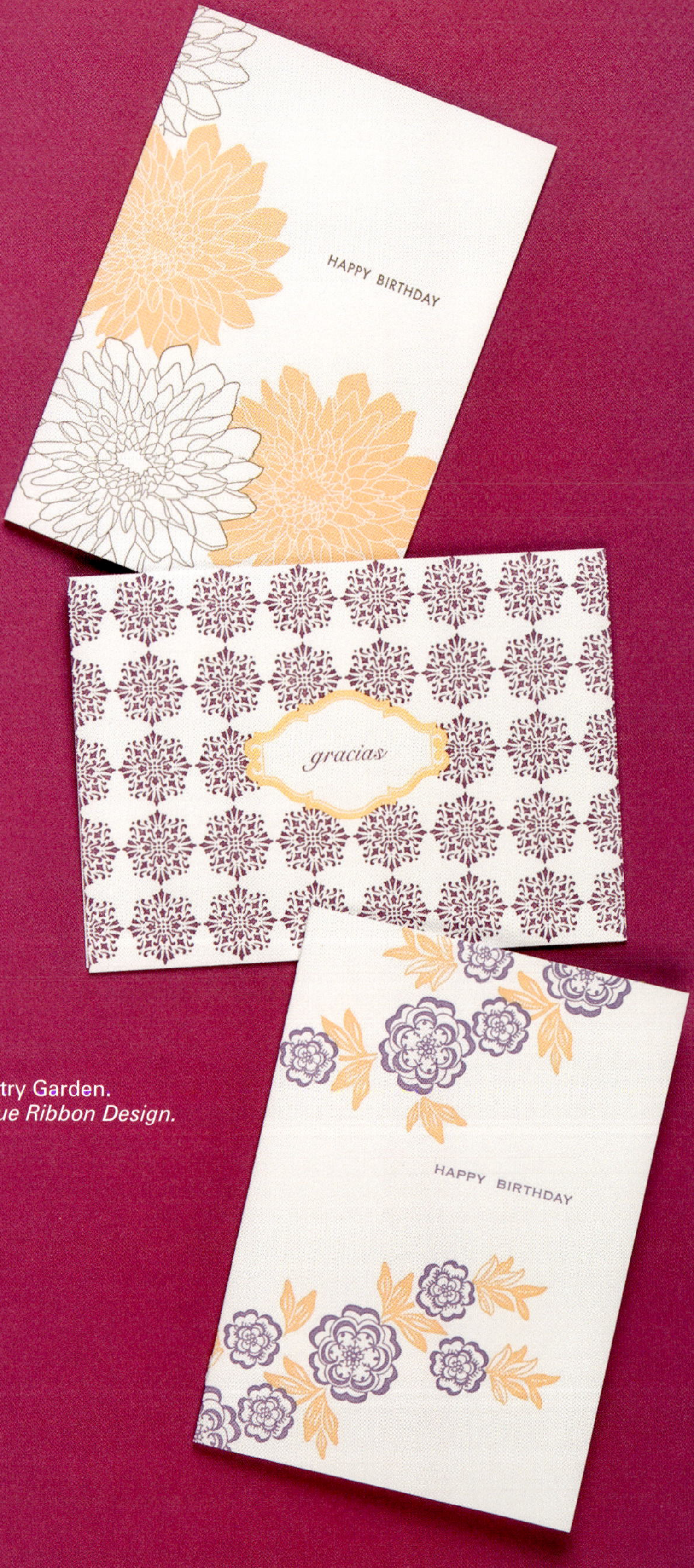

Dahlias, Gracias, and Country Garden. Letterpress. *Courtesy of Blue Ribbon Design.*

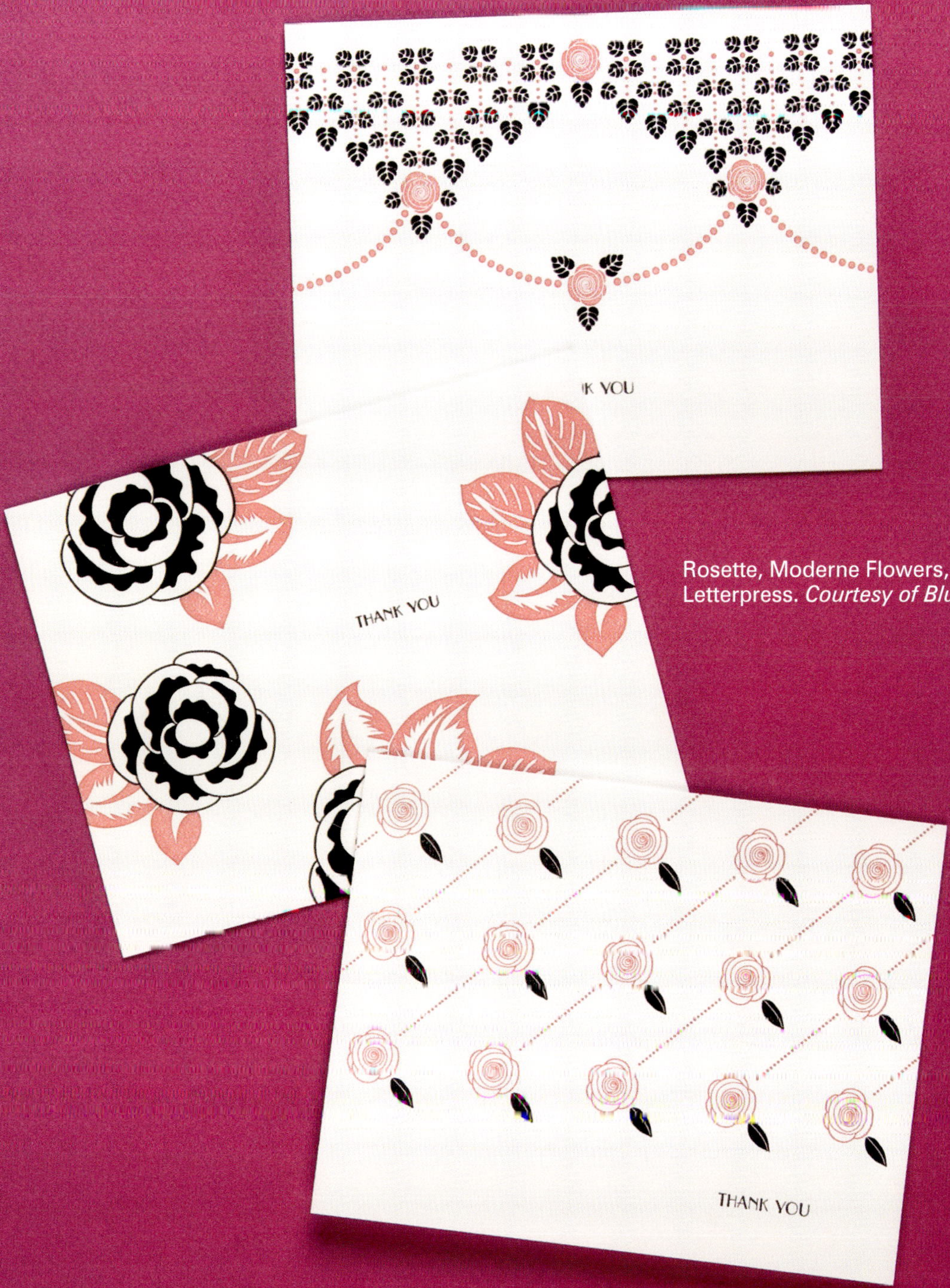

Rosette, Moderne Flowers, and Sorbet.
Letterpress. *Courtesy of Blue Ribbon Design.*

Bobbin

www.bobbindesigns.com

Jean Shackelford Johnson launched Bobbin (named after her great grandmother) at the 2006 National Stationery Show, but the idea came about when creating a final project while earning her MFA in fashion design at the Savannah College of Art and Design. Most recently she has relocated to Charlotte, North Carolina. Living in the South, wildlife, textiles, interior, and fashion design are all inspirations for Jean's work. She currently sells her line to retailers such as Kate's Paperie and Anthropologie. Bobbin prides itself on being eco-friendly and also adopts a manatee for every show order it receives.

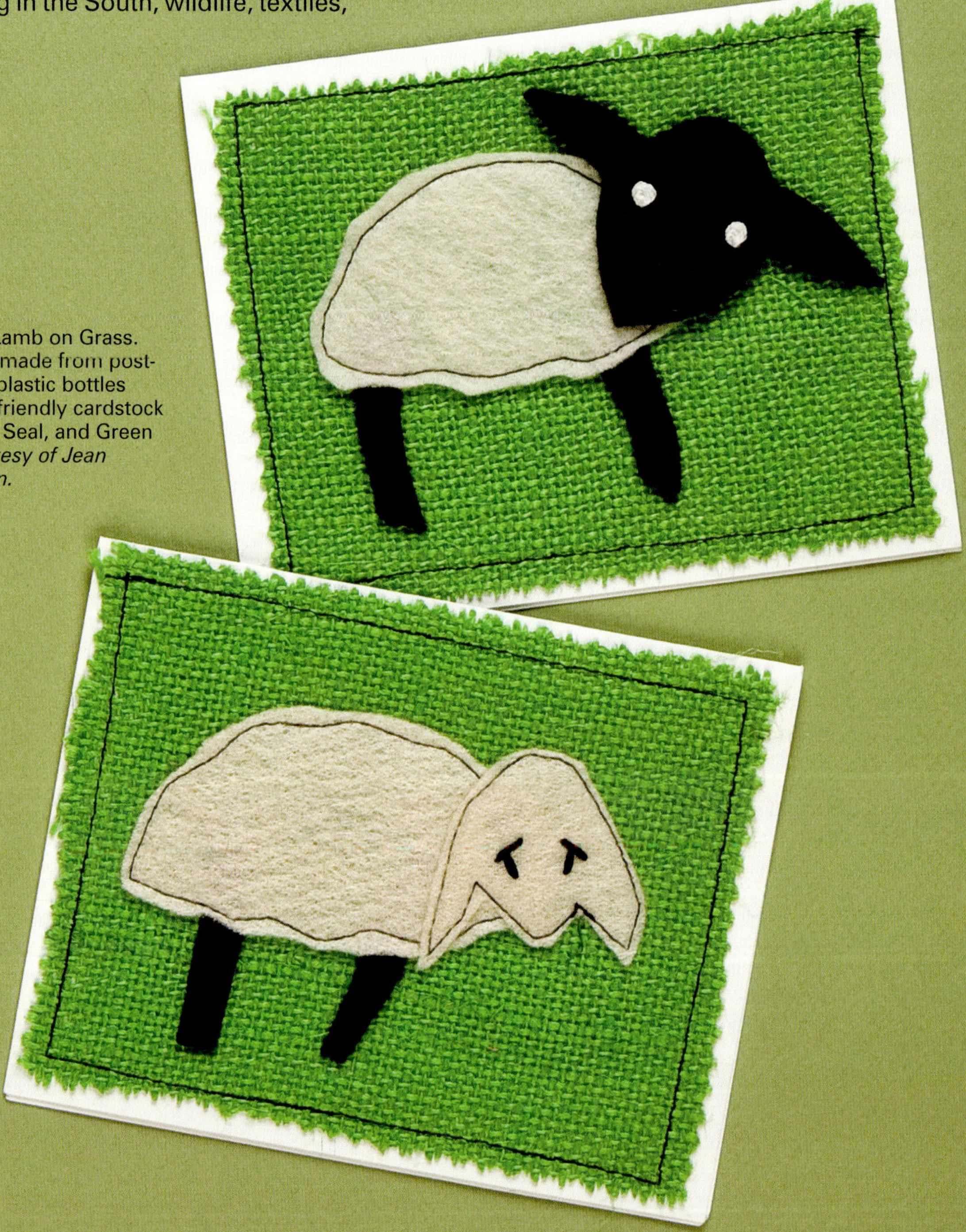

Goat on Grass and Lamb on Grass. Handmade with felt made from post-consumer recycled plastic bottles and sewn onto eco-friendly cardstock that has FSC, Green Seal, and Green E certification. *Courtesy of Jean Shackelford Johnson.*

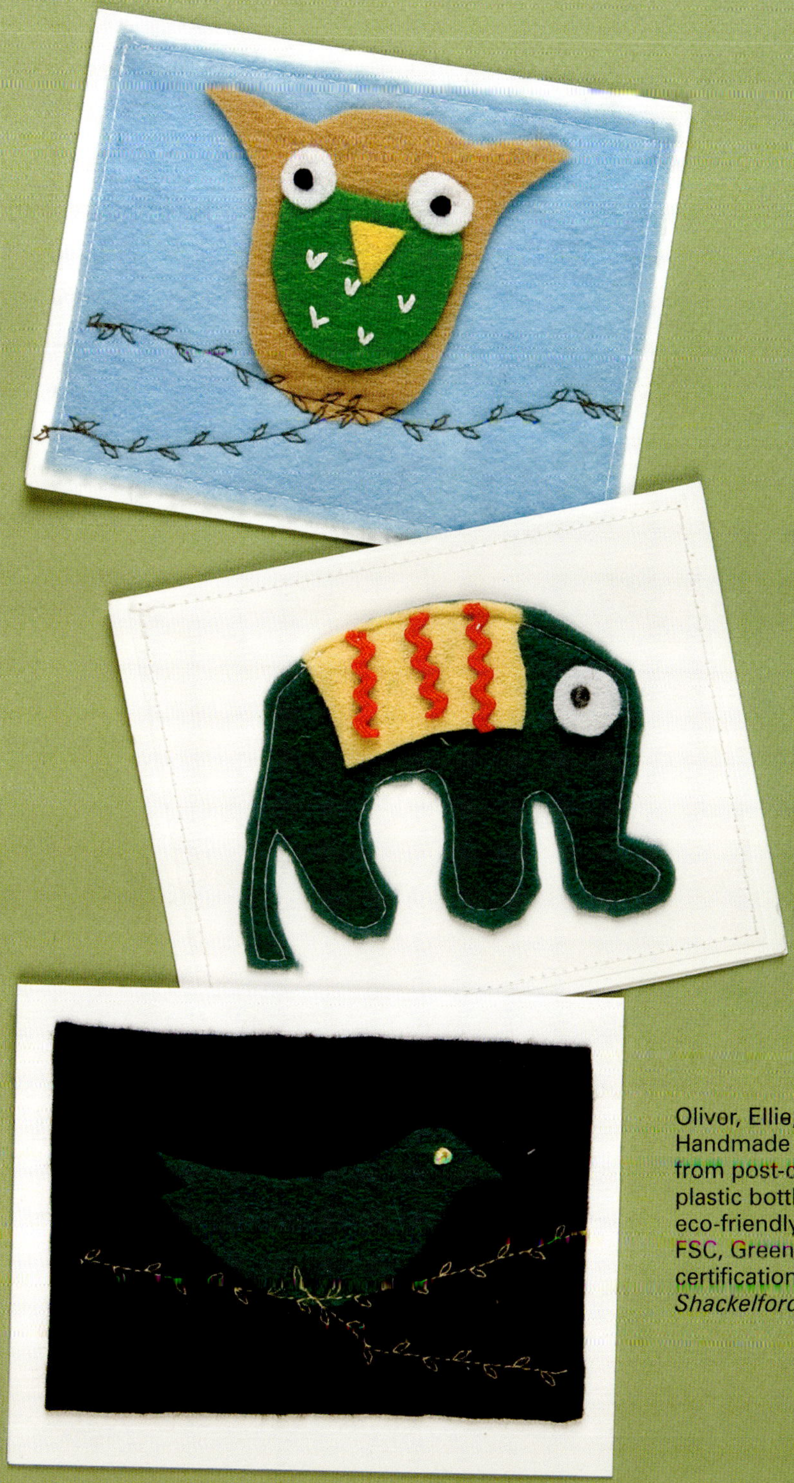

Oliver, Ellie, and Hardy. Handmade with felt made from post-consumer recycled plastic bottles and sewn onto eco-friendly cardstock that has FSC, Green Seal, and Green E certification. *Courtesy of Jean Shackelford Johnson.*

Carrot & Stick Press

www.carrotandstickpress.com

Susie Gelbron and Julie Walker founded Carrot & Stick Press in 2000. The two met at graduate school orientation and spent the first year of the program working collaboratively on a book project. After earning MFAs from the California College of Arts and Crafts, they started their company using a borrowed press in a drafty barn behind their professor's Berkeley home. Today, the company does all production on-site at their Oakland, California, studio, employing antique presses to produce their line of folded notes, gifts cards, and place cards. Their distinctive patterns are also available on offset printed notebooks, place mats, and photo cards. Their work has been featured in many national publications including *Vogue, Martha Stewart Living, Harper's Bazaar*, and *The New York Times*.

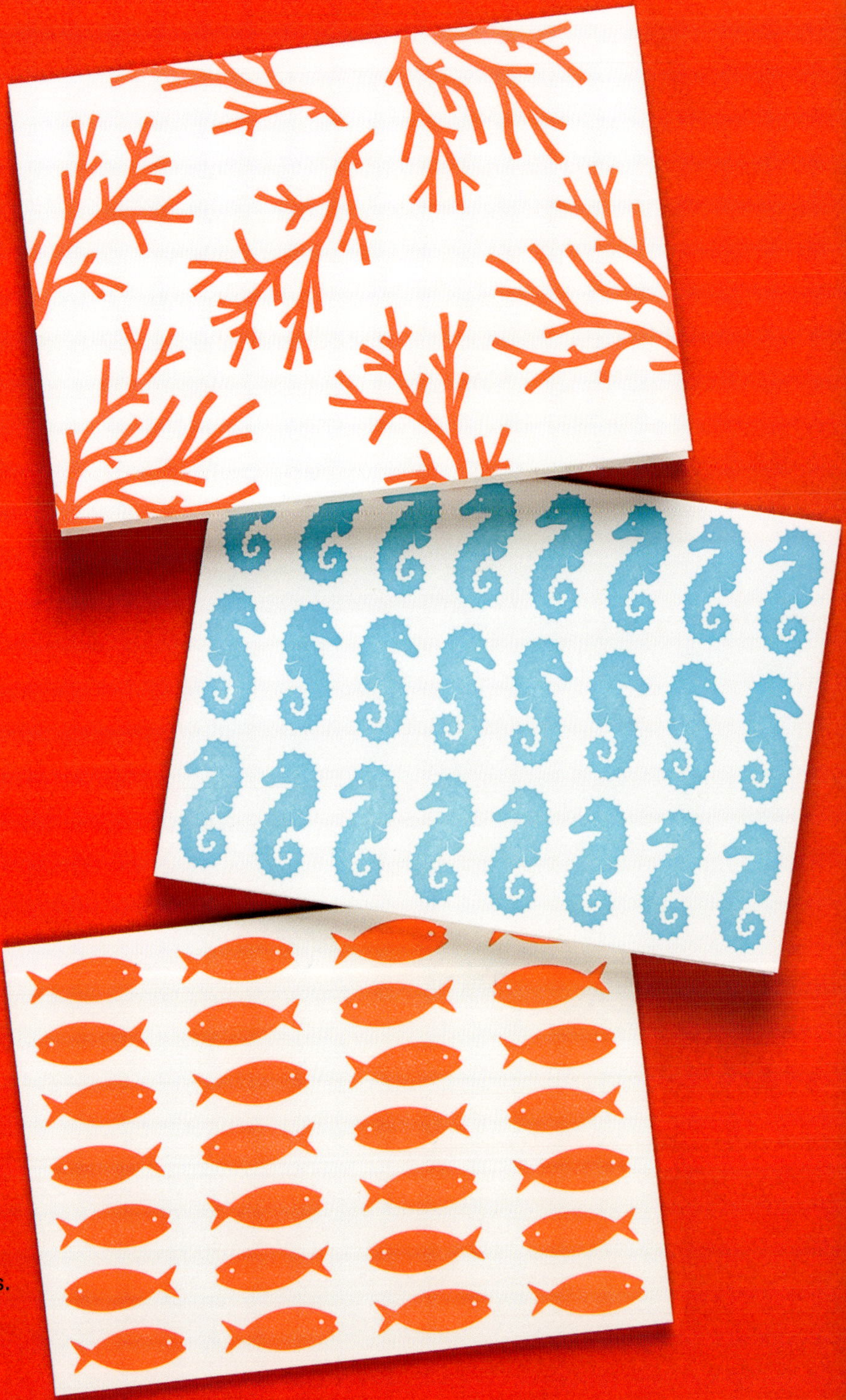

Coral, Seahorse, and Fish. Letterpress.
Courtesy of Carrot & Stick Press.

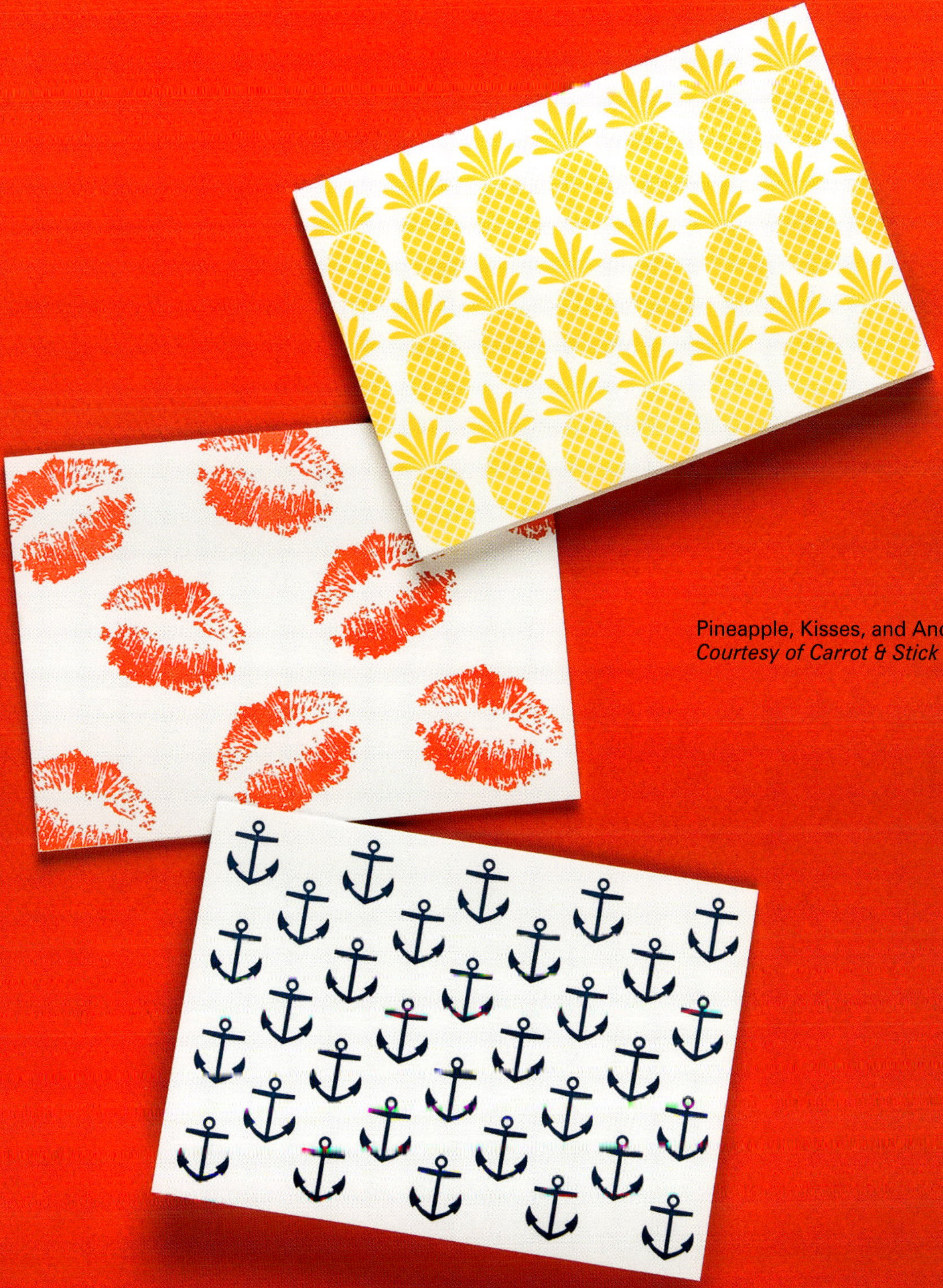

Pineapple, Kisses, and Anchor. Letterpress.
Courtesy of Carrot & Stick Press.

Cartolina Cards

www.cartolina.com

Fiona Richards launched Cartolina Cards in 2007. She lives and works in the quiet mountain town of Nelson, British Columbia. Her unique collages based on vintage imagery and type are inspired by her collections and travels around the world. Her cards have been featured in many magazines and newspapers including *Domino, Country Living, Vogue, The Washington Post,* and *Traditional Home*. Her cards are available all over the world, including Europe where she sells cards at some of the most chi chi stores such as Harrods, Harvey Nicholls, and Selfridges in London.

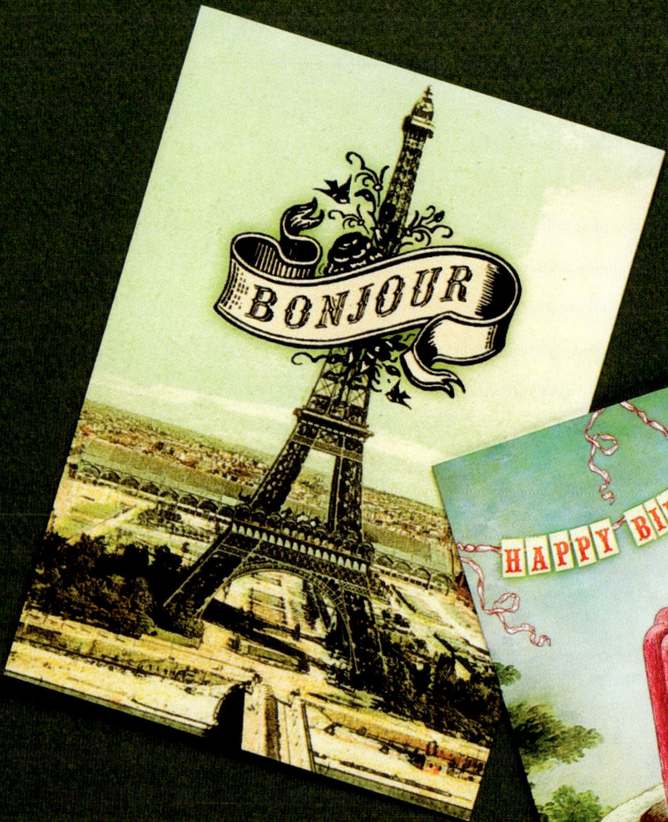

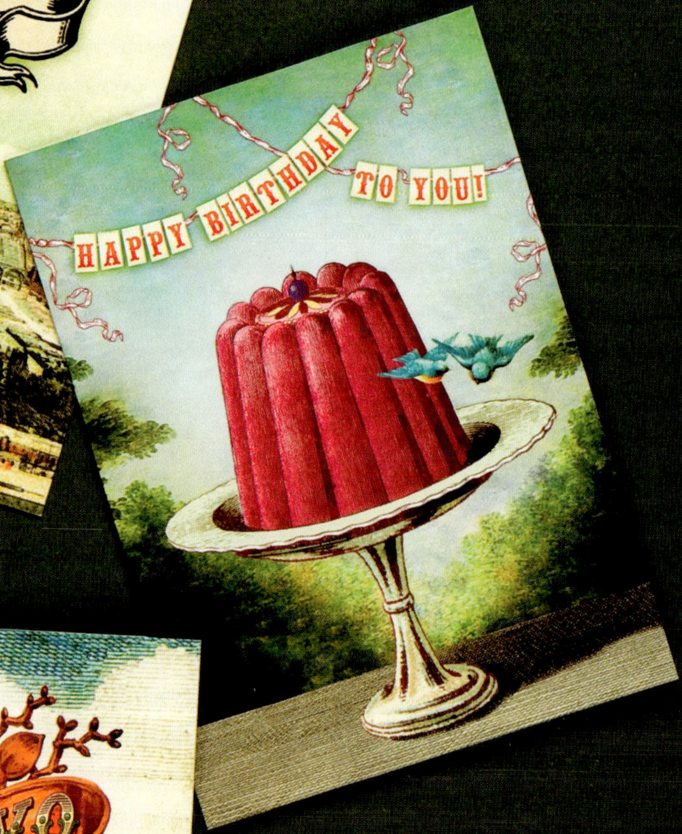

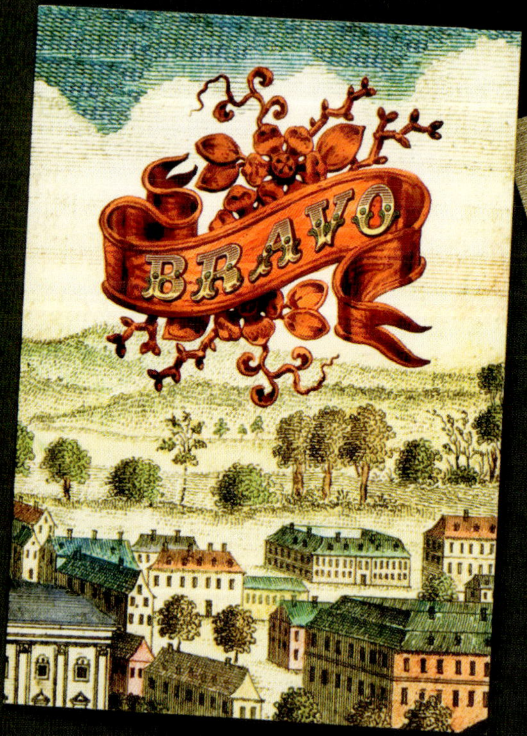

Bonjour, Happy Birthday To You, and Bravo. Printed on recycled paper. *Courtesy of Cartolina Cards.*

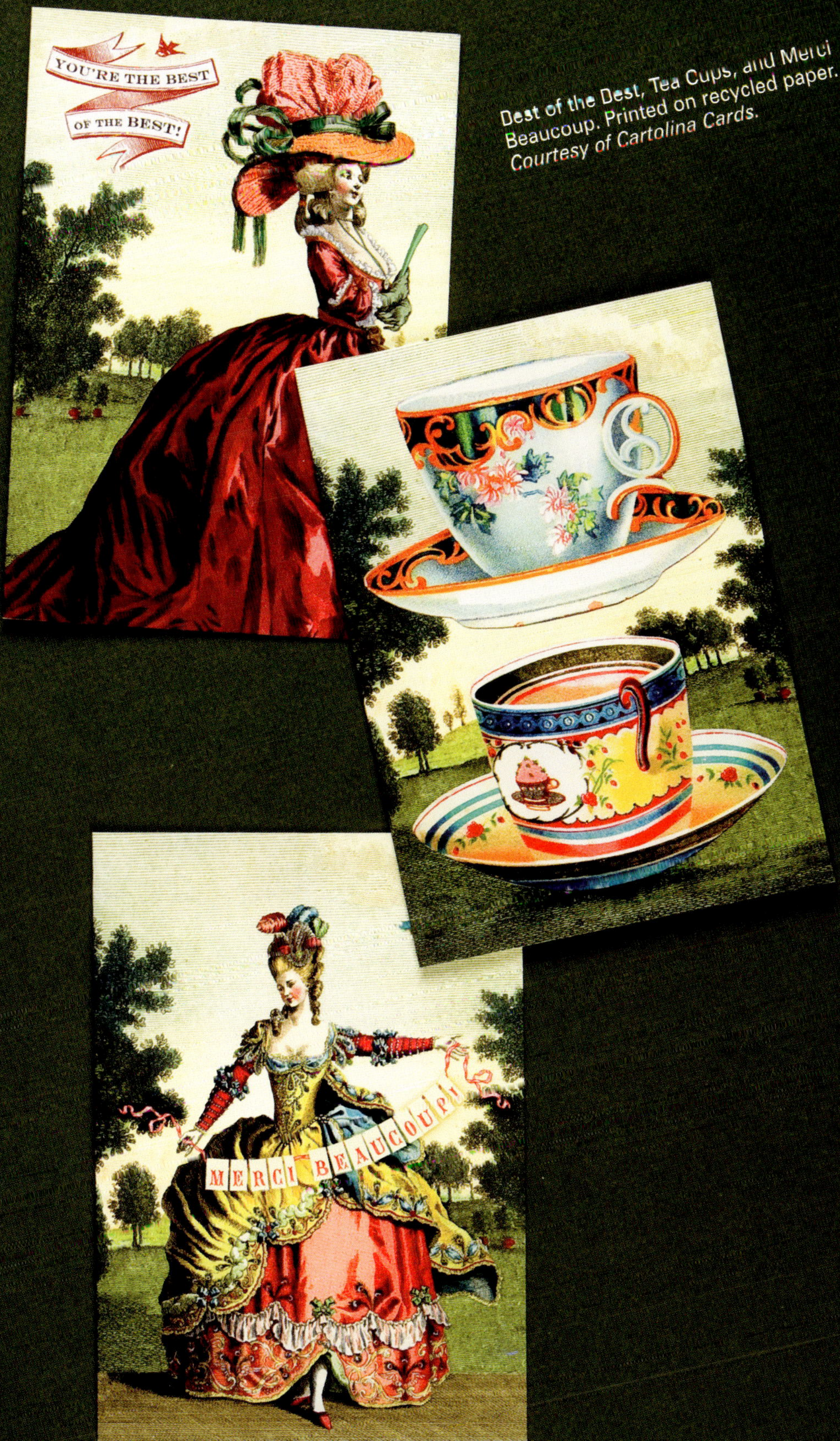

Best of the Best, Tea Cups, and Merci Beaucoup. Printed on recycled paper. *Courtesy of Cartolina Cards.*

Cheree Berry Paper

www.chereeberry.com

Prior to launching Cheree Berry Paper, in January 2006, Berry worked for four years as the associate art director at Kate Spade Paper, where she was in charge of the company's wedding and personalized stationery lines. It was at Kate Spade where Berry fostered her love for stationery. She then began her career at Pentagram, a premier New York City design firm. Her corporate clients included Stuart Weitzman, Jonathan Adler, Lilly Pulitzer, Winslow's General Store, and Crane & Co. She currently bases her company from St. Louis with a tight knit creative staff. In an office of five girls, there is always a lot to talk about ... last night's episode of "Glee," the newest style of Tom's shoes, and what great bands are passing through St. Louis.

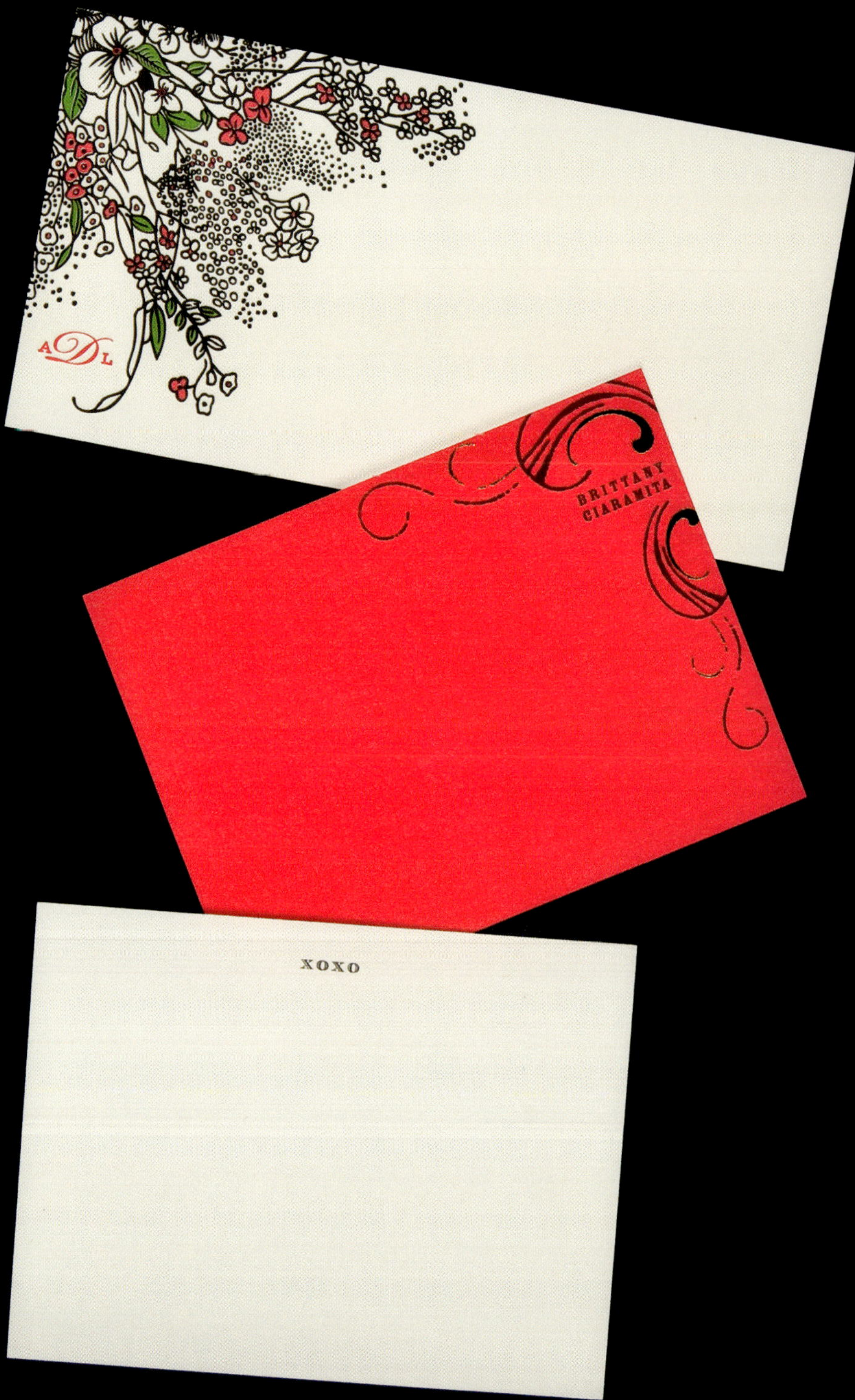

Signature Blossom Monarch, Fuchsia Wonka Swirl, and XOXO. Various printing methods including letterpress with foil stamping on double thick paper stock, engraving with hand painted edges, and flat printing. *Courtesy of Cheree Berry Paper.*

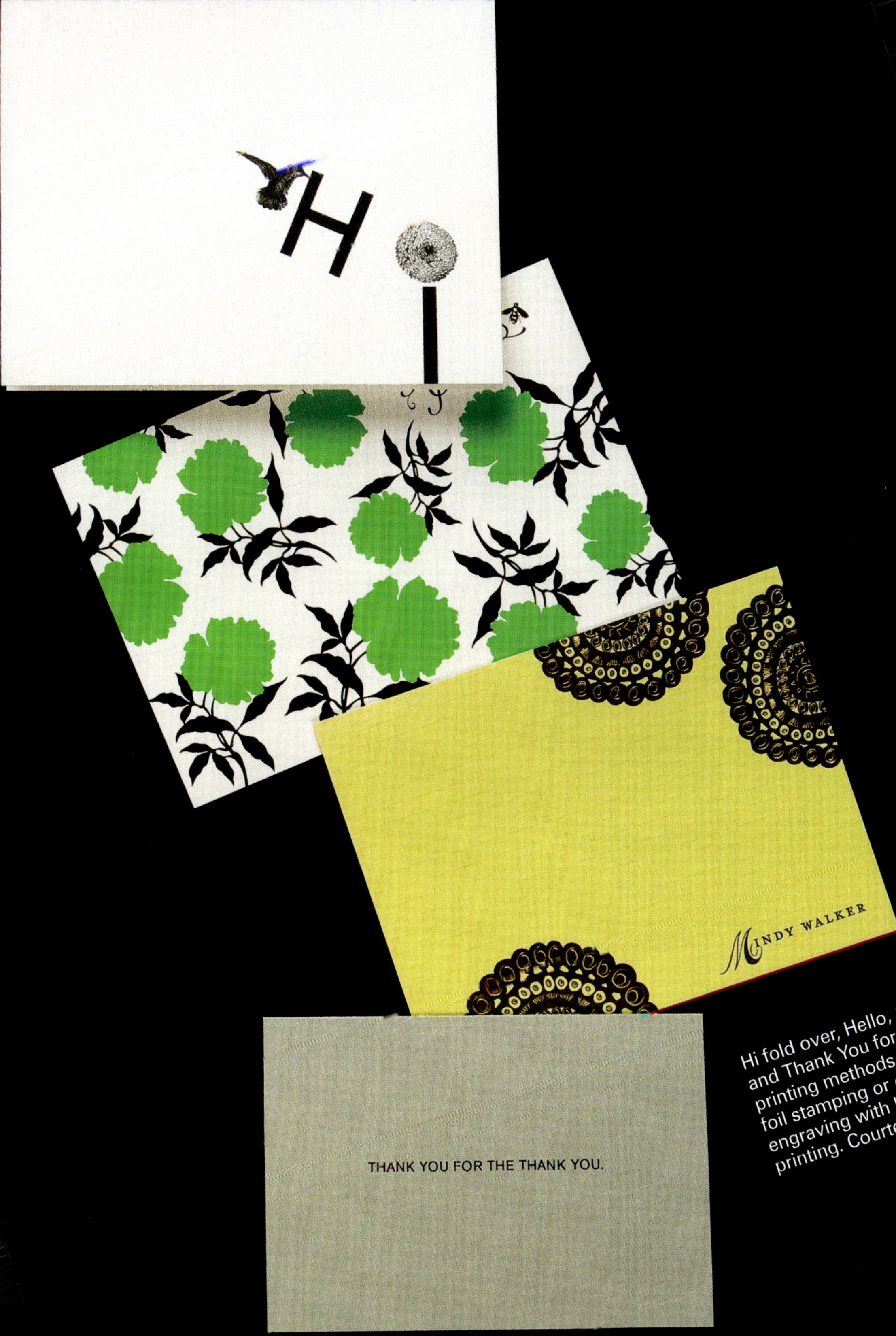

Hi fold over, Hello, Chartreuse Mosaic, and Thank You for the Thank You. Various printing methods including letterpress with foil stamping or double thick paper stock, engraving with hand painted edges, and flat printing. Courtesy of Cheree Berry Paper.

Dee & Lala

www.deeandlala.com

Dee & Lala was established in the spring of 2008. Christen Cutrona is "Dee," a family nickname given to her at birth by her older sister that was shortened from Christie Dee. She is an independent graphic designer who currently resides in South Pasadena, California. Mable Lee is "Lala," the designer and proprietor of Lala Press, a letterpress studio located in Los Angeles, California. When Christen and Mable met in 2007, they knew immediately that a collaboration was in their future. Today, Dee & Lala's original artwork and letterpress wares can be found in over 200 stores across the US and abroad. Their work has also been featured in *Los Angeles Magazine,* the *L.A. Times*, and on numerous blogs including *Paper Crave, Apartment Therapy, Dwell, and Cool Mom Picks.*

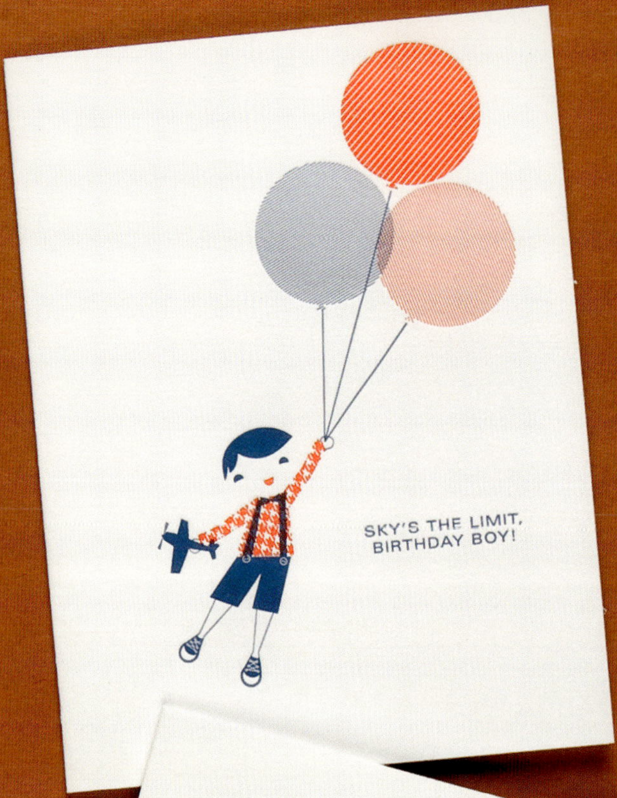

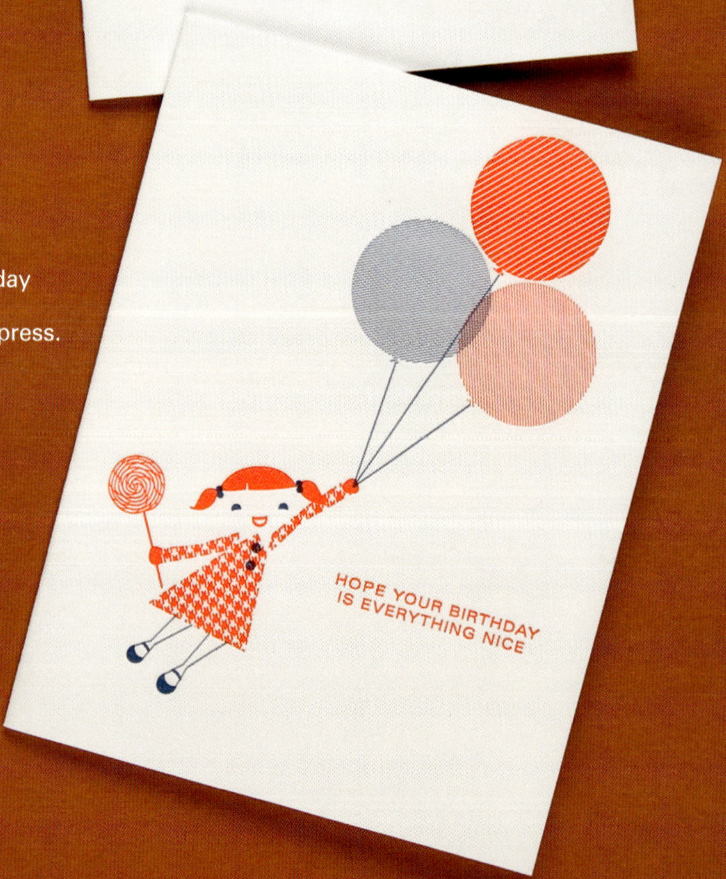

Birthday Boy 'Sky's the Limit Birthday Boy' and Birthday Girl 'Hope Your Birthday is Everything Nice.' Letterpress. *Courtesy of Dee & Lala.*

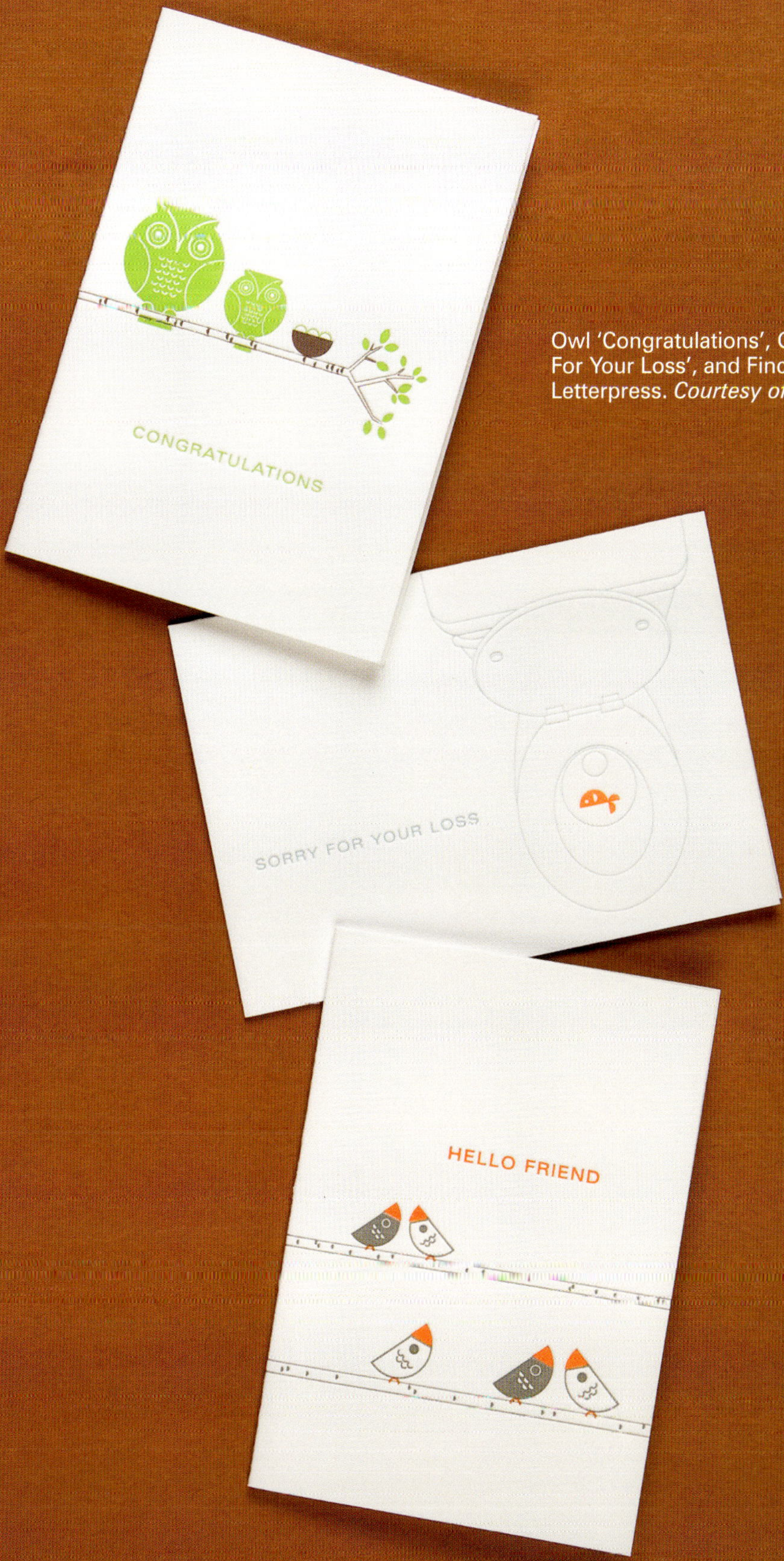

Owl 'Congratulations', Goldfish 'Sorry For Your Loss', and Finch 'Hello Friend'. Letterpress. *Courtesy of Dee & Lala.*

Escargot, Octopus, and Les Fleurs. Letterpress. *Courtesy of Delphine.*

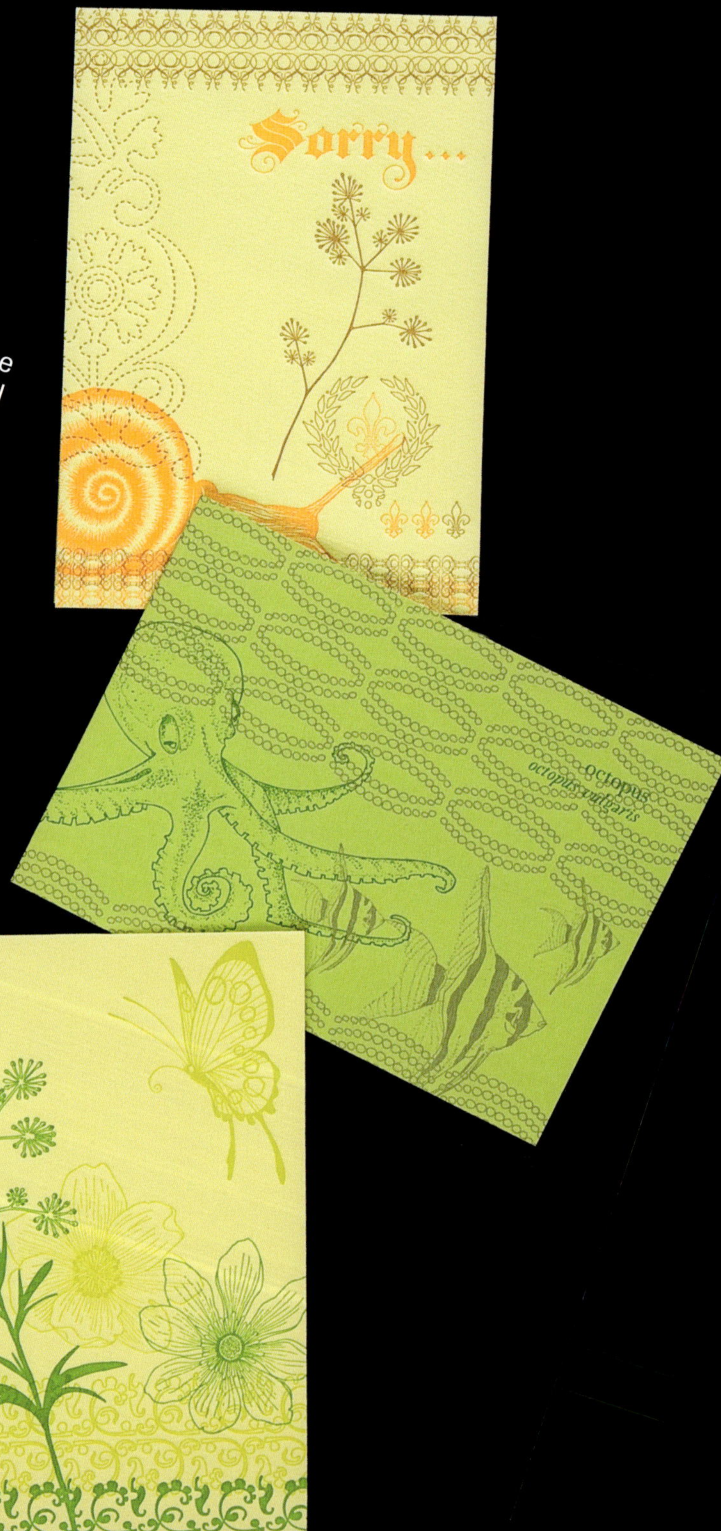

Delphine

www.delphinepress.com

Erika Firm has been creating since she was a tot. She was probably the only kid on the block to have, at age five, her own X-acto knife and t-square. Her first design job was the playbill for her fifth grade class production of *A Midsummer Night's Dream*. Prior to starting Delphine in 2003, Erika worked in the magazine, newspaper, and dotcom industries, as well as at a design studio, and at an independent literary book shop. She inherited her love of design from her mom, an artist (and former commercial artist/graphic designer/interior designer) and her love of marketing and business from her dad (an executive in the machine tool industry). She draws inspiration everywhere: nature, her family, her clients, movies, books, and travel. She loves paper, the written word, all shades of green, the sound of the surf, crepes, café au lait, weddings, and the smell of the pressroom.

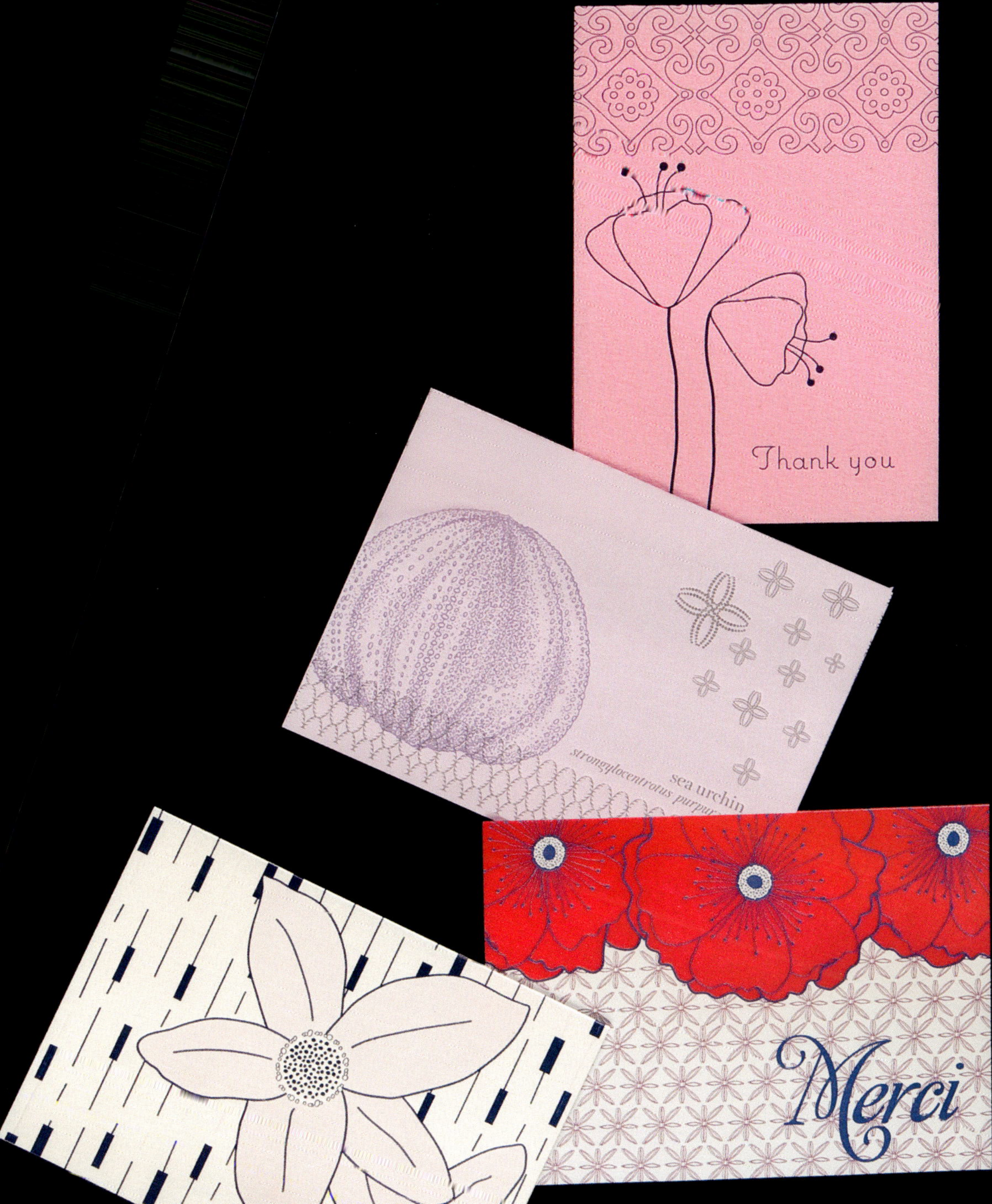

Anemone, Urchin, Viola, and Starlite Letterpress. *Courtesy of Delphine.*

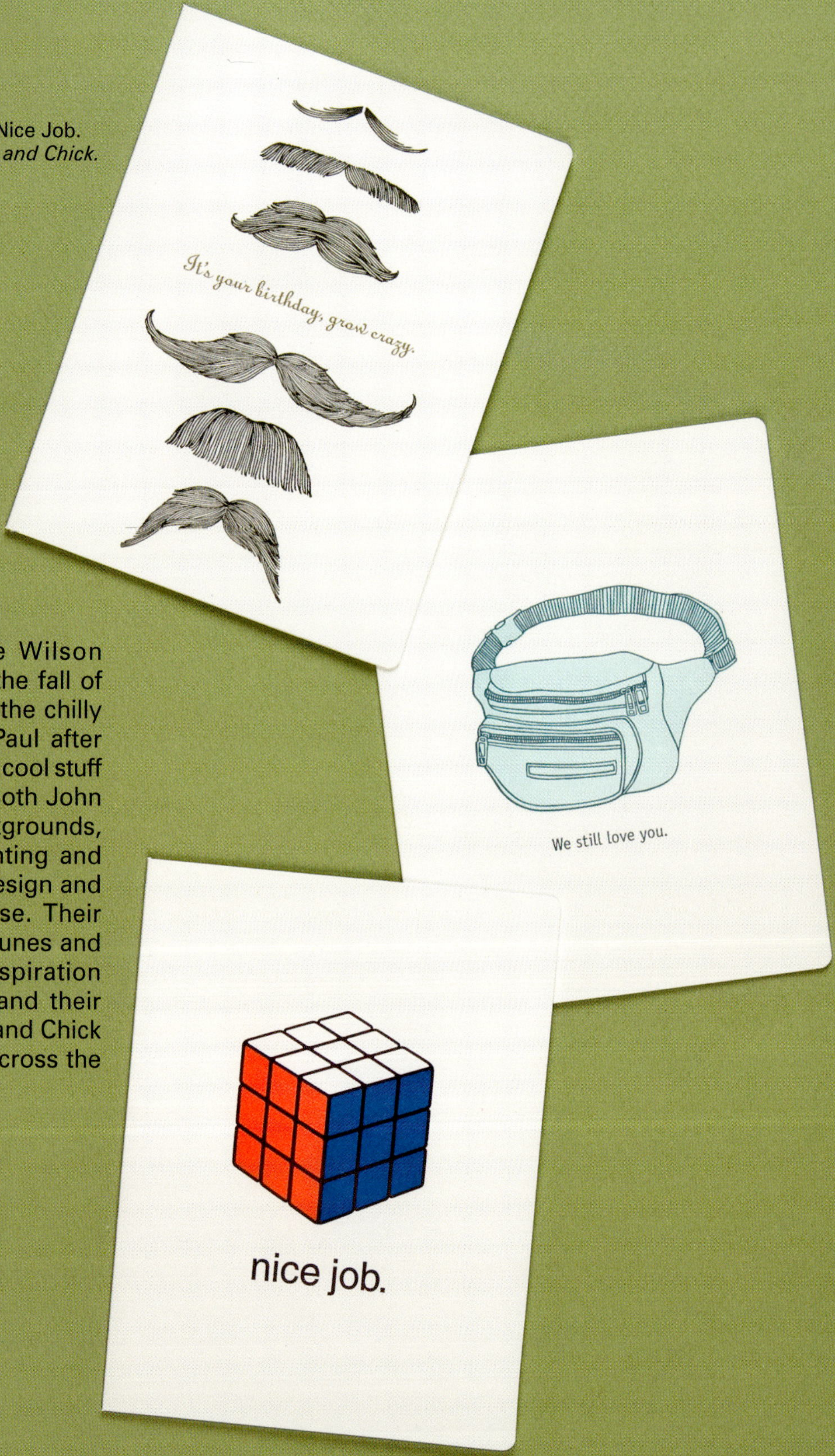

Grow Crazy, Fanny Pack, and Nice Job. Letterpress. *Courtesy of Dude and Chick.*

Dude and Chick

www.dudeandchick.com

John Gurtin and Katie Wilson started Dude and Chick in the fall of 2008. They joined forces in the chilly Minnesotan tundra of St. Paul after discovering a shared love for cool stuff and stationery sweetness. Both John and Katie have design backgrounds, as well as a history of printing and illustration. Together they design and produce every card in-house. Their days are spent listening to tunes and creating awesomeness. Inspiration comes from vintage style and their own sense of humor. Dude and Chick cards are carried at shops across the US and throughout the UK.

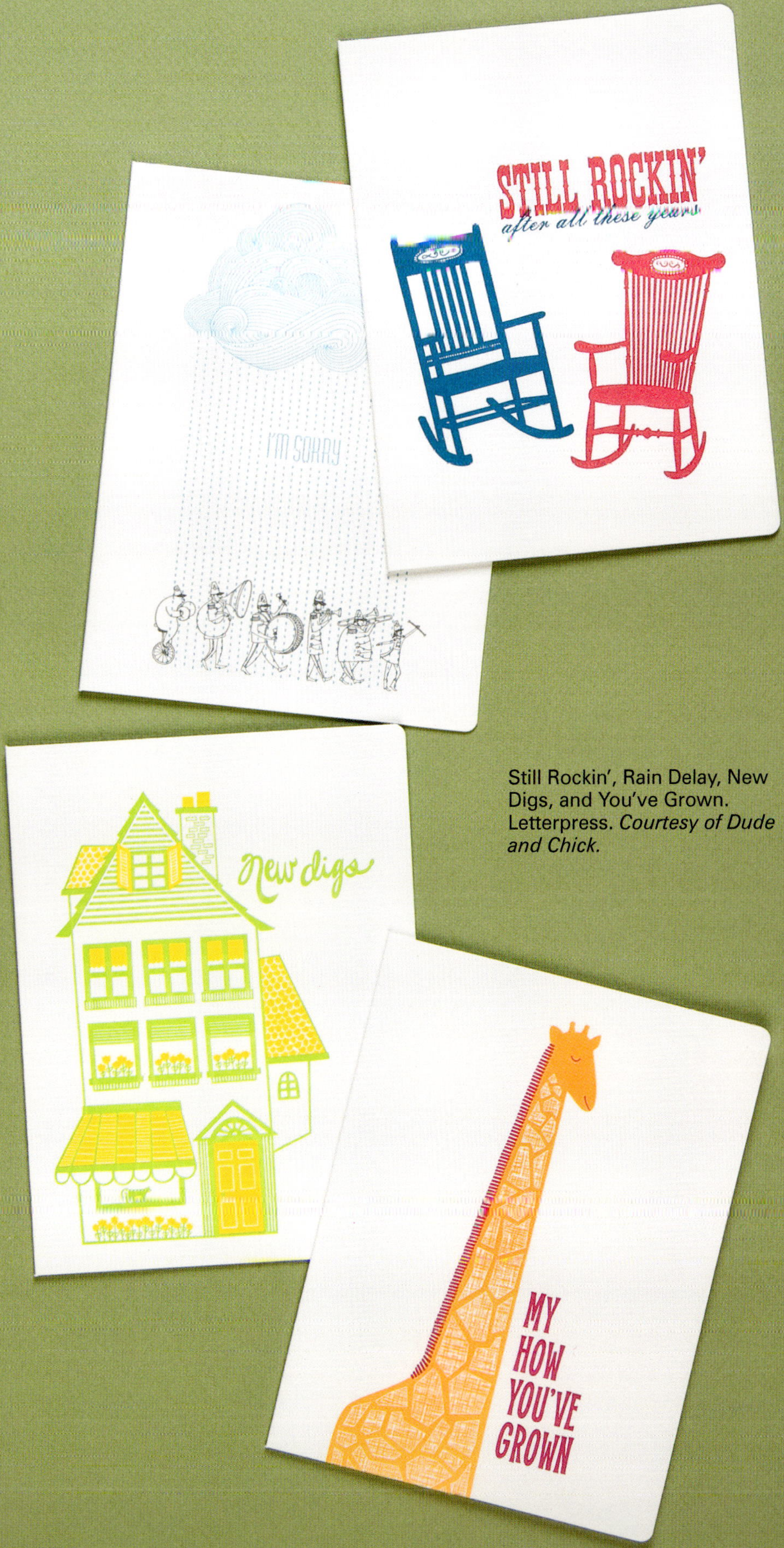

Still Rockin', Rain Delay, New Digs, and You've Grown. Letterpress. *Courtesy of Dude and Chick.*

Dutch Door Press

www.dutchdoorpress.com

Dutch Door Press is a letterpress and design studio founded in 2006 by Anna Branning and Mara Murphy. Their studio is located in the basement of a Victorian house in San Francisco's Haight-Ashbury district, where they print all of their greeting cards by hand on a 100-year-old Chandler and Price platen press. Their designs are inspired by the whimsical art of vintage children's books and the traditional folk art of Northern Europe and the Pennsylvania Dutch. They have published two works with Chronicle Books: a birthday calendar and a sticker and label book. Their greeting card designs have also been licensed in Japan. In their spare time they both enjoy drawing, painting, bird watching, observing nature in general, wandering in the woods, sewing, gardening, bookbinding, and playing with their children.

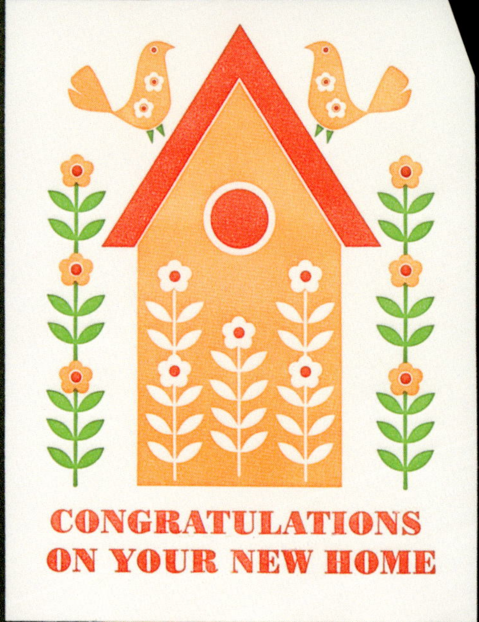

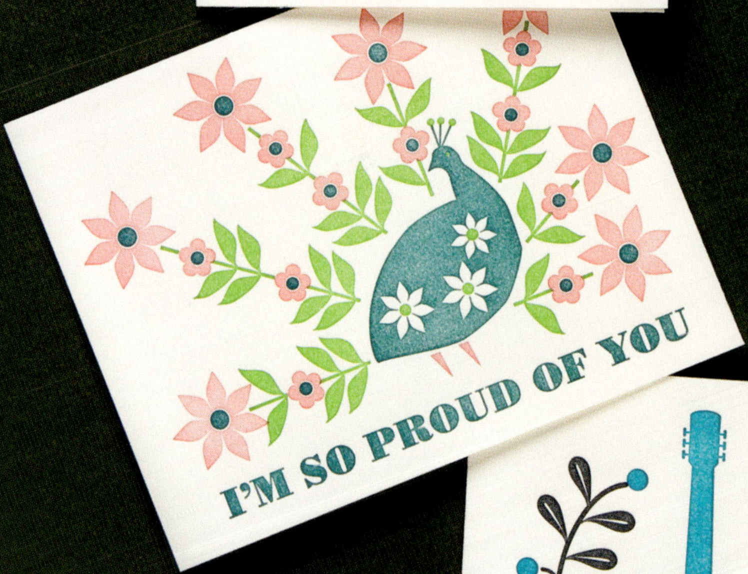

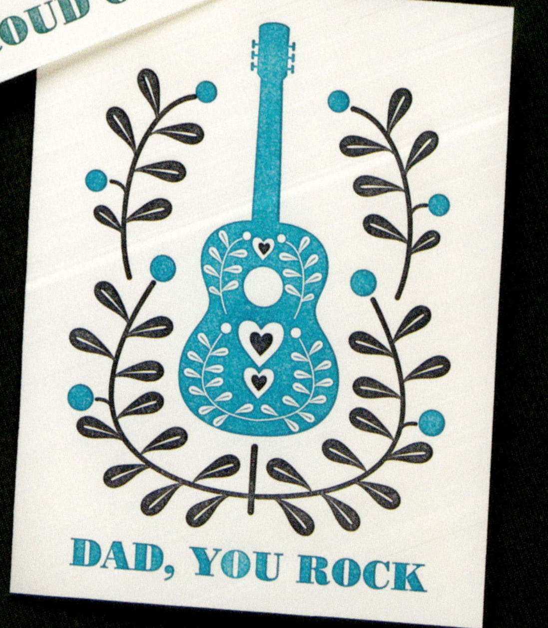

New Home, So Proud, and You Rock. Letterpress. *Courtesy of Dutch Door Press.*

Thank You, Happy Birthday, Birthday Wishes, and Hello. Letterpress. *Courtesy of Dutch Door Press.*

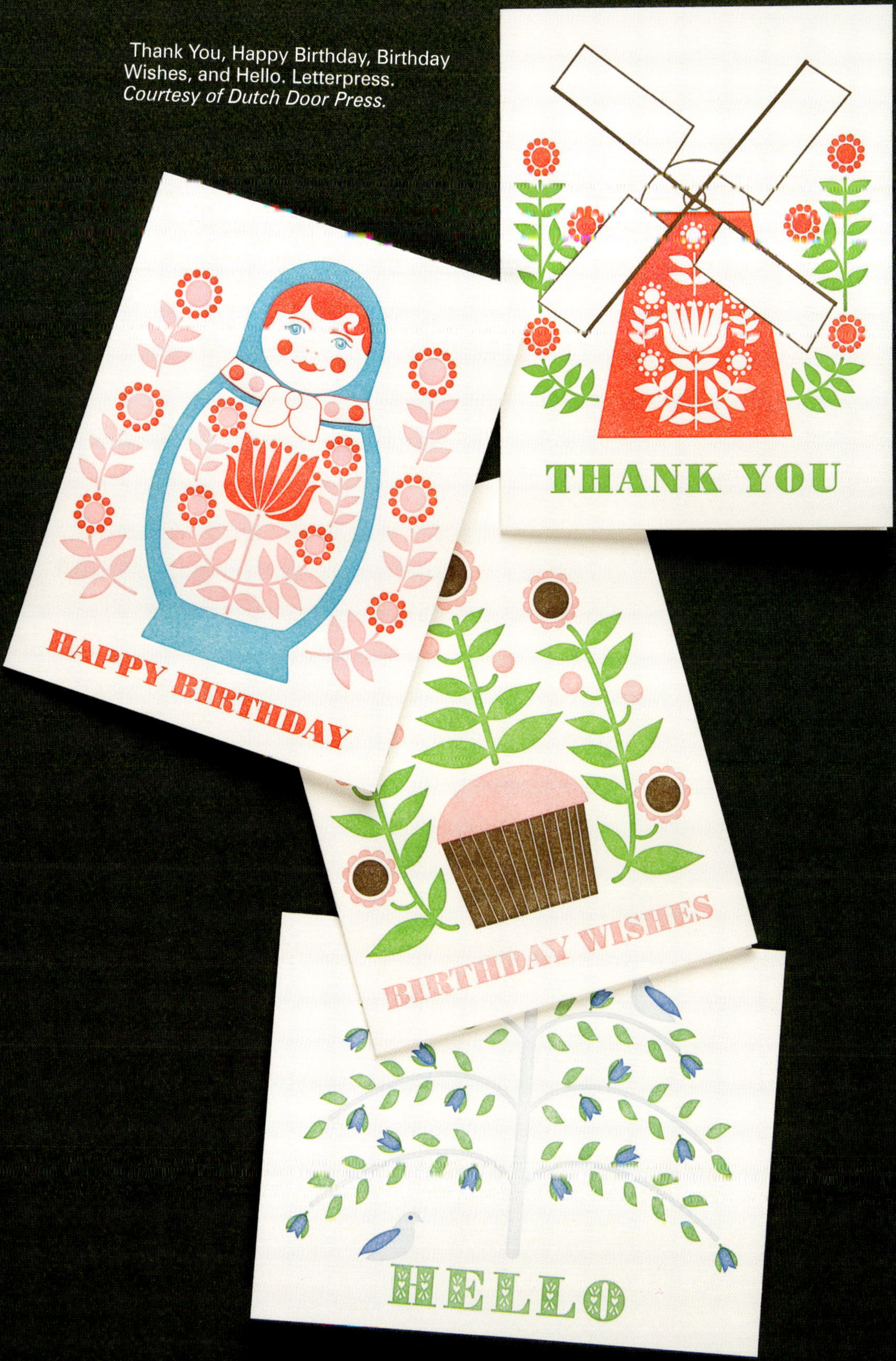

Quilt, Cats, Nature, and Dogs. Printed on 100% recycled paper. *Courtesy of Ecojot.*

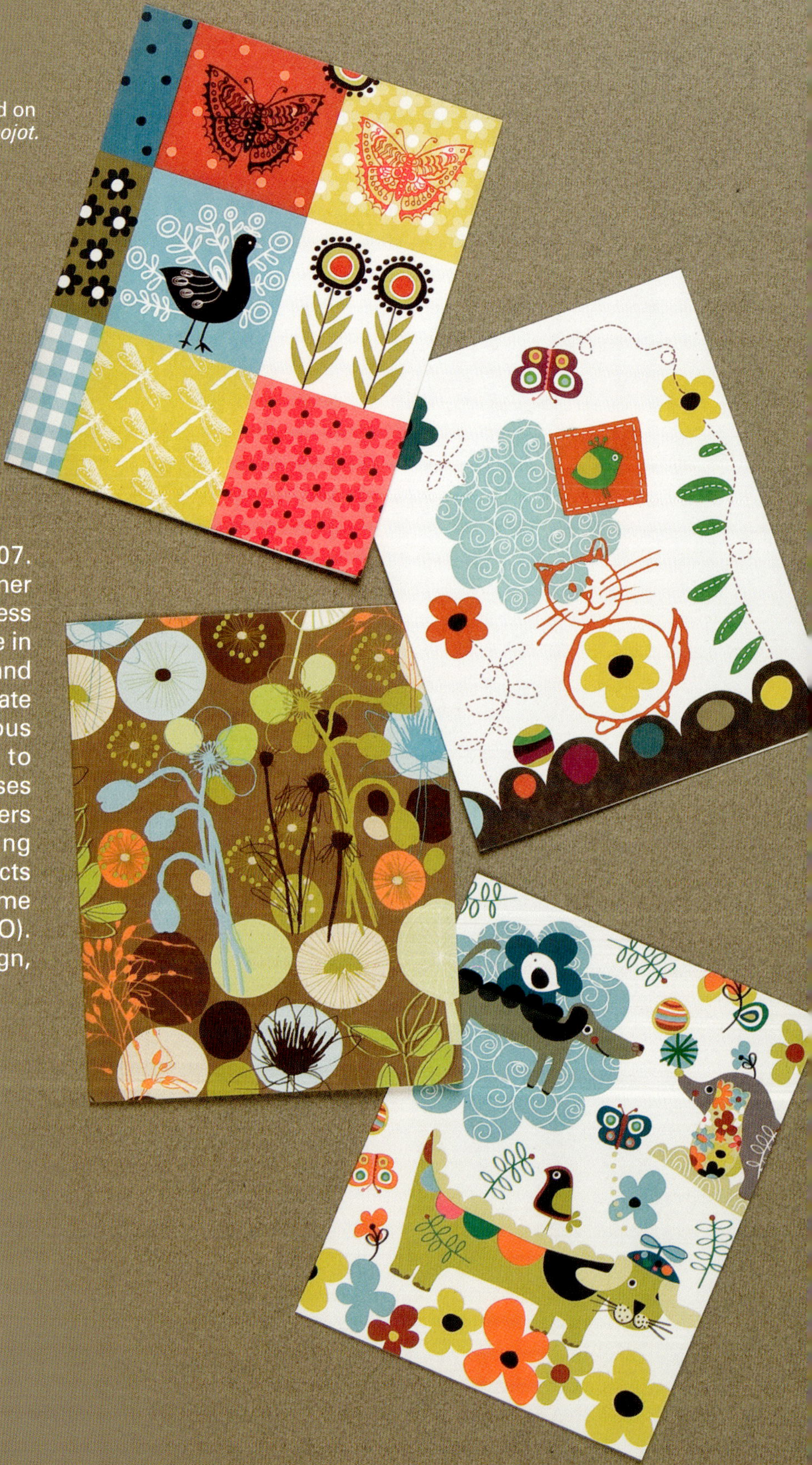

Ecojot

www.ecojot.com

Ecojot was established in 2007. Carolyn Gavin is the stationery designer for Ecojot, which is a family run business out of Toronto, Canada. They believe in producing ethically made products and giving back in some way. They donate books to children in need in various countries throughout the world to promote literacy. Carolyn also licenses her art through her agent, Lilla Rogers Studios. Her designs are now going onto such a wide variety of products from fabric (P&B Fabrics, Wild Thyme Collection) to scrap booking (K&CO). Her life revolves around family, design, color, pattern, and love.

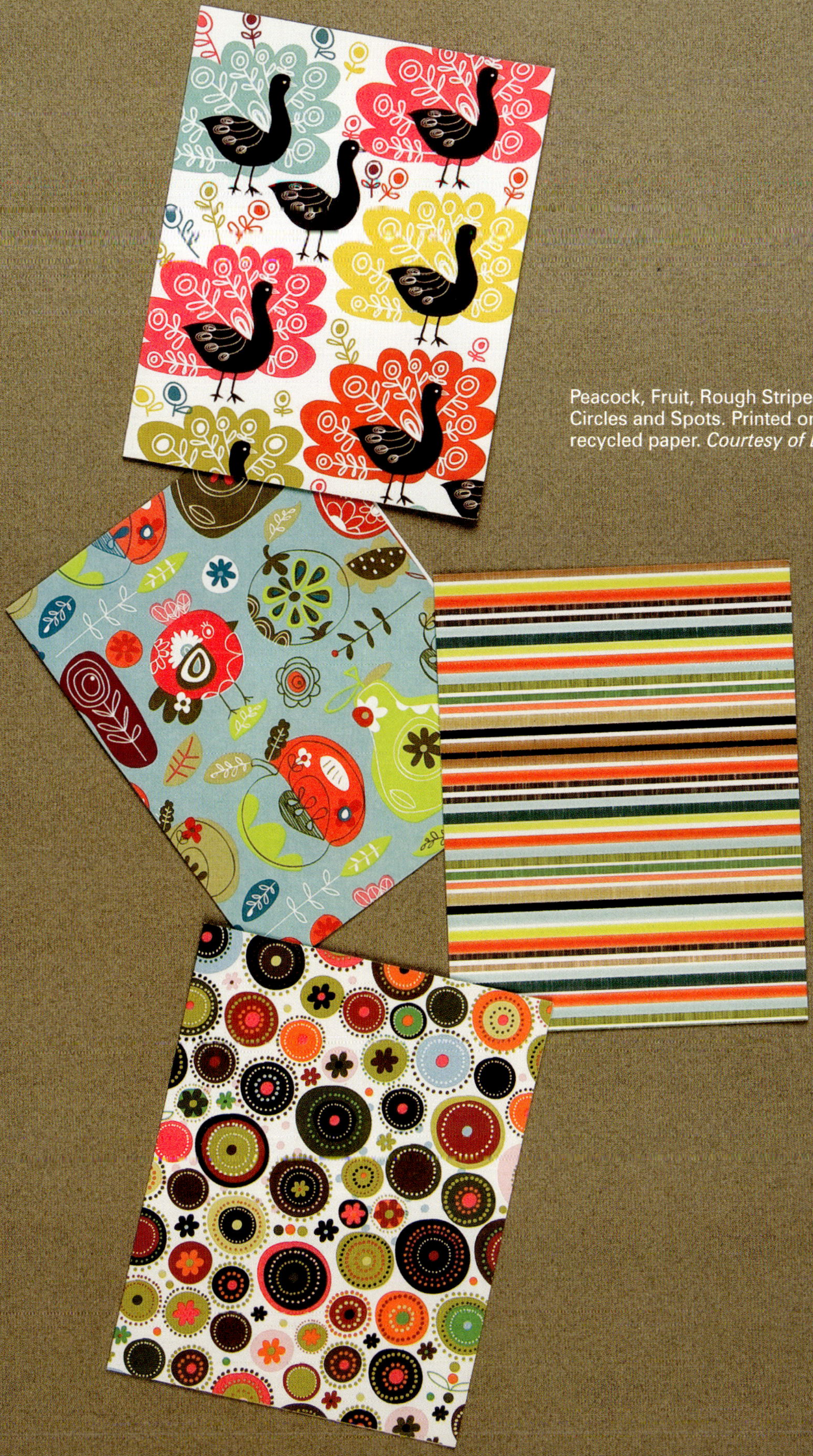

Peacock, Fruit, Rough Stripes, and Circles and Spots. Printed on 100% recycled paper. *Courtesy of Ecojot.*

enormouschampion

www.enormouschampion.com

Jordan Provost & Jason Wong founded enormouschampion in May 2008. Living and working in Brooklyn, New York, what began as a stationery line, has since been expanded into various other hard and soft goods. Along with custom work, the studio currently sells their products through various shops around the world. They have also licensed work with Urban Outfitters, Keds Collective, and are currently working on a few projects with various publishing houses. They find inspiration in everything from collected ephemera and their favorite childhood cartoons to nature and travels. They also have a love for photography, design/typography, and crafty folks. Some of their words to live by are "Be nice to everyone you meet...word-of-mouth goes a long way."

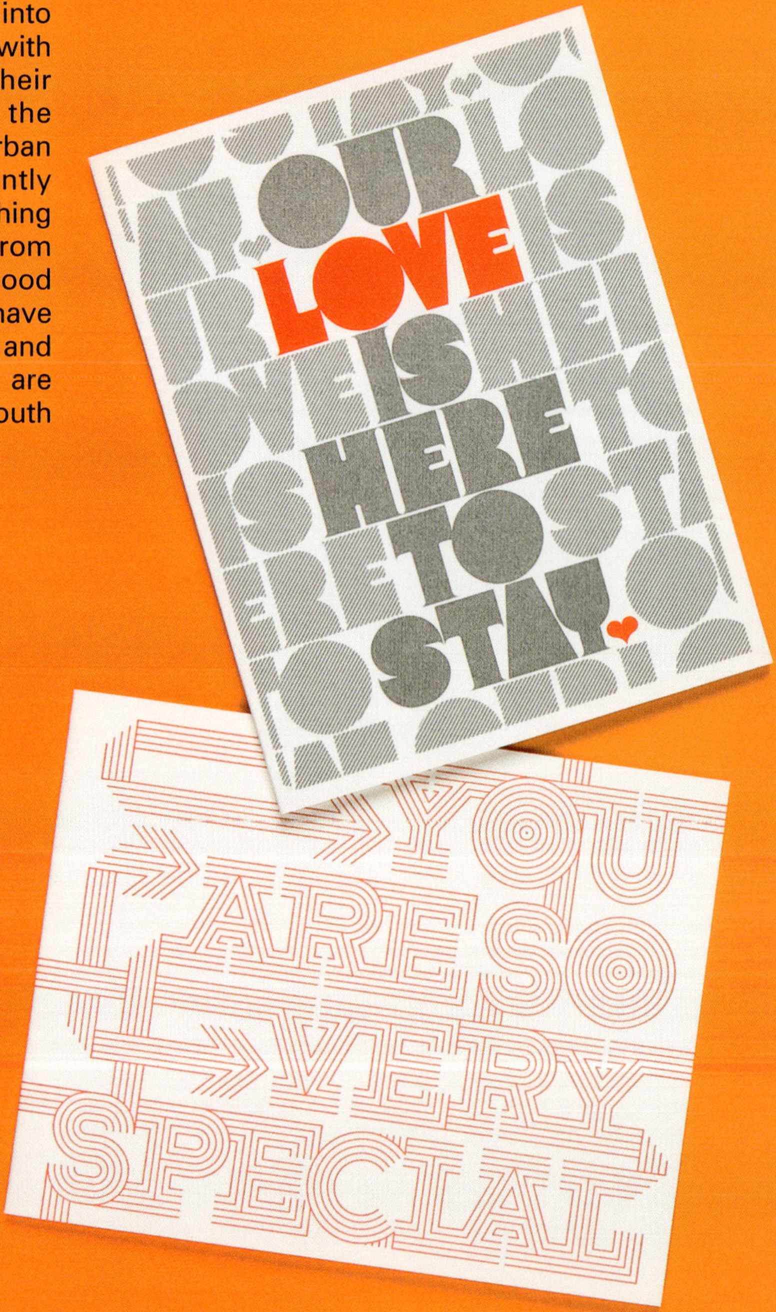

Our Love is Here to Stay and So Very Special. Silk screened with soy based inks and letterpress. *Courtesy of enormouschampion.*

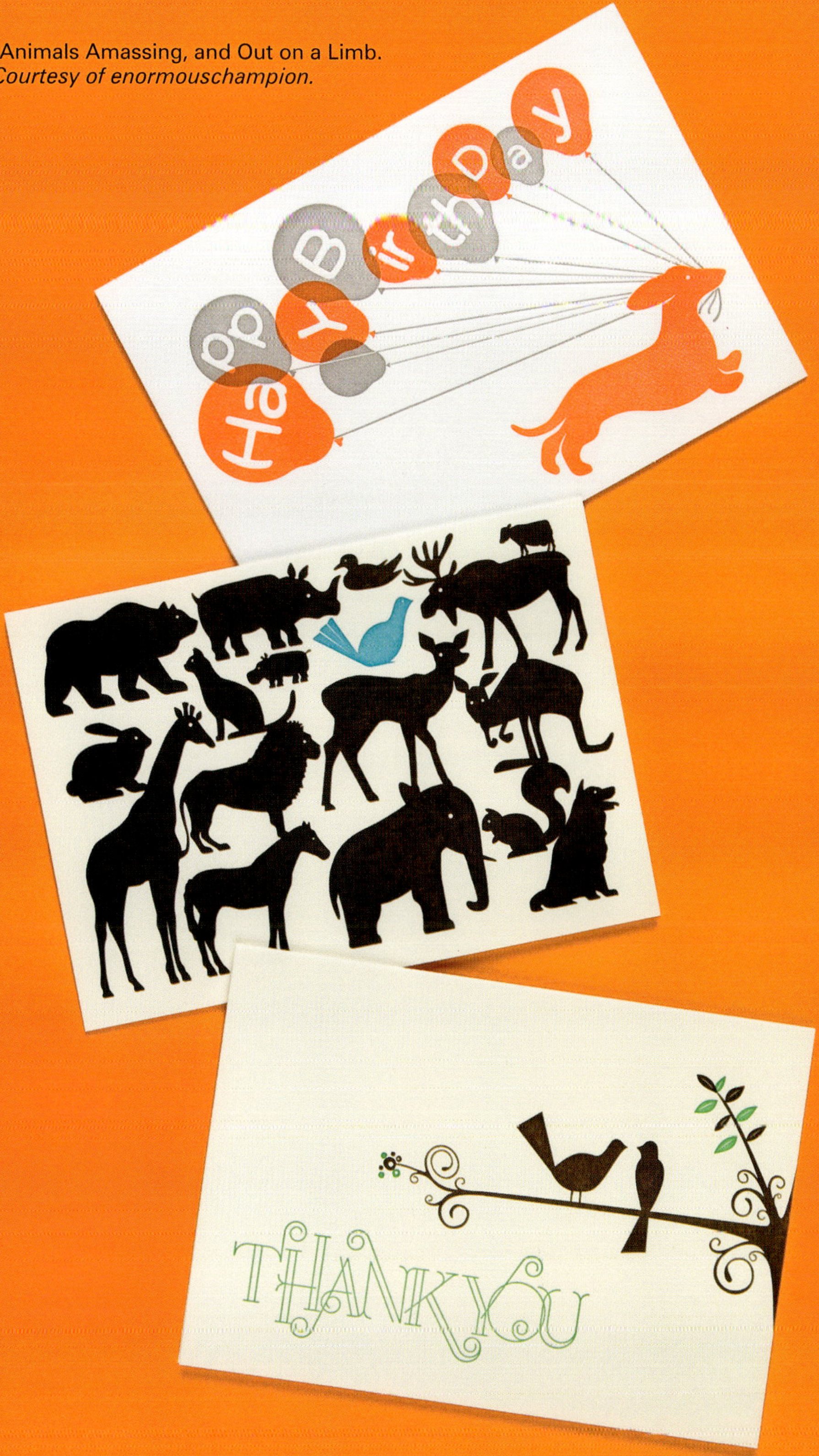

Balloon Day, Animals Amassing, and Out on a Limb. Letterpress. *Courtesy of enormouschampion.*

Fugu Fugu Press

www.fugufugupress.com

Prior to founding Fugu Fugu Press in July 2007, Shino Charlson was designing letterpress cards for another company she worked for between 2003 and 2006. She has always been an illustrator (www.shinoillustration.com), and found that she really enjoyed the design process for letterpress cards. Together, with her husband Ken, she runs their print shop from Pasadena, California. Her cards have been featured in: *Los Angeles Magazine, Angeleno Magazine, Metro New York, Stationery Trends Magazine, Design*Sponge, Apartment Therapy,* and the *L.A. Times Blog*.

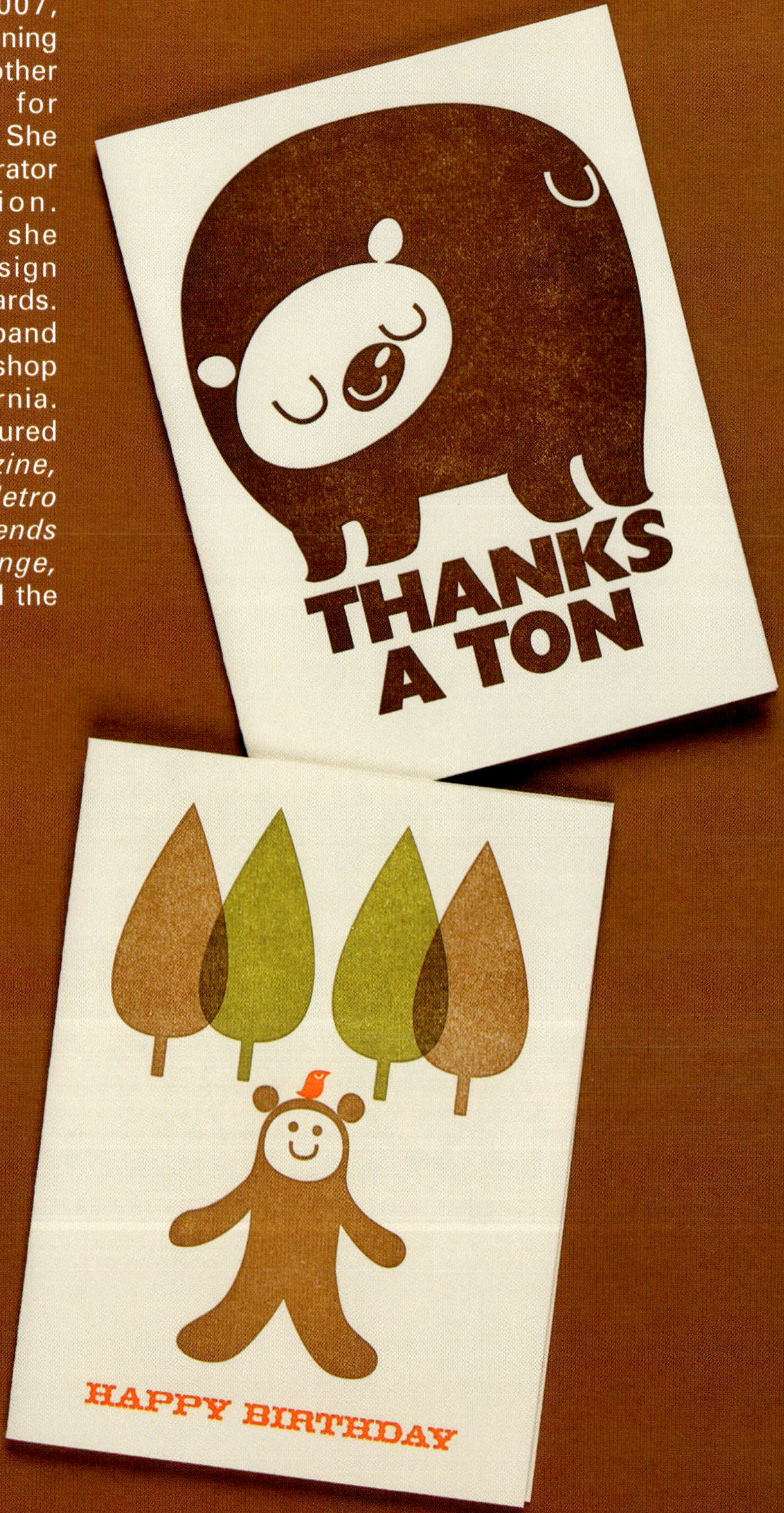

Birthday Bear in Woods and Thanks a Ton. Letterpress. *Courtesy of Ken and Shino Charlson.*

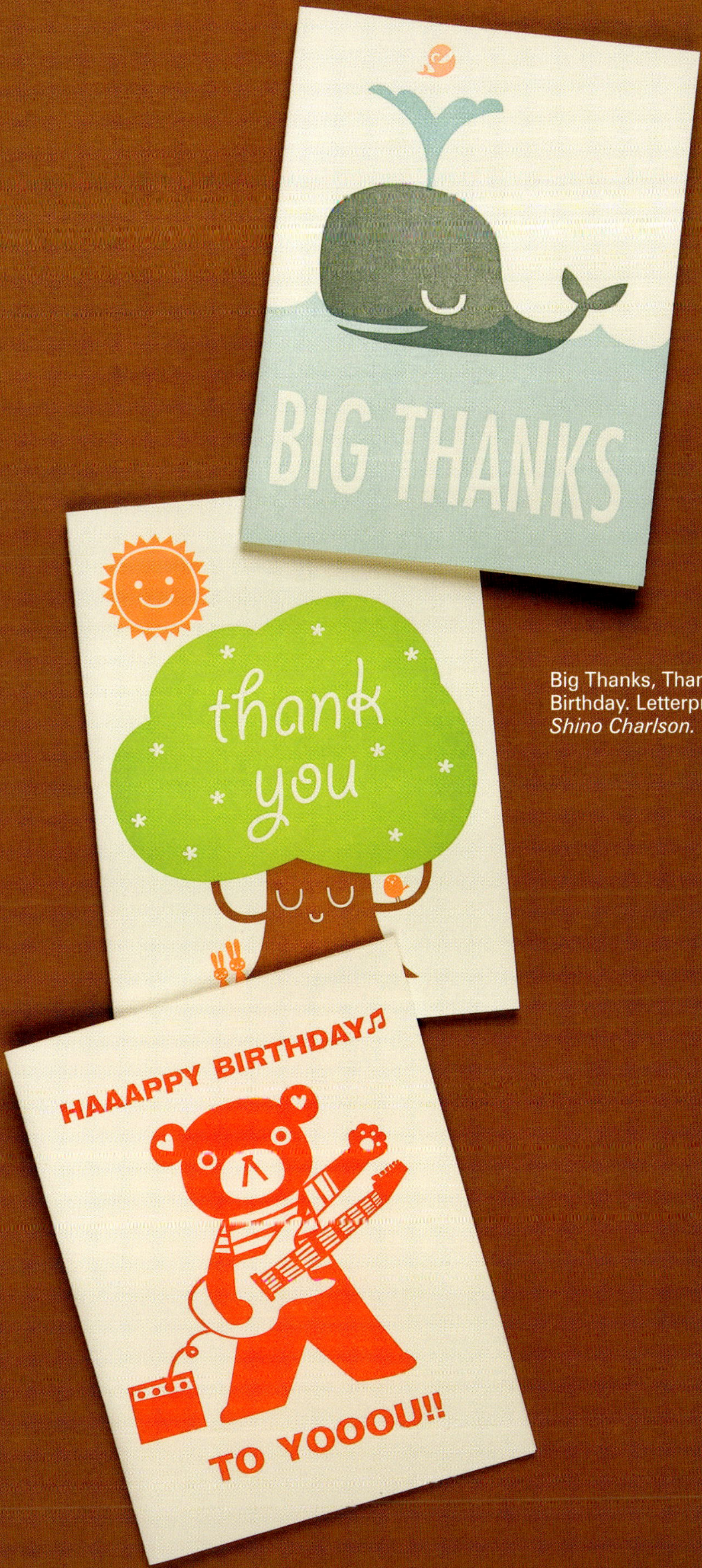

Big Thanks, Thank You Tree, and Rockin' Birthday. Letterpress. *Courtesy of Ken and Shino Charlson.*

Ghost Academy

www.ghostacademy.com

Megan Gray started developing her line in spring of 2008, but made her official debut at the Seattle Gift Show in August of 2008. She has always been a daydreamer, and has always had busy hands. Growing up, the only way she could focus in school was by doodling in the margins of her notebooks while simultaneously taking notes. In high school, she took every single art class her school offered, but no matter what medium she tried, she never found anything quite as satisfying as those simple, silly doodles. Before starting Ghost Academy, Megan had been a florist for twelve years. Even though she is busy printing during the week, she still does floral design for weddings on the weekends under the business name Honey and Poppies. They both indulge her passion for color, her love of working with her hands, and her all around crush on anything lovely.

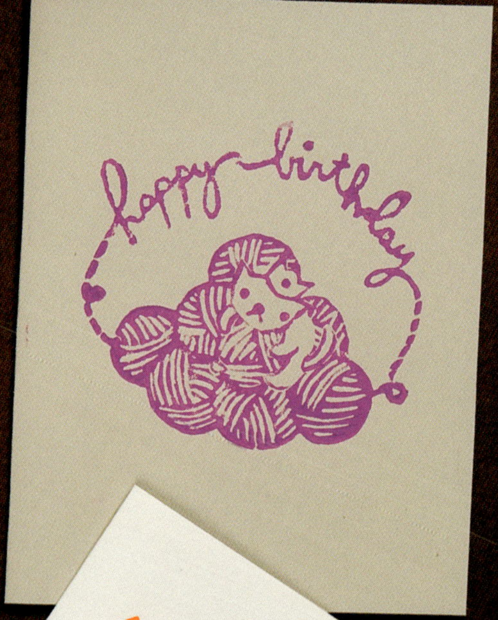

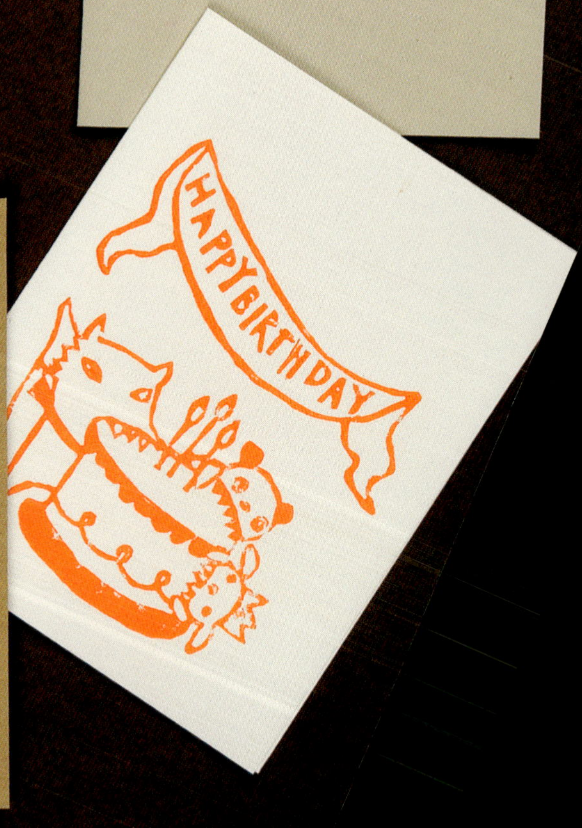

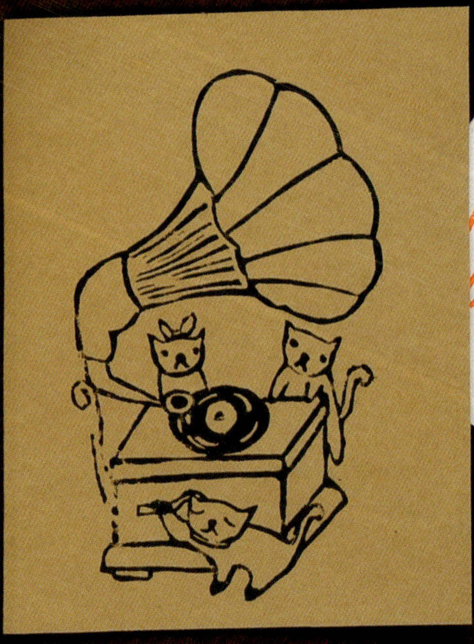

Birthday Yarn, Cake Eaters, and Kitty Savants. Hand printed on 100% recycled paper. *Courtesy of Megan Gray.*

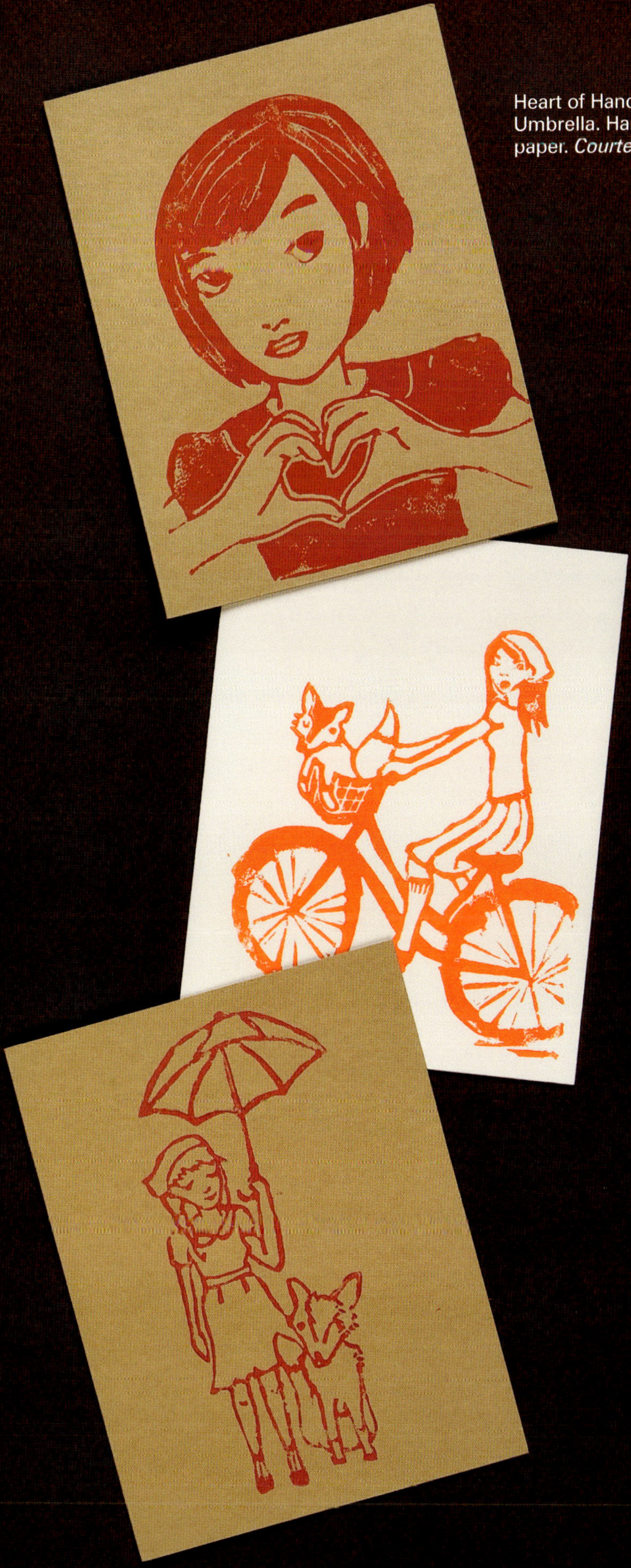

Heart of Hands, Foxy Bicycle, and Foxy Umbrella. Hand printed on 100% recycled paper. *Courtesy of Megan Gray.*

Ink + Wit

www.inkandwit.com

Tara Hogan worked as a web and print designer for many years in house until arriving one fine day in her own office running a one-woman show. The show turned into an impressive client list and licensing contracts with *House Beautiful Magazine*, Babysoy, Cardstore.com, Great Arrow Graphics, Graphique de France, Pinball Publishing, Bella Figura, and Babybe Organics. Her design business, INK+WIT, grew out of a desire and passion to create conceptual, organic, elegant, and simple designs with an illustrative impression. Her designs have been seen on blogs such as *Dwell.com, Apartment Therapy, Design*Sponge, Decor8, TimeOut NY, Dooce, and Real Simple*.

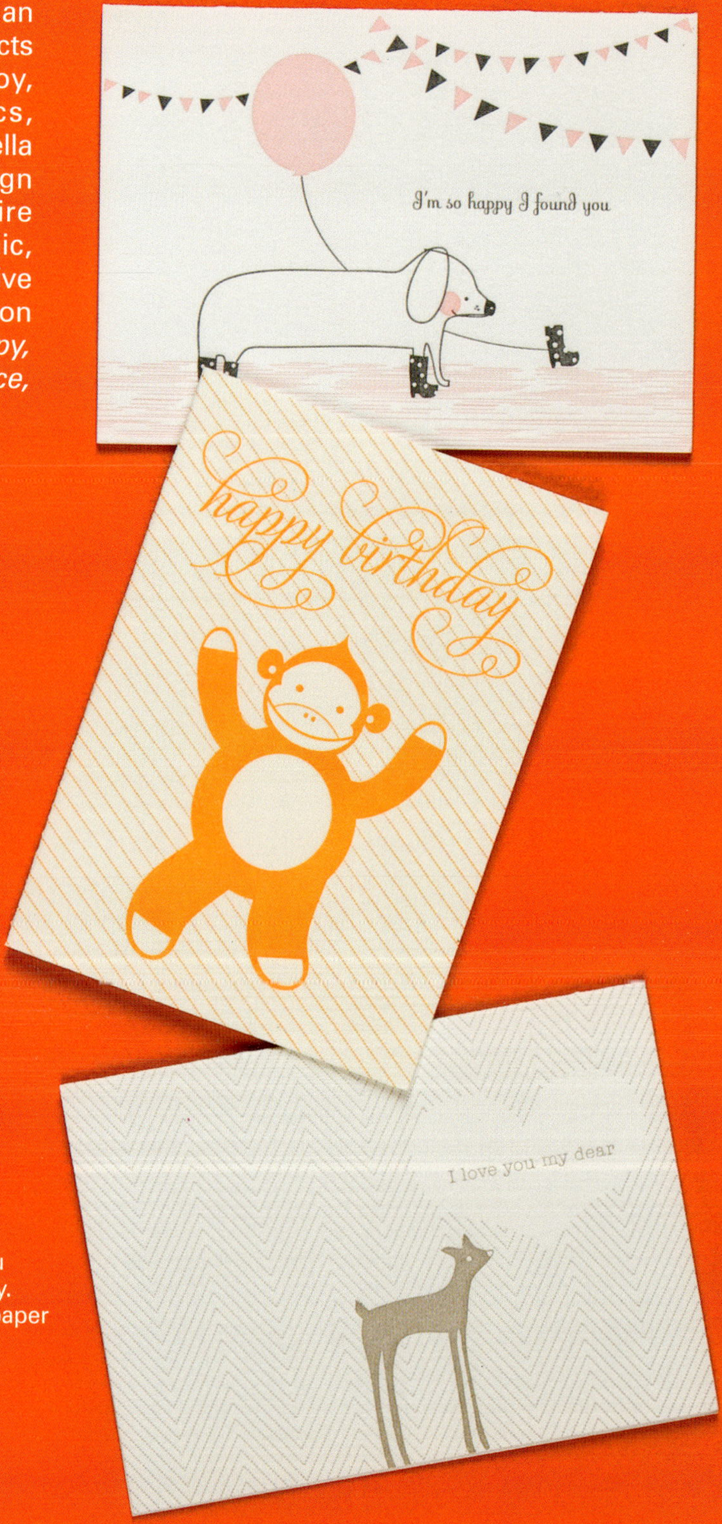

I'm So Happy I Found You, I Love You My Dear, and Happy Birthday Monkey. Letterpress printed on 100% cotton paper made of tree free fibers. *Courtesy of INK+WIT.*

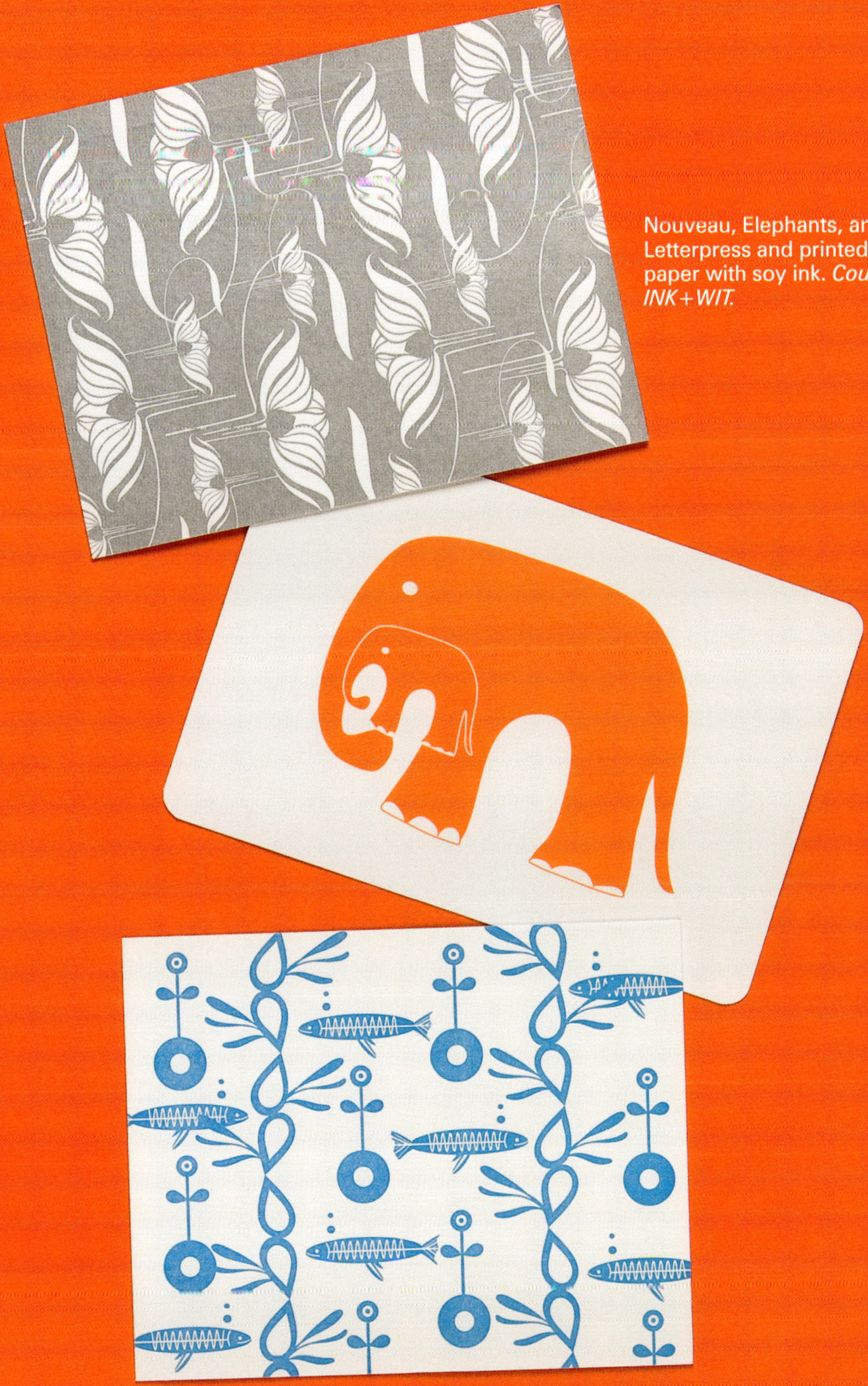

Nouveau, Elephants, and Blue Fish. Letterpress and printed on recycled paper with soy ink. *Courtesy of INK+WIT.*

Birdhouse and Spotted Owl. Inkjet printed on FSC certified paper. *Courtesy of Marie Perkins, Inkjet Designs.*

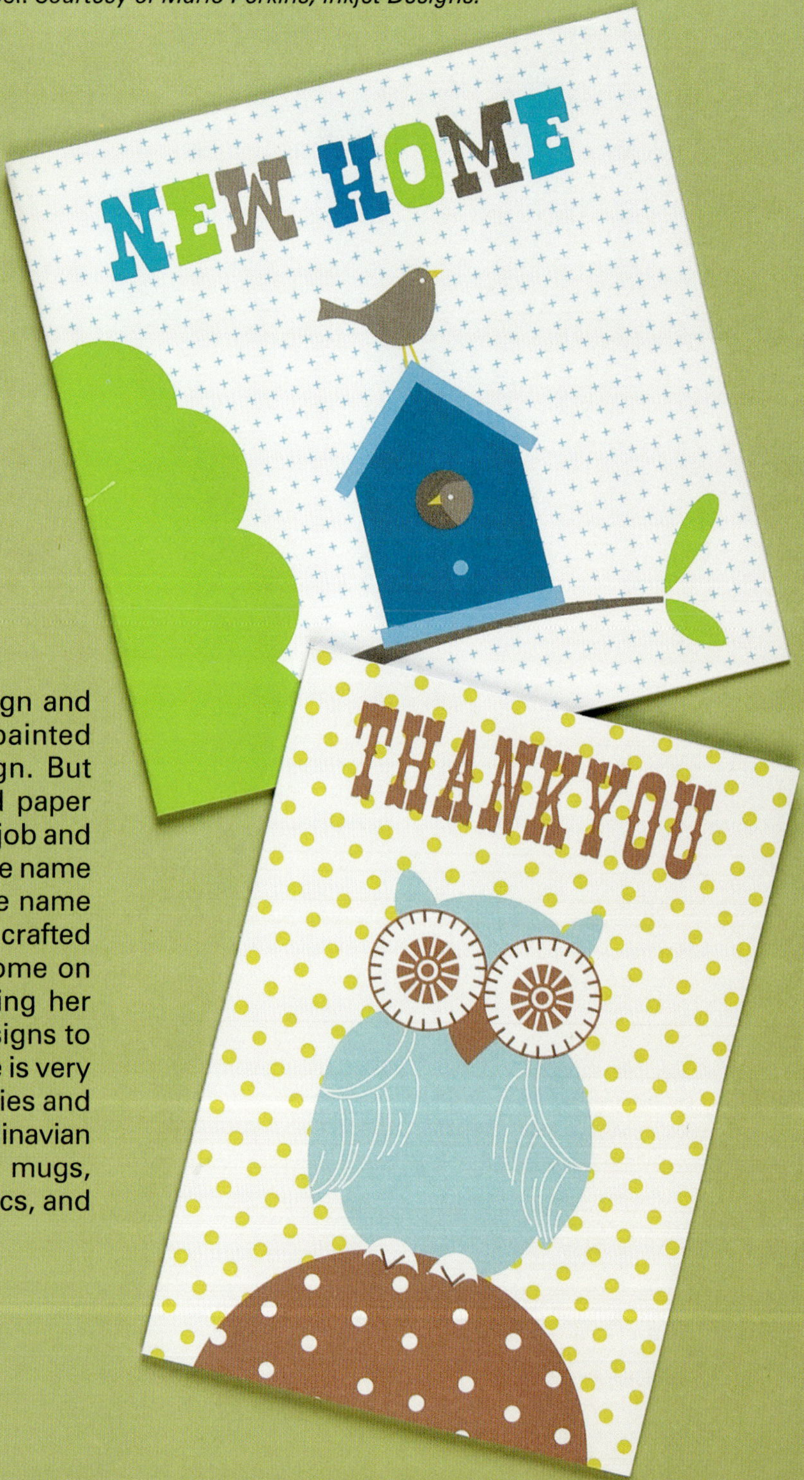

Inkjet Designs

www.inkjet-designs.com
www.inkjet.etsy.com

Marie Perkins studied graphic design and illustration before going into hand painted ceramics and then later textile design. But it was a love of cards, stationery, and paper goods that led her to leave her full time job and take the plunge to go freelance under the name 'Inkjet Designs' in 2007. (She chose the name Inkjet because at first all of her hand crafted products and cards were printed at home on her trusty inkjet printer). Since debuting her company, she has sold or licensed designs to Paperchase, Soul UK, and Cardmix. She is very much inspired by designs from the sixties and seventies and loves Japanese and Scandinavian design. She collects and photographs mugs, vintage ceramics, retro wallpaper, fabrics, and patterns and prints that catch her eye.

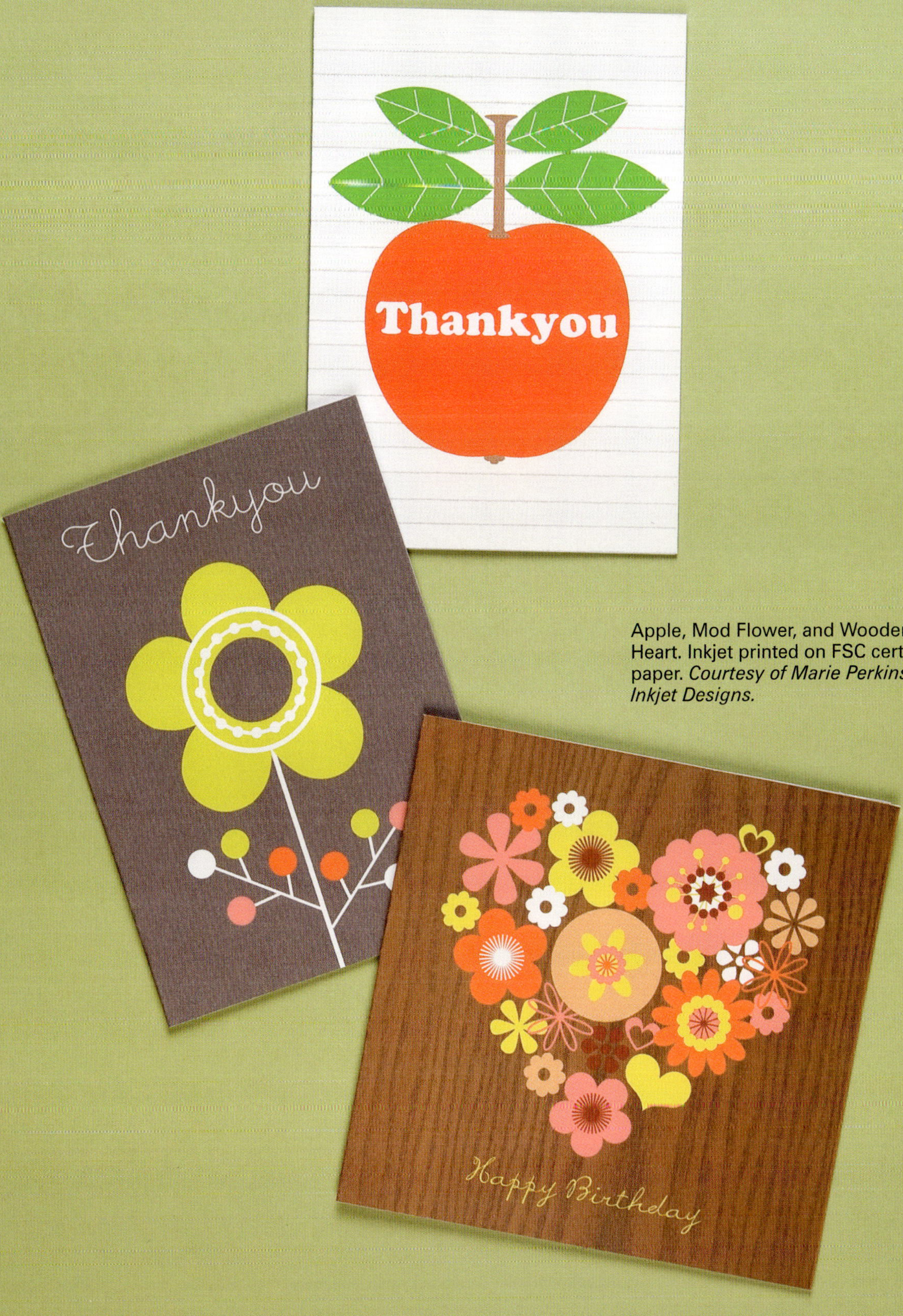

Apple, Mod Flower, and Wooden Heart. Inkjet printed on FSC certified paper. *Courtesy of Marie Perkins, Inkjet Designs.*

Julianna Smith Illustration

www.juliannasmith.com

Julianna Smith started her own company called Parlez-Vous Greeting Cards in 2001. Within a few years, her cards were available in over 1,000 stores and boutiques nationwide. In 2006, she stepped out of the manufacturing business and began licensing her designs to Recycled Paper Greetings and Papyrus. She currently designs and illustrates greeting cards from her home studio outside of Portland, Oregon, with her creative husband and two tireless children. Her work is a combination of gouache, pencil, and digital illustration. She is very much inspired by vintage fabric designs and old-fashioned children's books. For more of Julianna's inspirations, visit her blog, www.underthetuliptree.typepad.com.

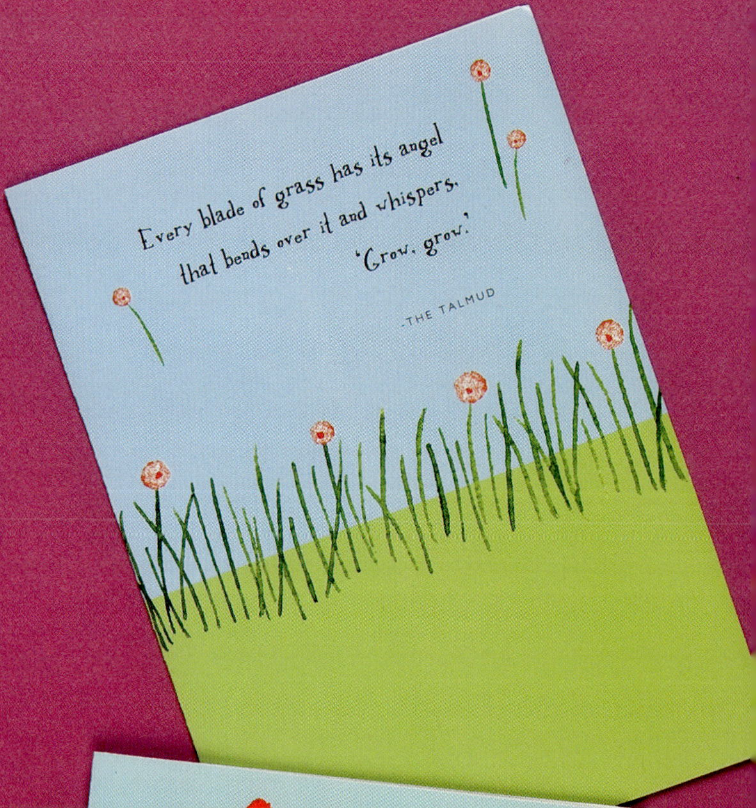

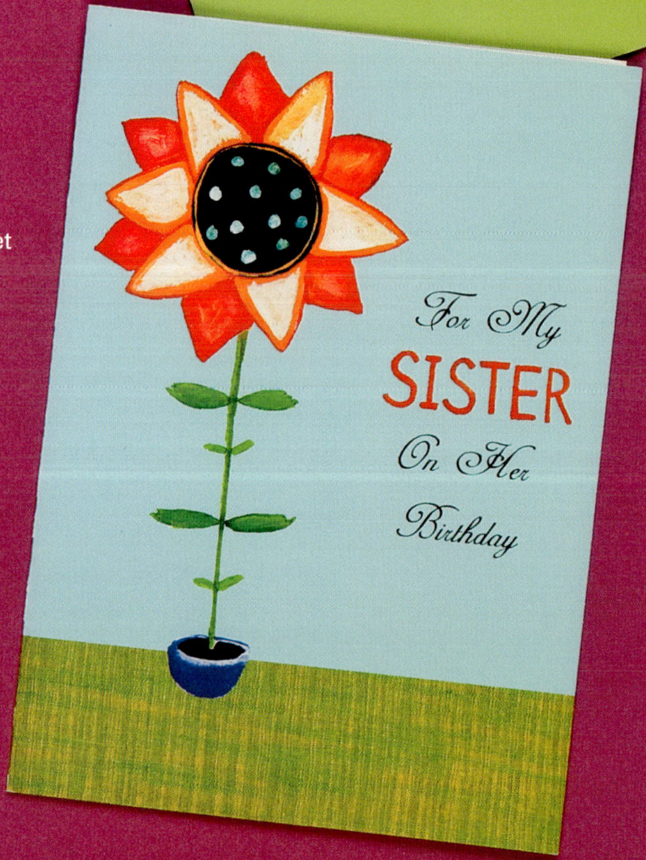

Encouragement and Birthday Sister. Offset Printed. *Courtesy of Julianna Smith.*

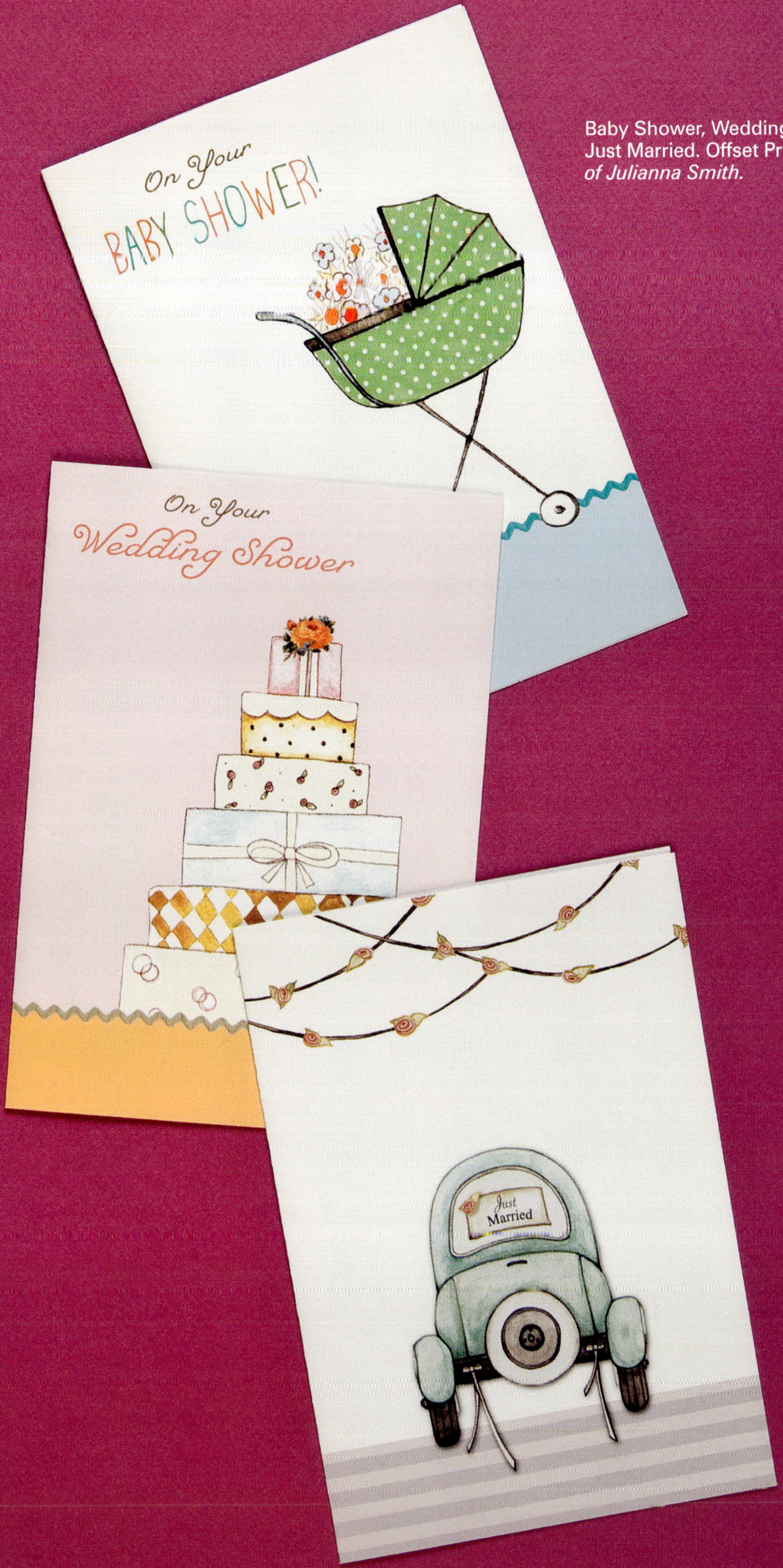

Baby Shower, Wedding Shower, and Just Married. Offset Printed. *Courtesy of Julianna Smith.*

Kate & Birdie Paper Co.
www.kateandbirdie.com

Gloria Wall, artist and creative director for Kate & Birdie Paper Co. is known for her hand-drawn style, using only original illustrations and patterns for Kate & Birdie's paper goods and canvas prints. A self-taught artist, Gloria founded Kate & Birdie in Winnipeg, Canada, in 2004, on the top floor of an old sewing factory in one of North America's oldest commercial districts. With her love of color, illustration and design, starting a creative enterprise was a lifelong dream. Paired with a long family line of entrepreneurs, it also meant it was a natural fit. Gloria also finds time to license her custom invitations, announcements, and holiday cards exclusively for Tiny Prints.

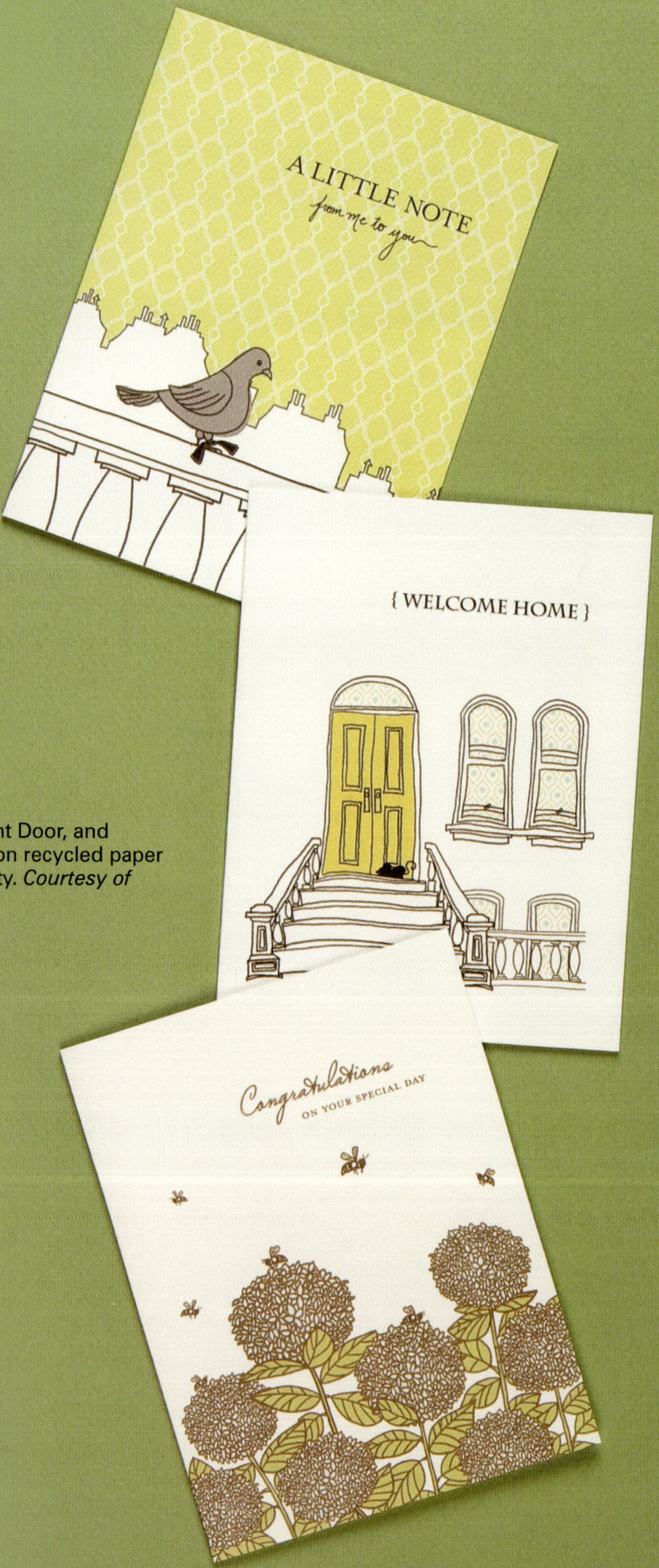

Messenger Pigeon, New Home Front Door, and Wedding Day Hydrangeas. Printed on recycled paper made with wind-generated electricity. *Courtesy of Gloria Wall.*

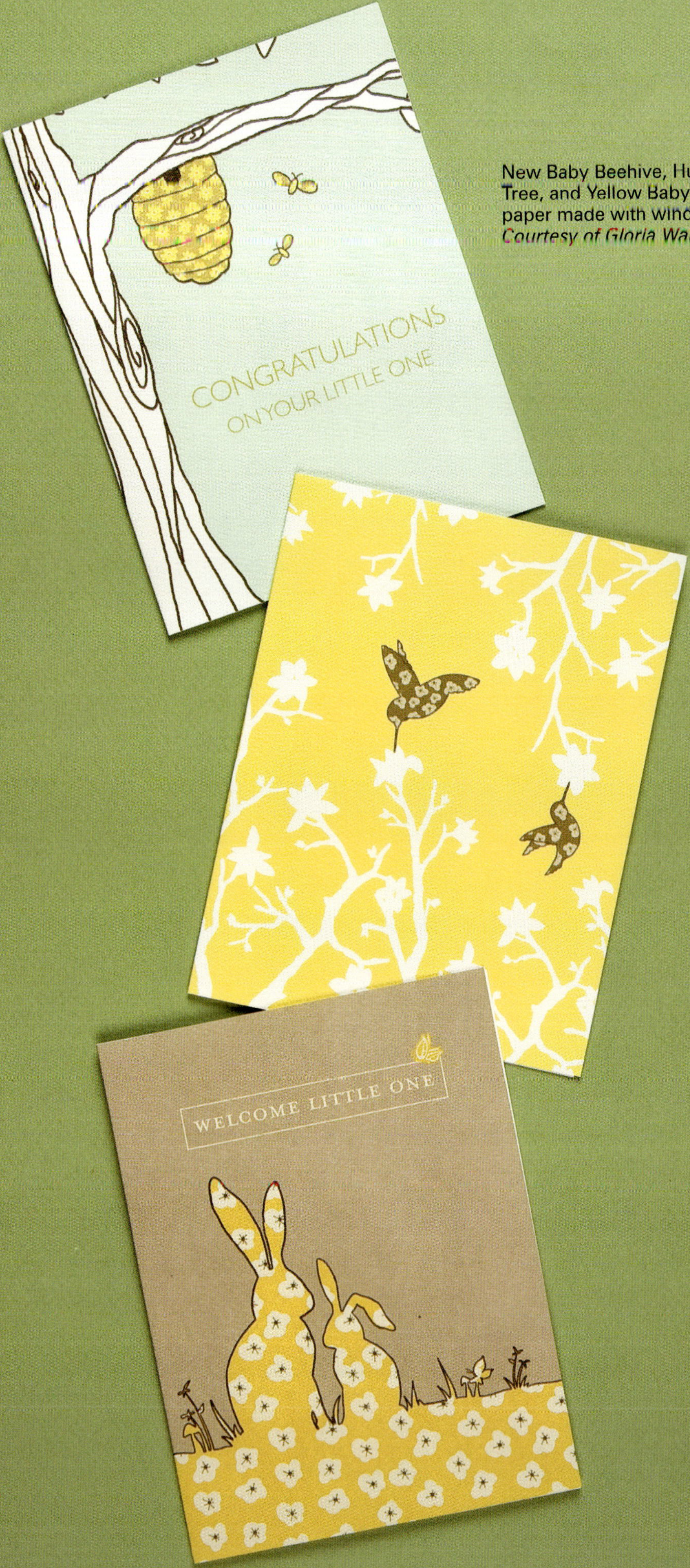

New Baby Beehive, Hummingbirds and Magnolia Tree, and Yellow Baby Bunnies. Printed on recycled paper made with wind-generated electricity. *Courtesy of Gloria Wall.*

La Familia Green

www.lafamiliagreen.com

Mollie Green grew up among the tumbleweeds and cotton fields of Lubbock, Texas. After moving to the Midwest in high school, she completed a BFA in painting and printmaking at the School of the Art Institute of Chicago. Graduation forced the lesson of how to live and work as an artist, which meant retail by day and artist by night. Attempting to integrate retail skills with artistic training and a love of multiples led to the birth of La Familia Green in 2005. She wanted to make stationery and journals that were completely handmade and special yet accessible. She loves the immediacy and intimacy of cards. She also loves that she can easily and quickly express her interests through this medium. La Familia Green personalized photo cards and notes are available on Cardstore.com and Mollie has also collaborated on book projects with Chronicle Books.

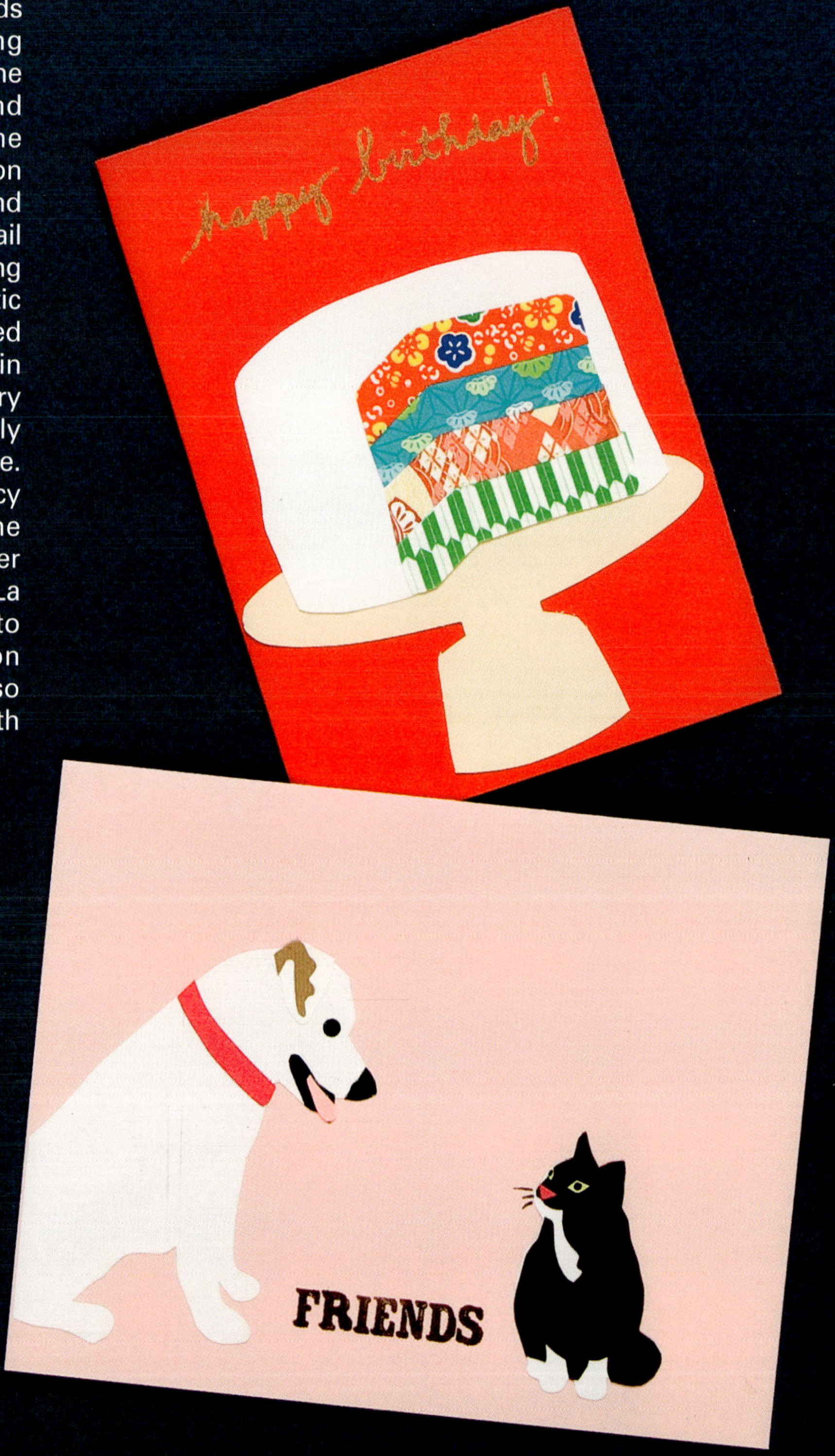

Birthday Cake and Friends. Handmade with hand cut paper and gocco printing. *Courtesy of La Familia Green.*

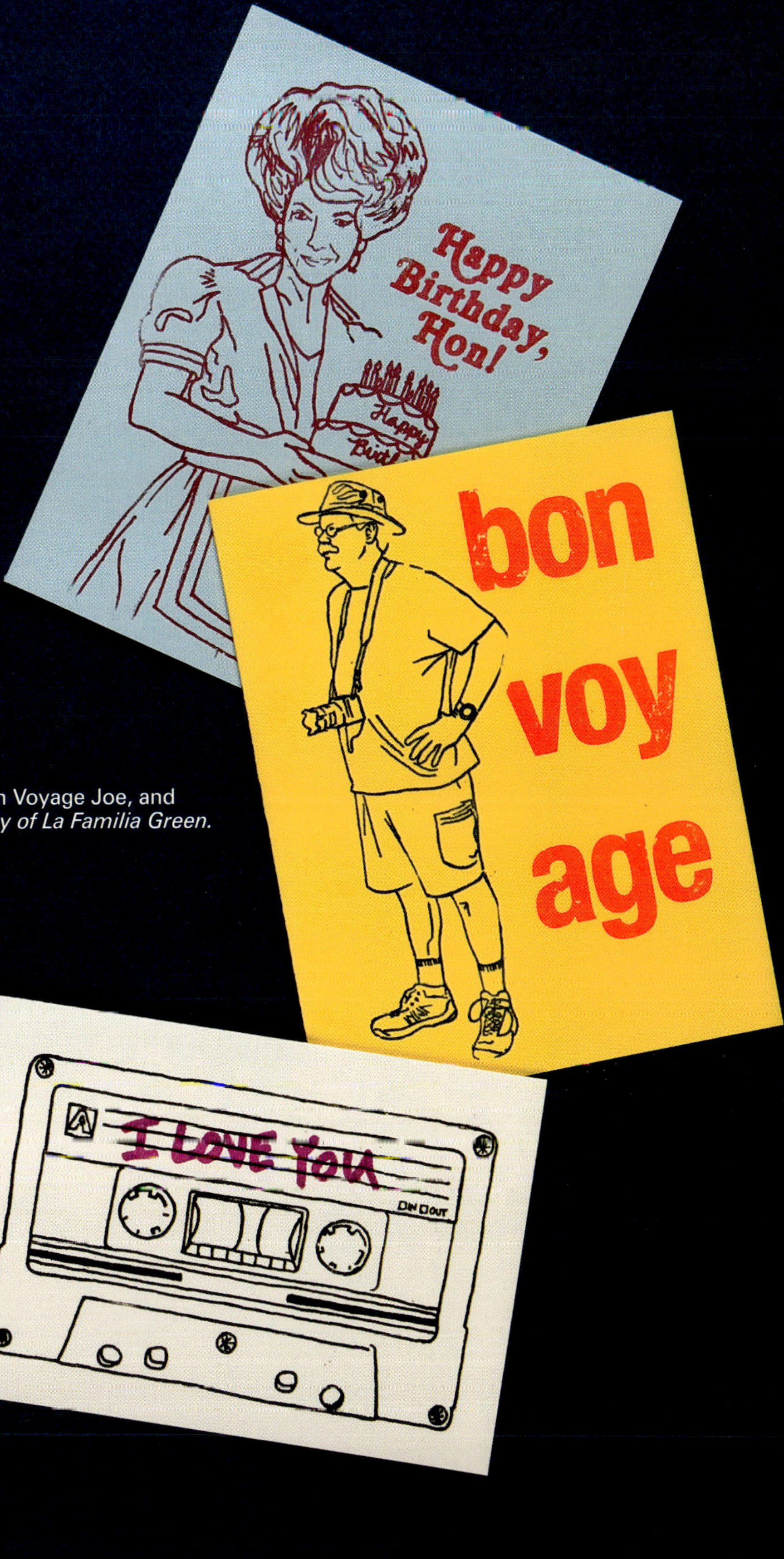

Happy Birthday Hon, Bon Voyage Joe, and Mixtape. Gocco. *Courtesy of La Familia Green.*

Maginating
www.maginating.com

Ever since he could hold a pencil, Brad Woods has been drawing, designing, and Maginating, a verb he invented as a child to describe imaginative play. Brad eventually earned two degrees in animation and began a fifteen-year career in the industry. Not entirely satisfied despite his many years in film and television, Brad became drawn to the handmade: the thick creases of paper, the clank of cast iron, and the scent of ink fresh from the can. He began to move away from ephemeral digital wizardry toward the tactile old-world craftsmanship of letterpress printing. In 2006, Maginating was born. Brad is particularly influenced by George Nelson's groundbreaking designs for Herman Miller, Alexander Girard's clever playfulness and uninhibited use of color, and Charles and Ray Eames' technical ingenuity.

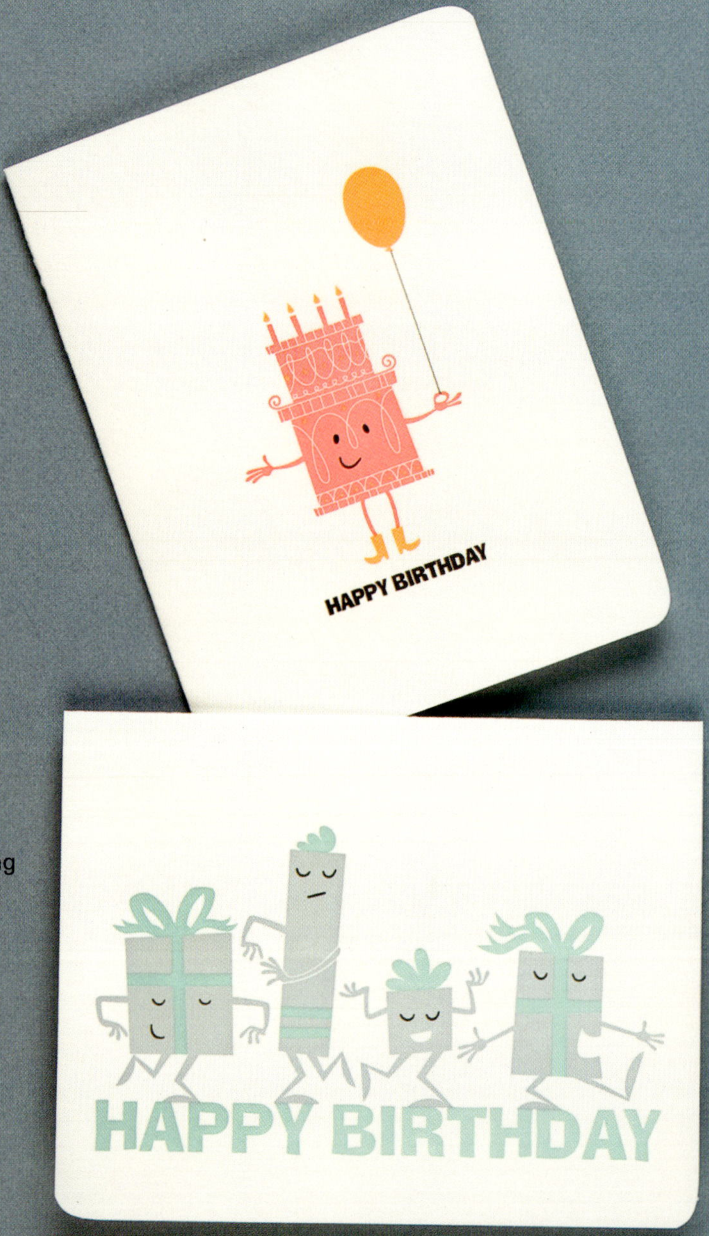

Birthday Cake Man and Dancing Gifts. Letterpress. *Courtesy of Maginating.*

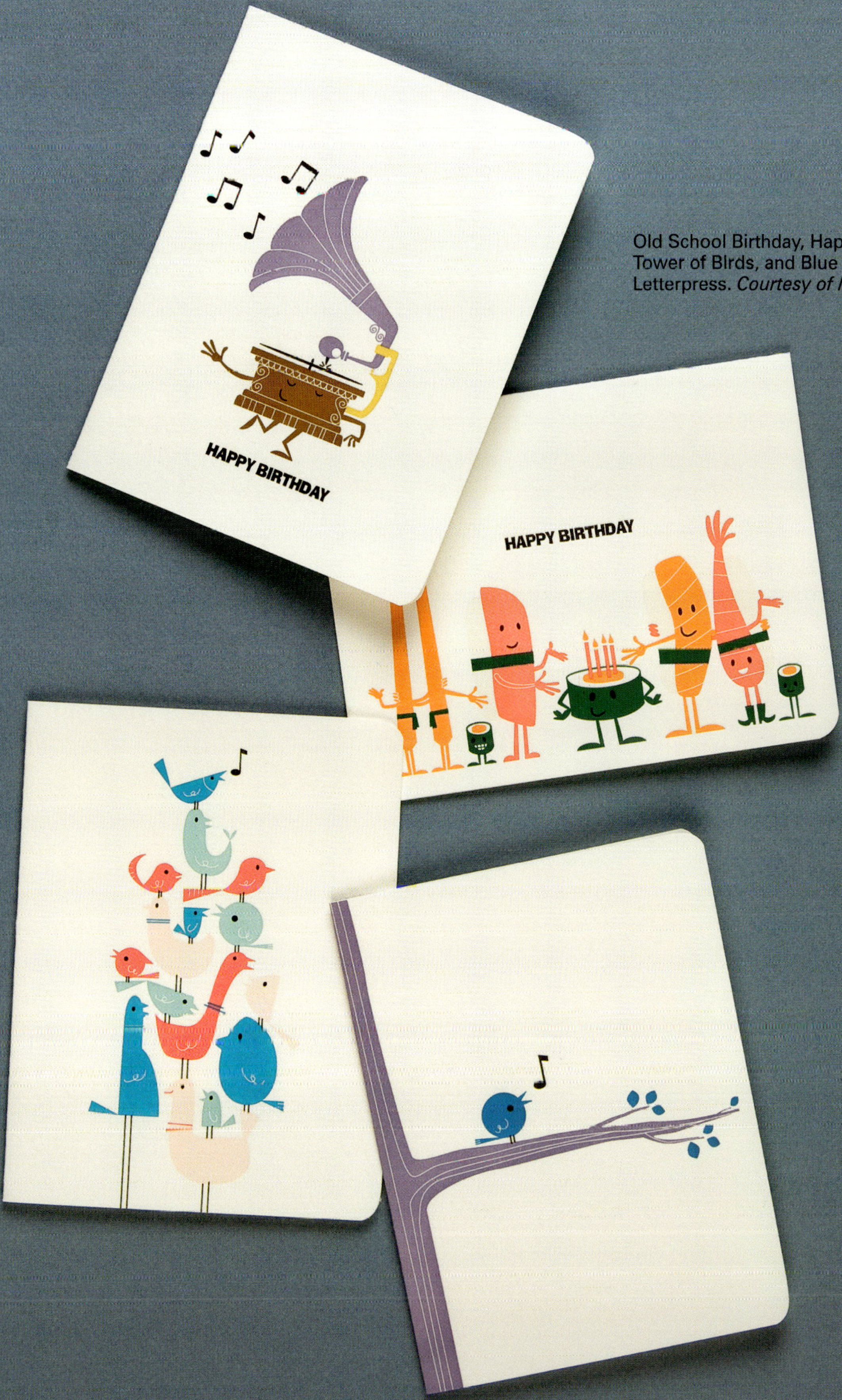

Old School Birthday, Happy Sushi to You, Tower of Birds, and Blue Bird of Happiness. Letterpress. *Courtesy of Maginating.*

Marzipan Inc. & Fin Roe
www.marzipaninc.com
www.finandroe.com

As a young girl, Lori Dunbar would joke about someday ruling the world with a business of her own. It all started when she created her wedding invitations in the fall of 2001. Finding that she loved the process, her dream business started to emerge. After her wedding, she created a small line of greeting cards and approached several stores for their input. To her delight, nearly every store she visited placed orders for her handcrafted originals. Soon her little business was bustling. After six years in business, Lori decided to start a new division of her company which focused on customizable products such as photo announcements, invitations, calling cards, and more. She named the new division Fin + Roe after her two young boys (Finley & Rowan). In 2010, Marzipan Inc. partnered with the Whitney English company to distribute and fulfill her custom line of announcements and invitations under the brand name Citrus & Clover.

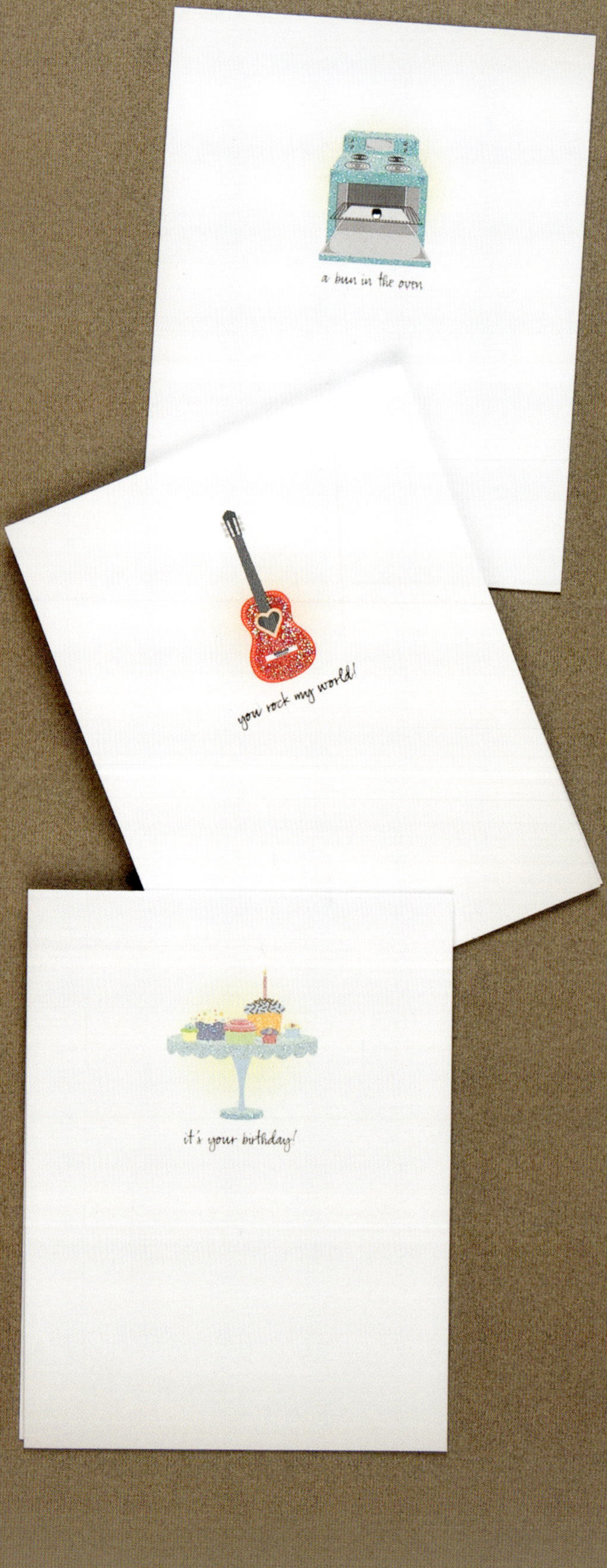

Josie, London, and Nadia. Printed on FSC certified paper using soy based inks and hand embellished with glitter. *Courtesy of Lori Dunbar.*

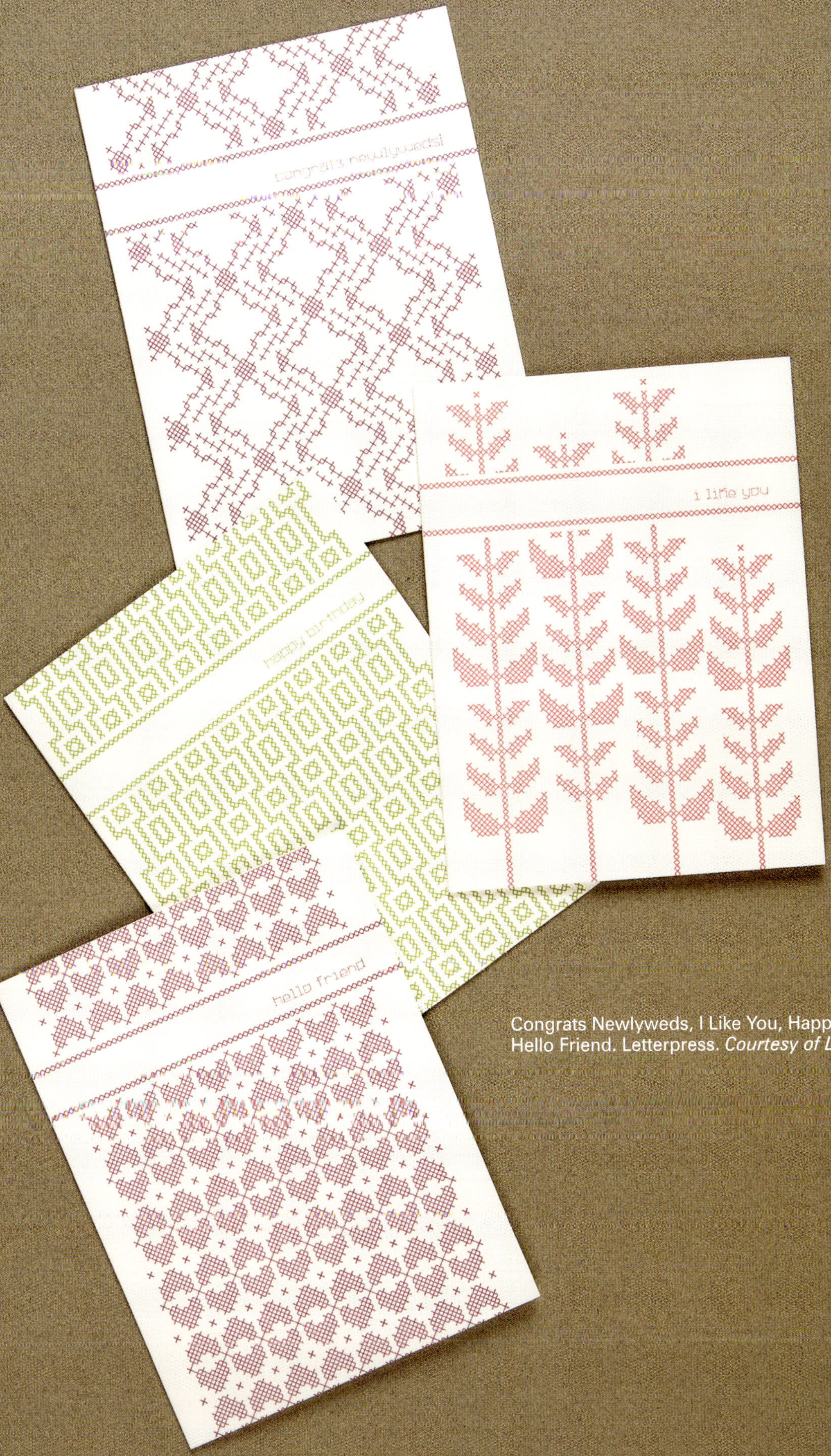

Congrats Newlyweds, I Like You, Happy Birthday, and Hello Friend. Letterpress. *Courtesy of Lori Dunbar.*

Modern Printed Matter

www.modernprintedmatter.com

Anna Cote has always designed and made her own cards and invitations, but she made it official by starting her own business in January of 2005. She has a real love of paper and hand written correspondence and uses her own photography to create modern organic illustrations. She became a stationery artist after being unsatisfied with her career as an environmental engineer and wanting to live what she loves. Her designs are sold at over 300 retail locations, and has been featured in *HOW, Country Living, The Martha Stewart Show, Design*Sponge*, and various other publications and blogs. Her studio and retail store is located in Rhode Island where she lives with her husband, son, and two kitties.

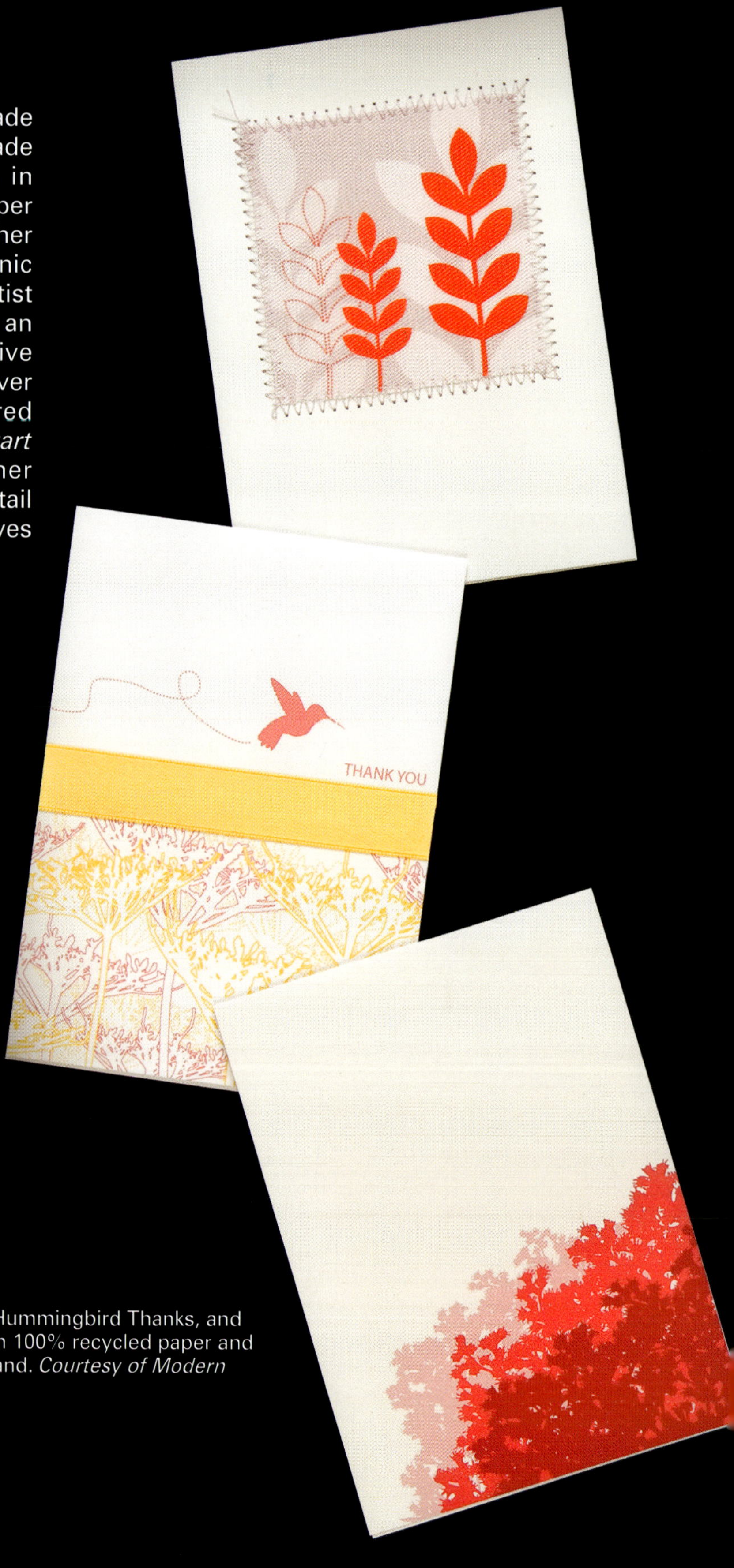

Stitched Leaves, Hummingbird Thanks, and Shrubs. Printed on 100% recycled paper and embellished by hand. *Courtesy of Modern Printed Matter.*

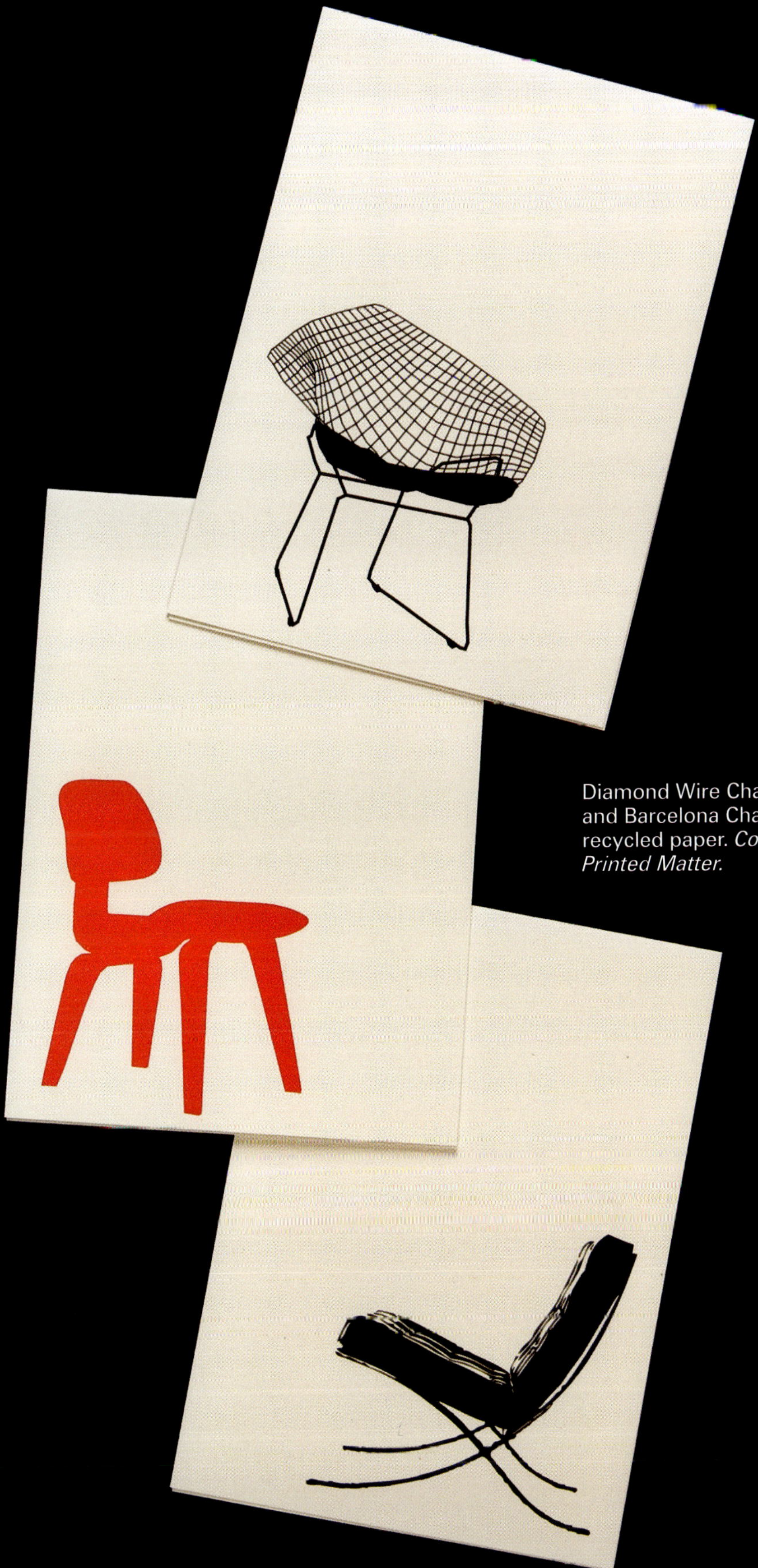

Diamond Wire Chair, Plywood Chair, and Barcelona Chair. Printed on 100% recycled paper. *Courtesy of Modern Printed Matter.*

Morris & Essex

www.morrisessex.com

Eliza Jane Curtis started selling t-shirts around 2001 and switched to stationery in 2007 because she was living overseas and it was easier to mail stationery than t-shirts. She has always loved making her own valentines and birthday cards so it felt pretty natural to start making them in batches and selling them. Eliza grew up in rural Maine, moved to New York to study design and lived there for a number of years. Then she moved to Buenos Aires, Argentina, for a few years and has just recently moved back to rural Maine again, coming full circle. Her work has been featured on well-known blogs and websites and has sold at Kate's Paperie locations in Manhattan, as well as a number of other boutiques around the world.

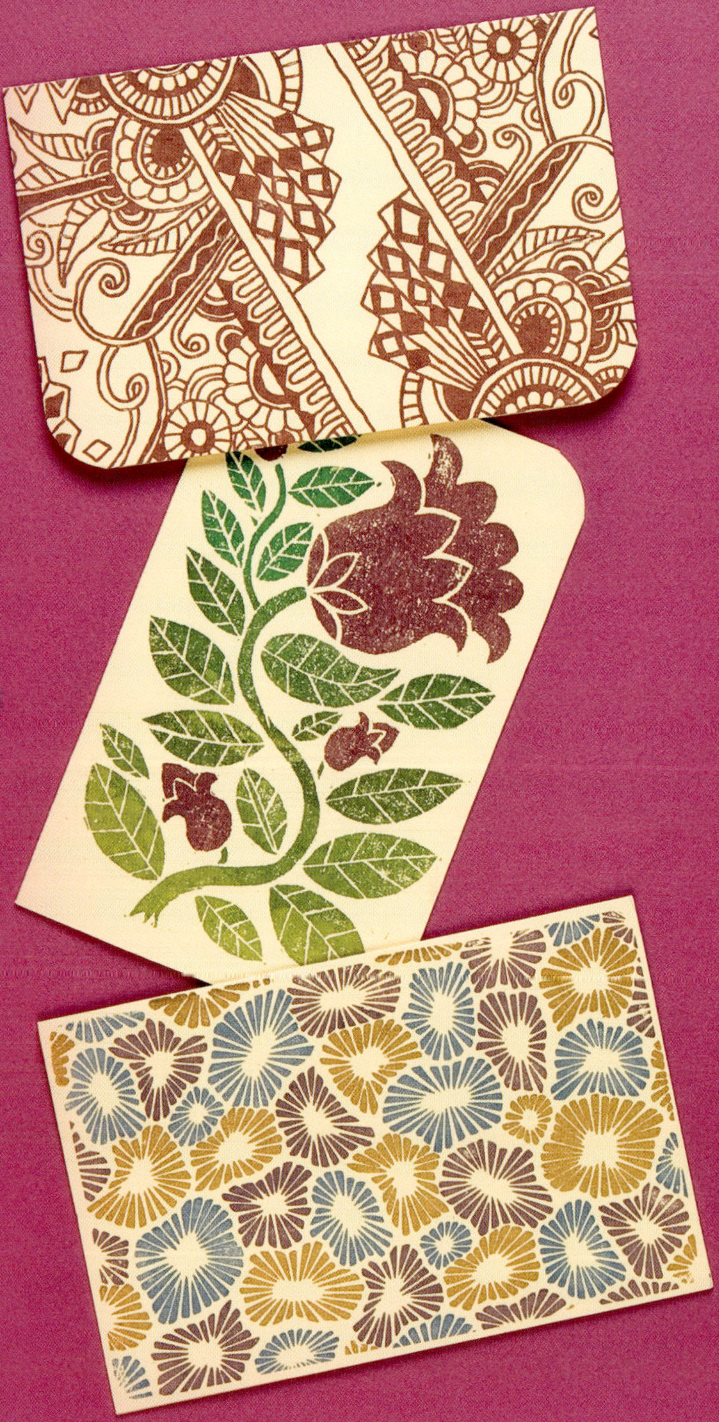

Curitiba, Linocut Vine, and Starburst. Hand printed on Fabriano Elle Erre paper. *Courtesy of Morris & Essex.*

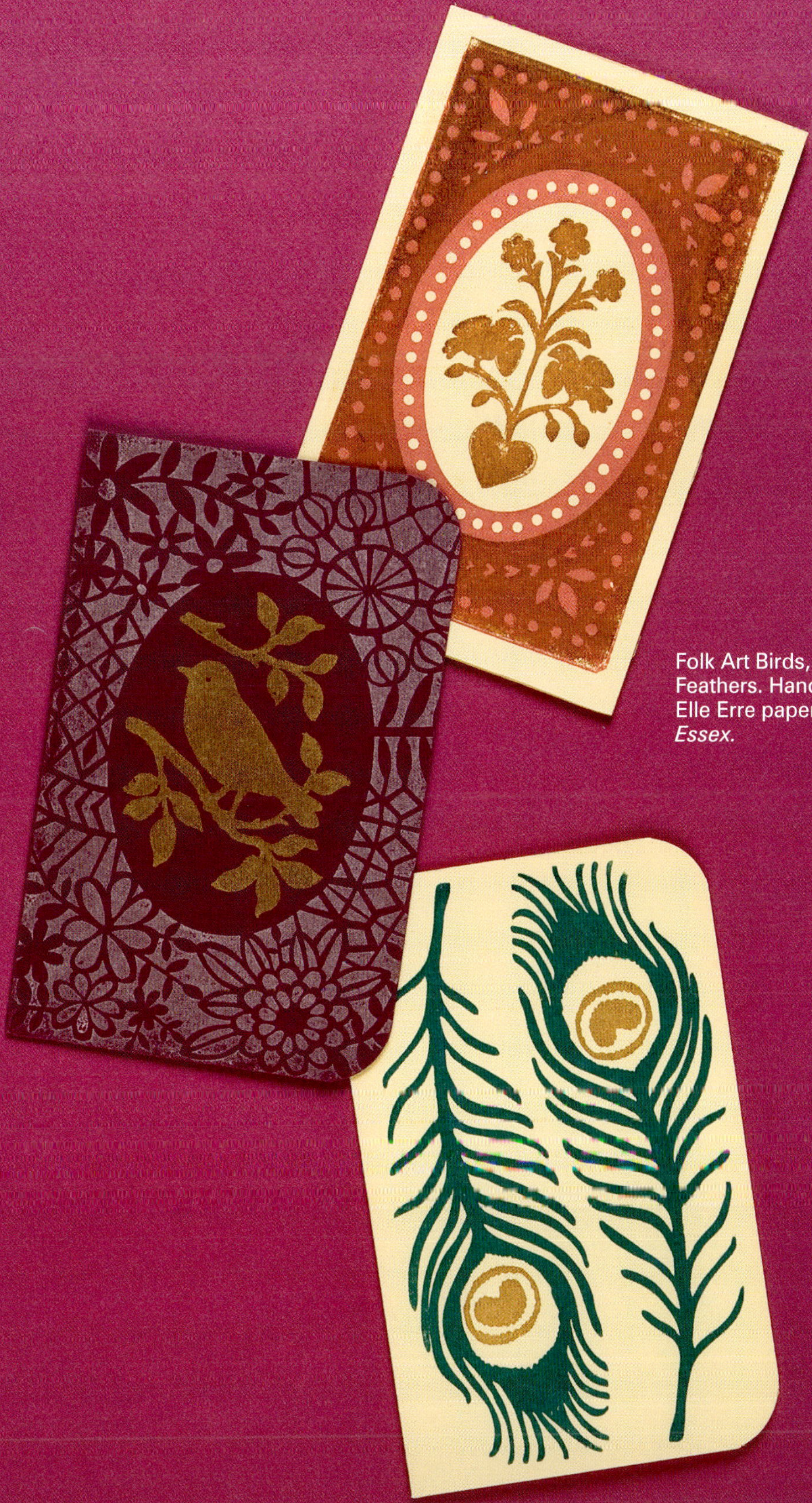

Folk Art Birds, Gold Bird, and Peacock Feathers. Hand printed on Fabriano Elle Erre paper. *Courtesy of Morris & Essex.*

Motormouthpress, LLC

www.motormouthpress.com

Laurie Coughlin, the artist behind Motormouthpress, LLC, first used the name "Motormouthpress" as her press name while earning her MFA in Book Arts/Printmaking at The University of the Arts in Philadelphia. Her first love is making books. She enjoys the entire process from making the paper to printing the pages with text and/or imagery to binding the book. She has always wanted to share her good design sensibilities with others, but books can be expensive to manufacture. So she thought she could translate her designs easily to greeting cards, and thus Motormouthpress was transformed into Motormouthpress, LLC in September of 2004 only a few short years after graduation. In addition to her own card line, Laurie also licenses her work for Cardstore.com and Mayfairlane, LLC.

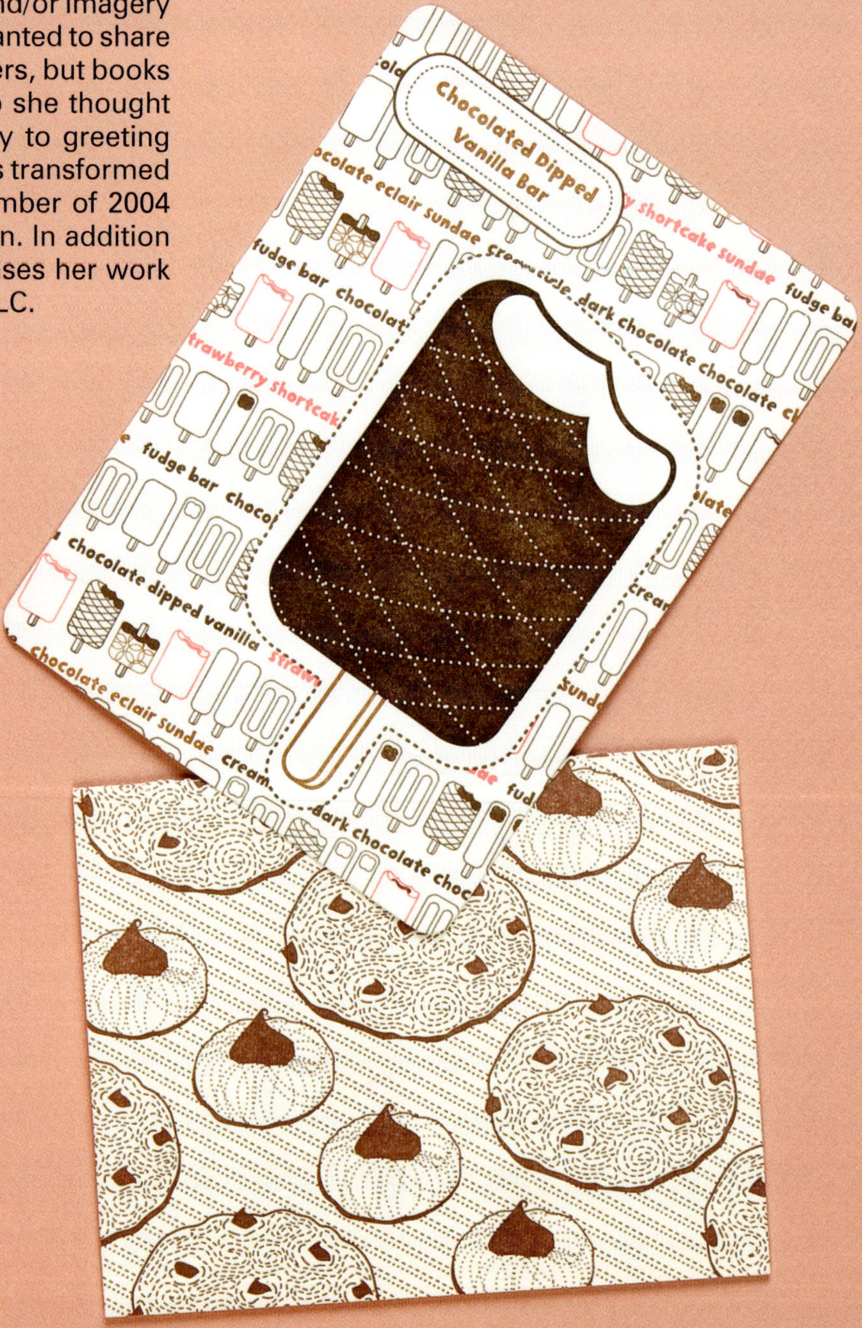

Chocolate Dipped Vanilla Bar and Chocolate Chip Cookies. Letterpress. *Courtesy of Motormouthpress, LLC.*

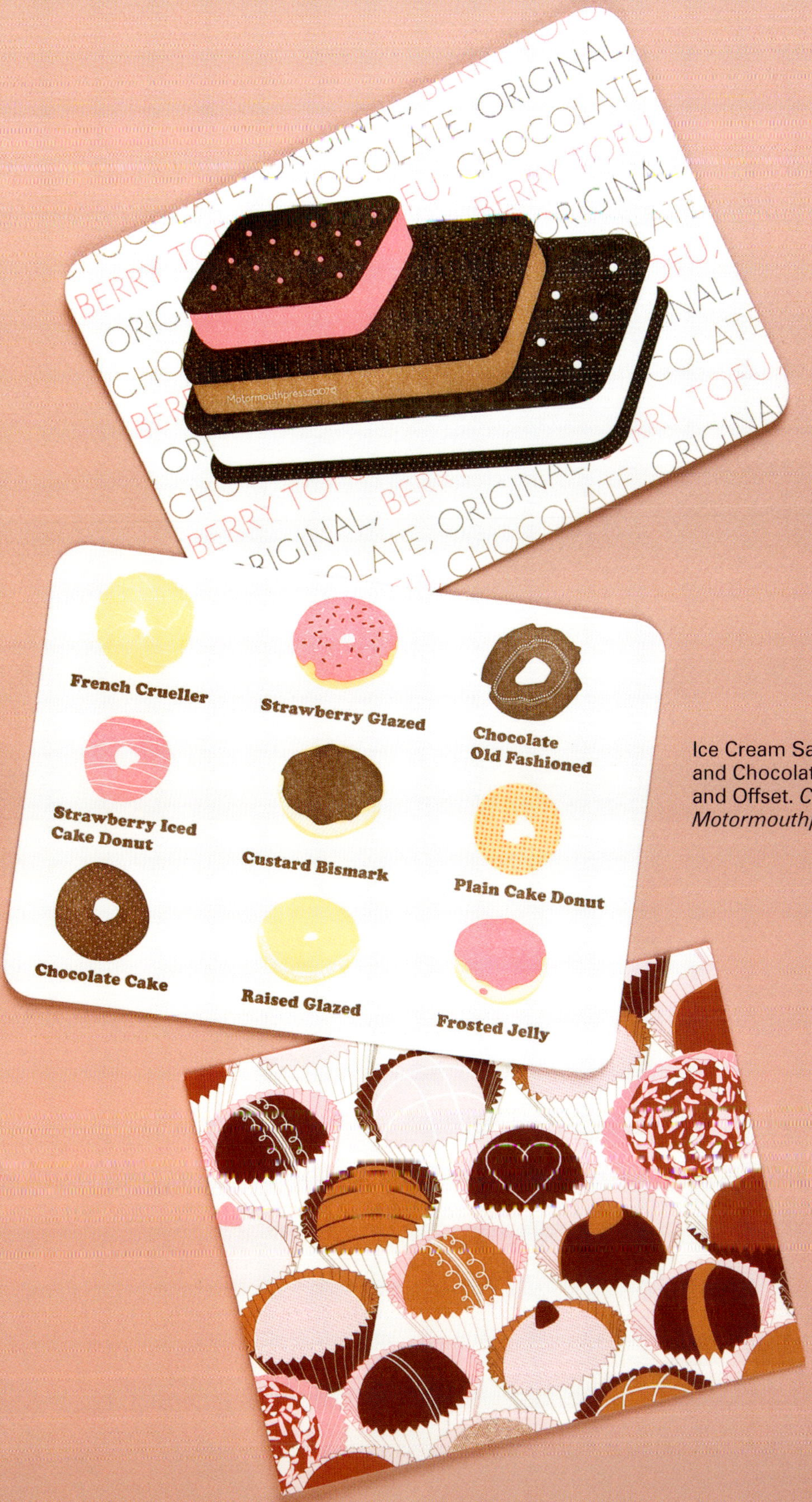

Ice Cream Sandwiches, Donuts, and Chocolate Box. Letterpress and Offset. *Courtesy of Motormouthpress, LLC.*

Mr. Boddington's Studio

www.mrboddington.com

Established in 2007, Mr. Boddington's Studio is a quirky little stationery shop among the tall buildings of New York City. The studio draws inspiration from classic art and tradition, applying it to modern concepts and design. In Mr. Boddington's spare time, he enjoys sailing the West Indies, discovering exotic papers and inks, and Bombay gin and tonics with bread and orange marmalade.

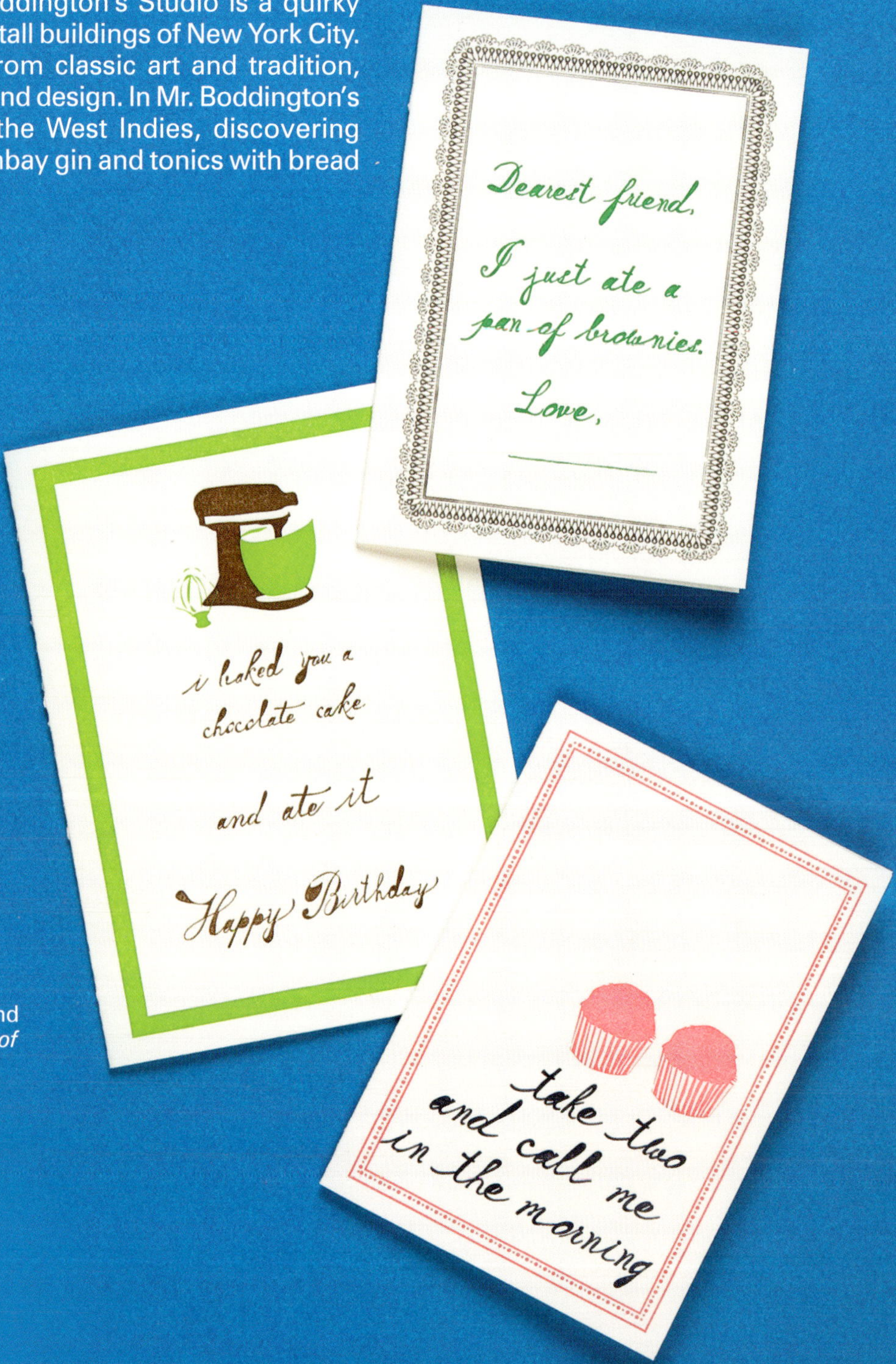

Pan of Brownies, Bake a Cake, and Take Two. Letterpress. *Courtesy of Mr. Boddington's Studio.*

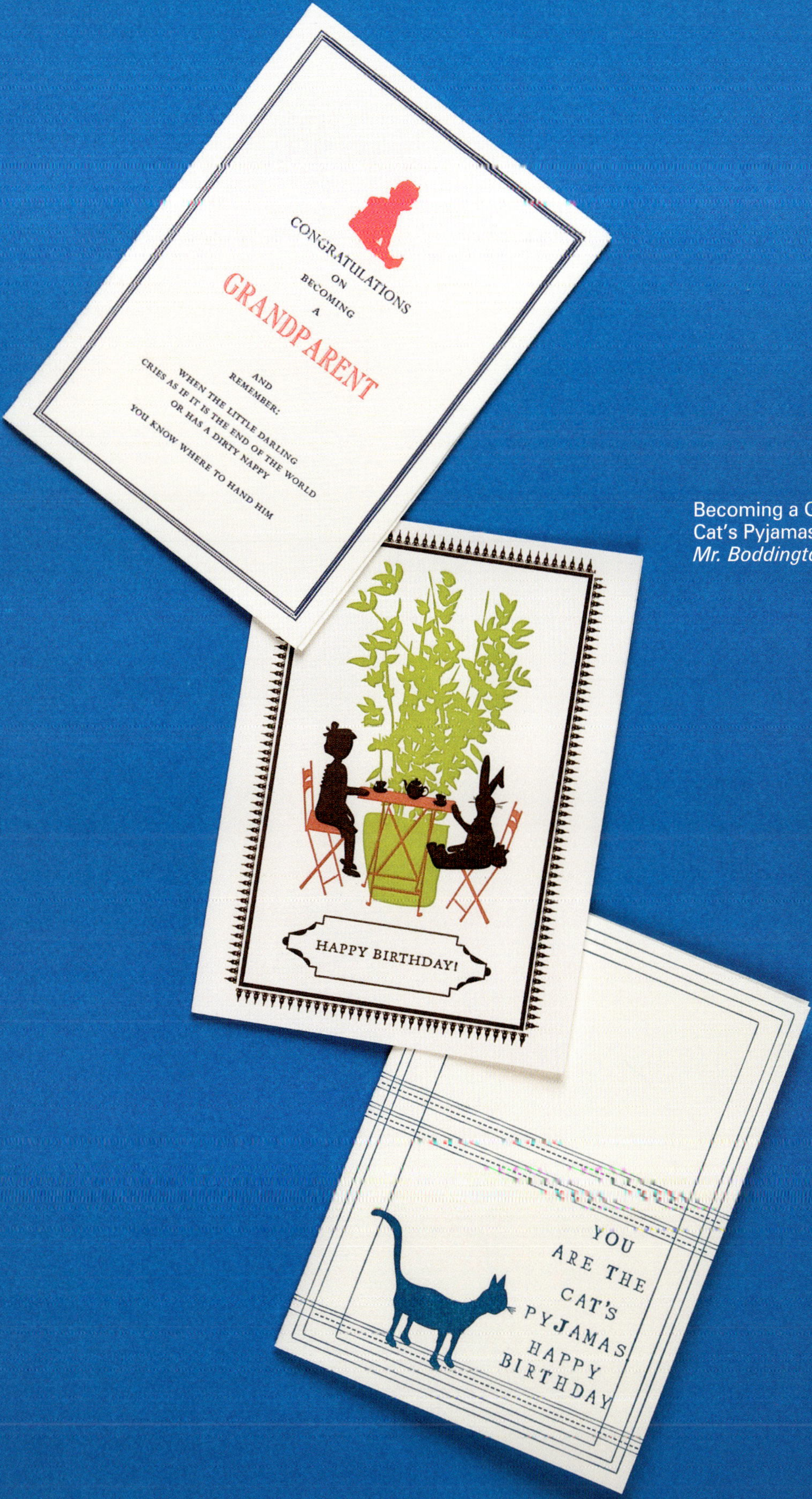

Becoming a Grandparent, Tea Party, and Cat's Pyjamas. Letterpress. *Courtesy of Mr. Boddington's Studio.*

Natalie Eden
www.natalieseden.com

Natalie was drawing at the age of three and never stopped. Together with her talented husband Keith and years of design experience in the Seattle, Washington, area, the couple launched a collection of eco-friendly, hand embellished cards in 2004. Natalie Eden has been featured in magazines, including *Seattle Bride, Mary Engelbreit,* and *Lucky Magazine* ... to name a few. Both Keith and Natalie find inspiration in classic children's books, vintage interior shops, while traveling, and from their two young children, who provide constant inspiration.

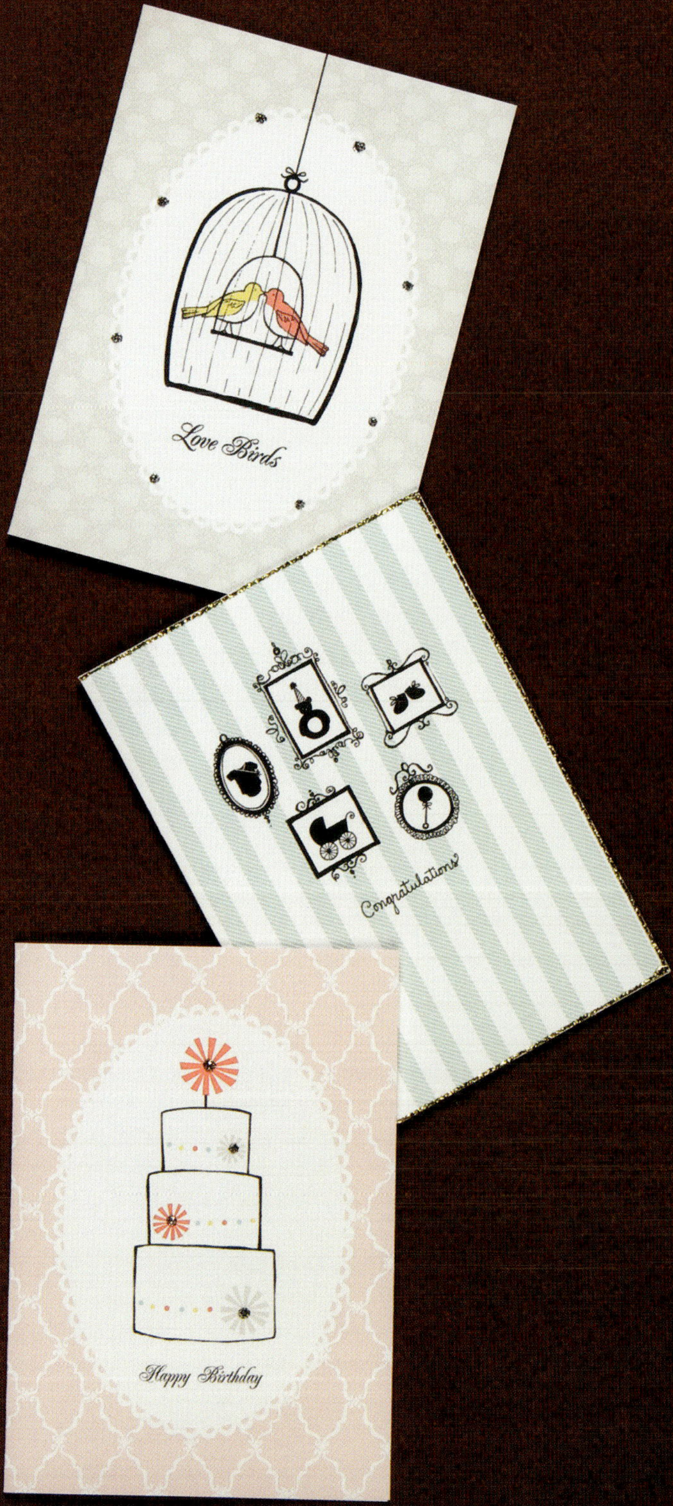

Love Birds, Bebe Frame, and Cake. Handmade with Glitter. *Courtesy of Natalie Eden.*

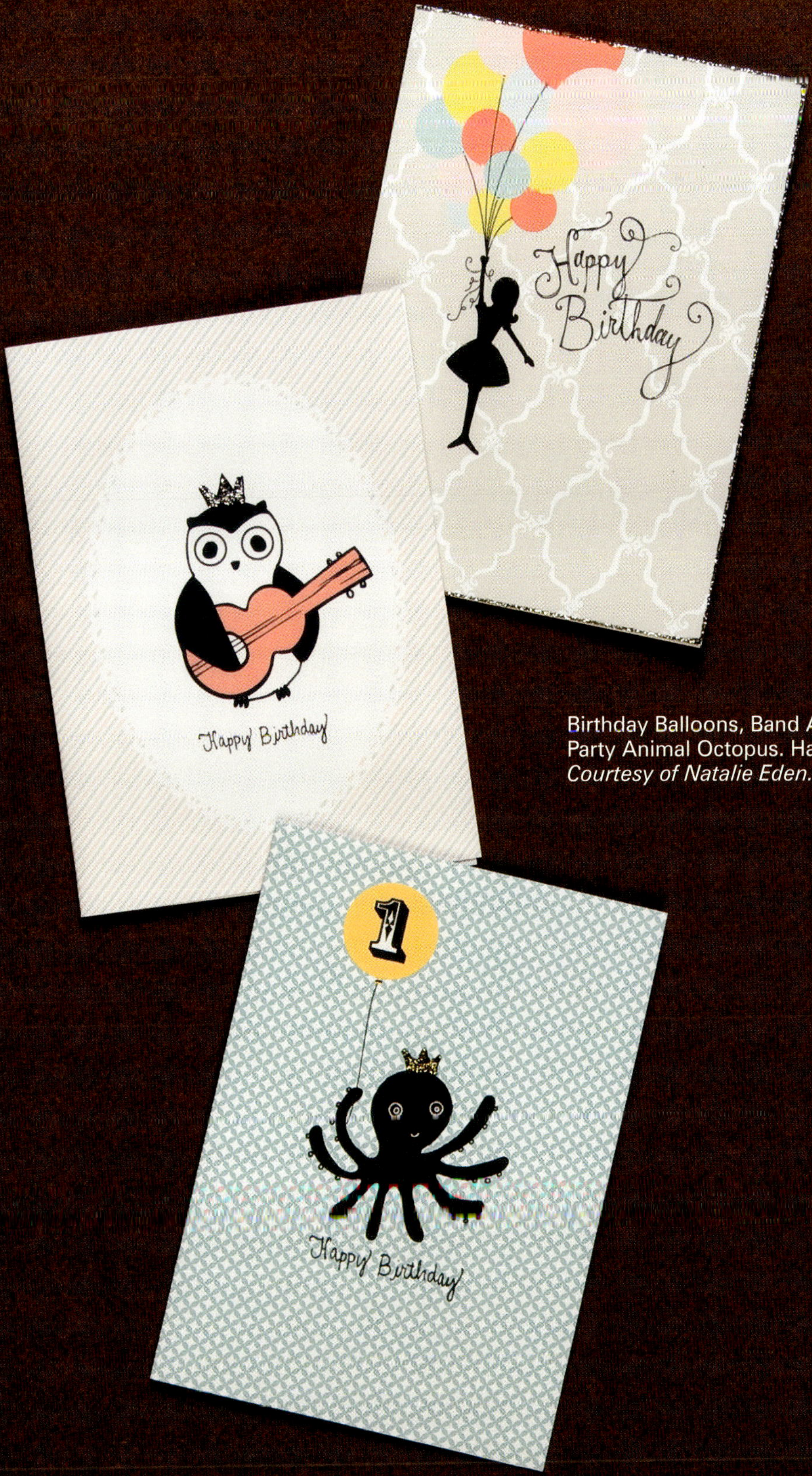

Birthday Balloons, Band Animal Owl, and Party Animal Octopus. Handmade with Glitter. *Courtesy of Natalie Eden.*

Night Owl Paper Goods

www.nightowlpapergoods.com

Jennifer Tatham and Alan Henderson became serious about starting a company in 2005 and quit their full time jobs a few years later (Jennifer in Sepetember 2007 and Alan in January 2008). Having grown up surrounded by the rural landscapes of Kentucky and Iowa, both Alan and Jennifer had a fondness for collection stamps, trading stickers, and recycling paper scraps into handmade cards and notebooks. With a similar passion for craftsmanship and detail, the pair has cultivated a style they like to call modern yet folksy. Based out of Birmingham, Owlabama, their work can now be found in over 700 shops across the United States as well as in over 150 shops internationally. They also license their artwork to Tiny Prints, an online retailer of custom cards and custom photo greetings. Night Owl Paper Goods has even been spotted on "The Today Show."

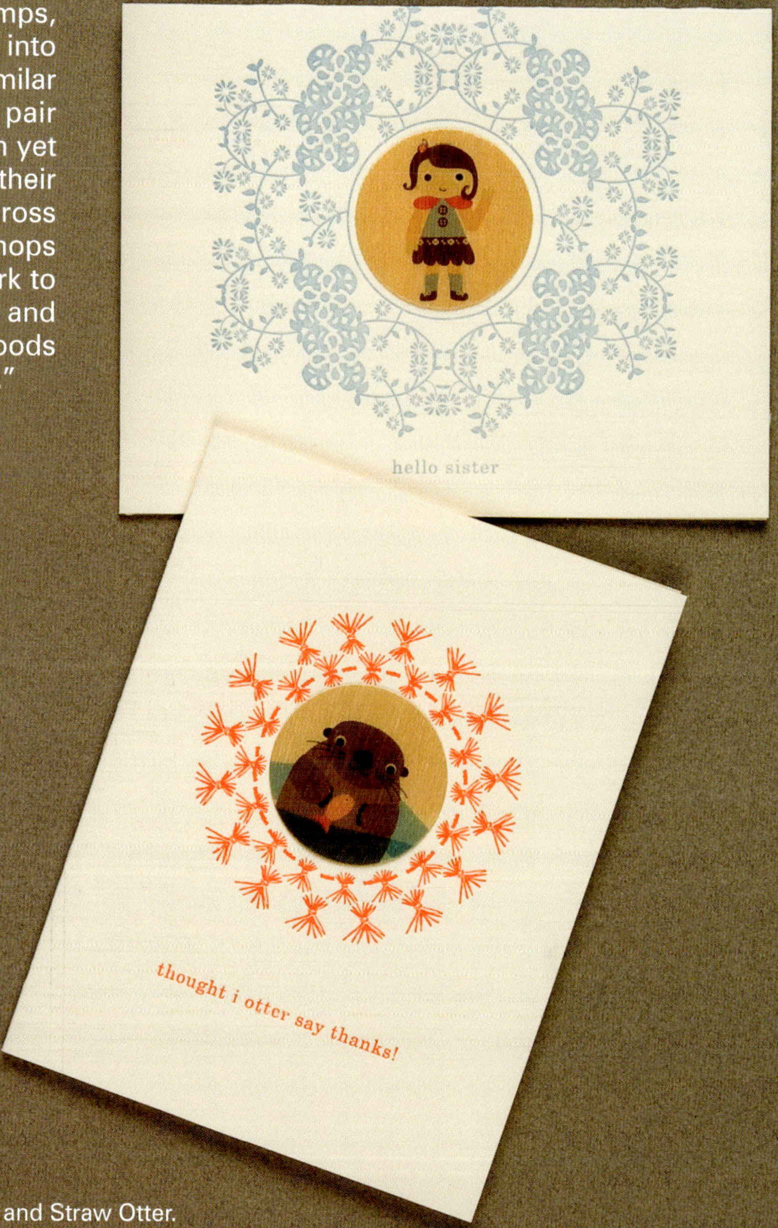

Folksy Floral Sister and Straw Otter. Letterpress printed on 100% reclaimed and recycled cotton with sustainably harvested wood embellishments. *Courtesy of Night Owl Paper Goods.*

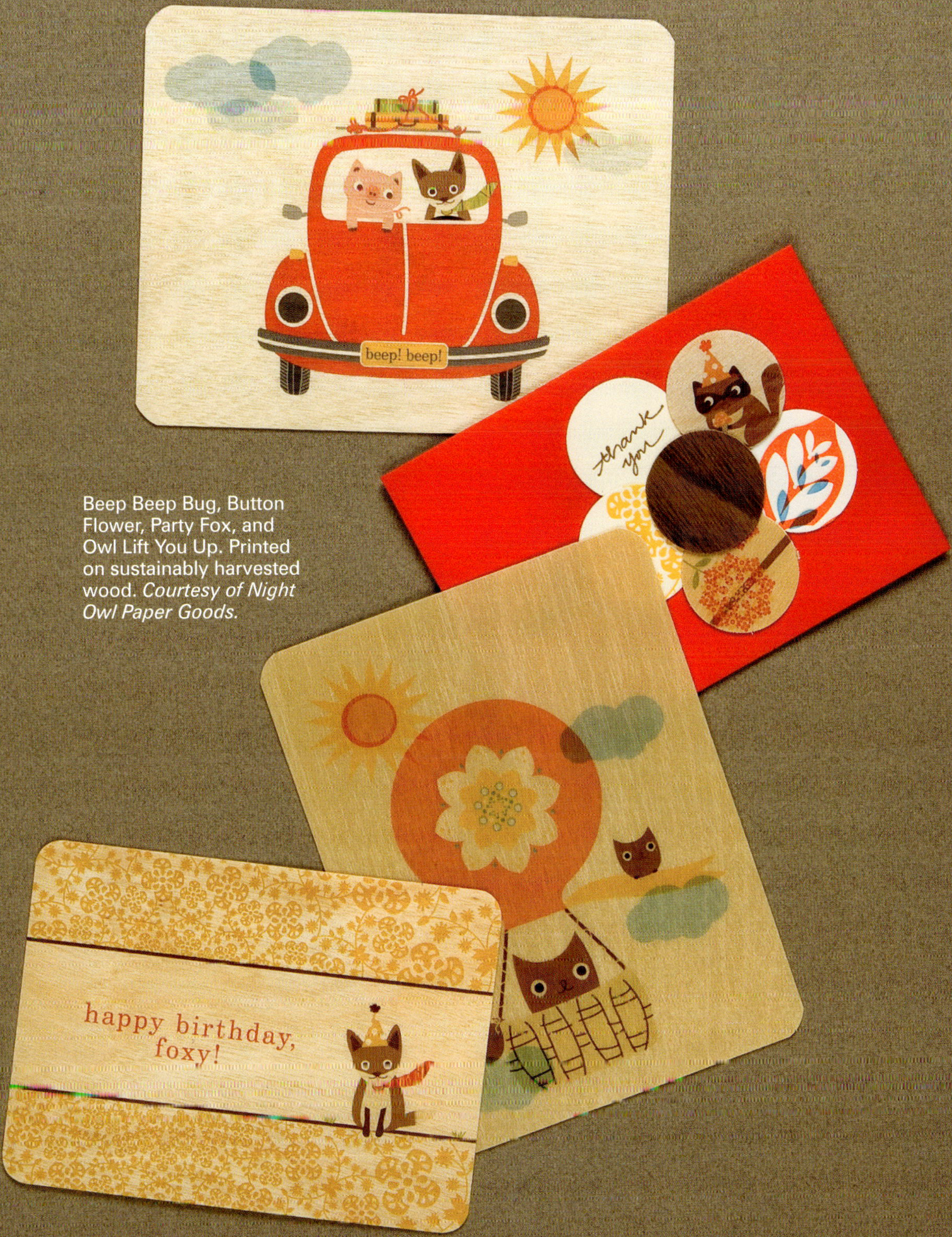

Beep Beep Bug, Button Flower, Party Fox, and Owl Lift You Up. Printed on sustainably harvested wood. *Courtesy of Night Owl Paper Goods.*

Old School Stationers

www.oldschoolstationers.com

Brian Reed has been designing stationery since 1995, but in the late 1990s computers swept into the printing world making his skills in darkroom prepress obsolete. Rather than ride the new wave of technology, he decided to go back about one hundred years and in 2003 bought his first Chandler and Price Letterpress Printer. One year later, together with his wife Amy, Brian started a small letterpress studio in Portland, Oregon, called Old School Stationers, where they specialize in the design and production of letterpress cards and wall prints. They feel that the subtle imperfections in hand work only enhance the beauty of the design. Hand drawn and crafted design work found in illustrations, old signage, block prints, and ironwork greatly inspires them. Another big source of inspiration comes from time spent in nature. Some of their favorite design ideas have occurred while gardening, camping, and hiking.

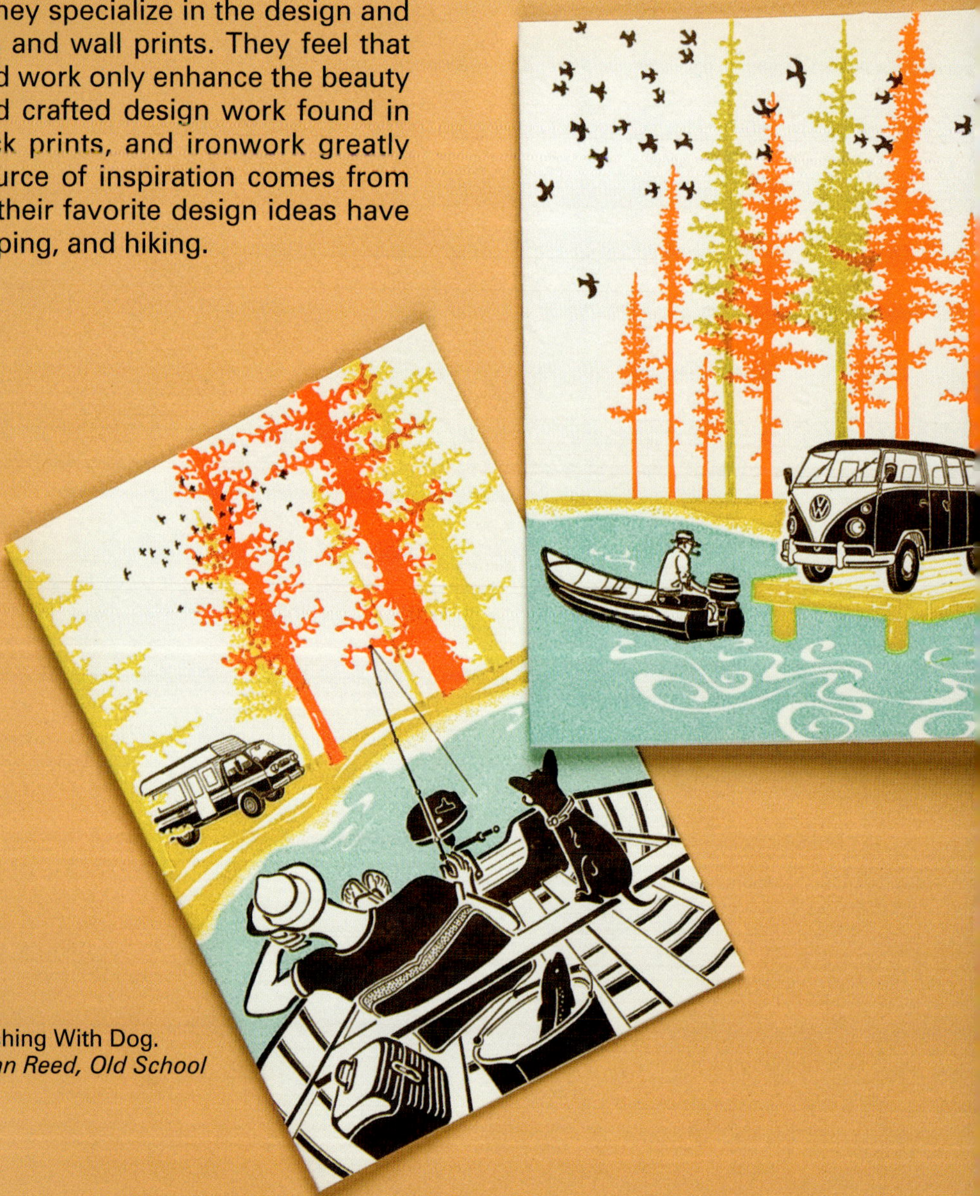

Volkswagen Camper and Fishing With Dog. Letterpress. *Courtesy of Brian Reed, Old School Stationers.*

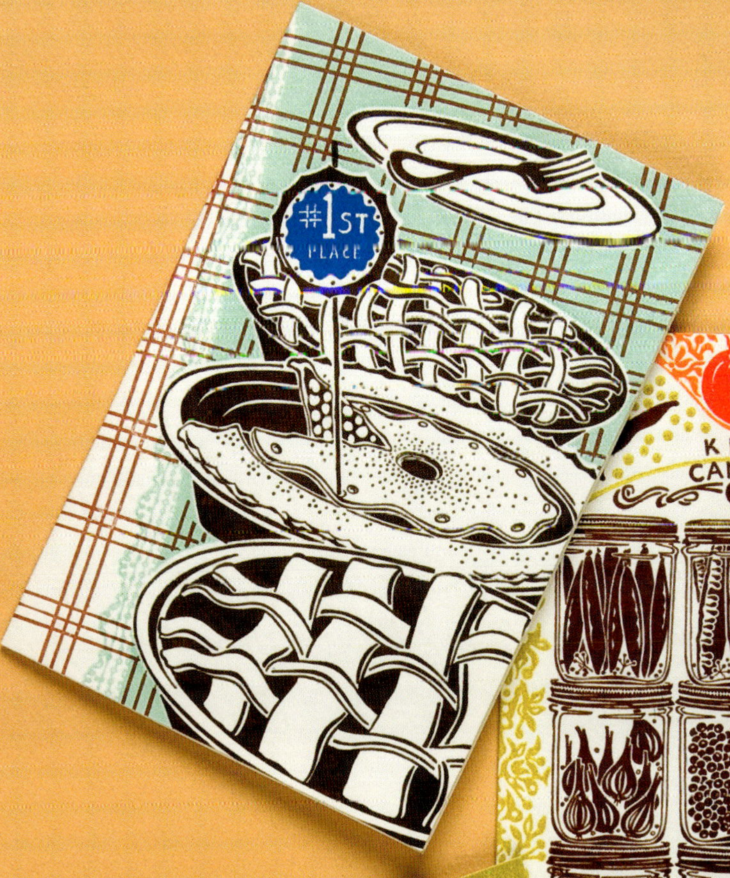

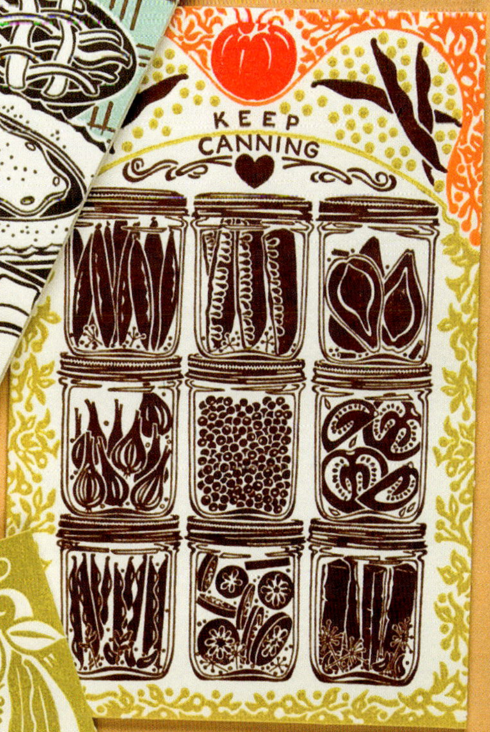

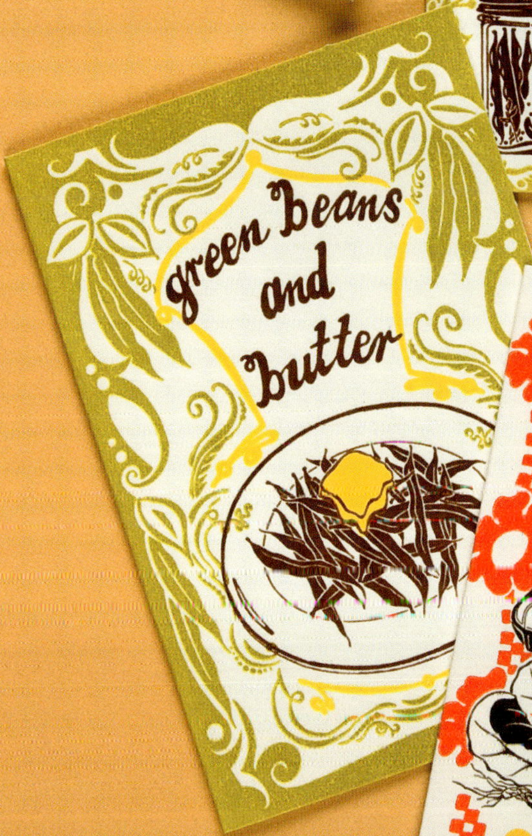

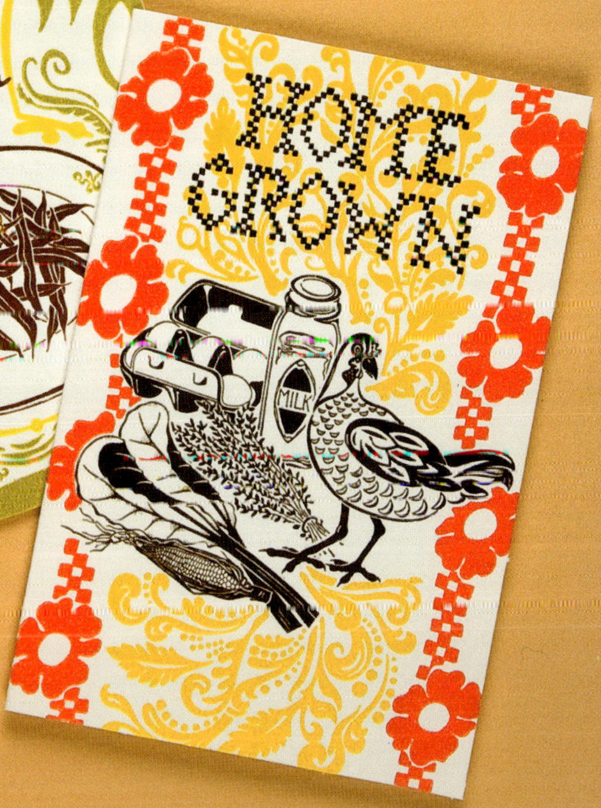

First Place Pie, Keep Canning, Green Beans and Butter, and Home Grown. Letterpress. *Courtesy of Brian Reed, Old School Stationers.*

Happy Birthday, I Miss You, Cheer Up, and Thinking of You. Letterpress. *Courtesy of Old Tom Foolery.*

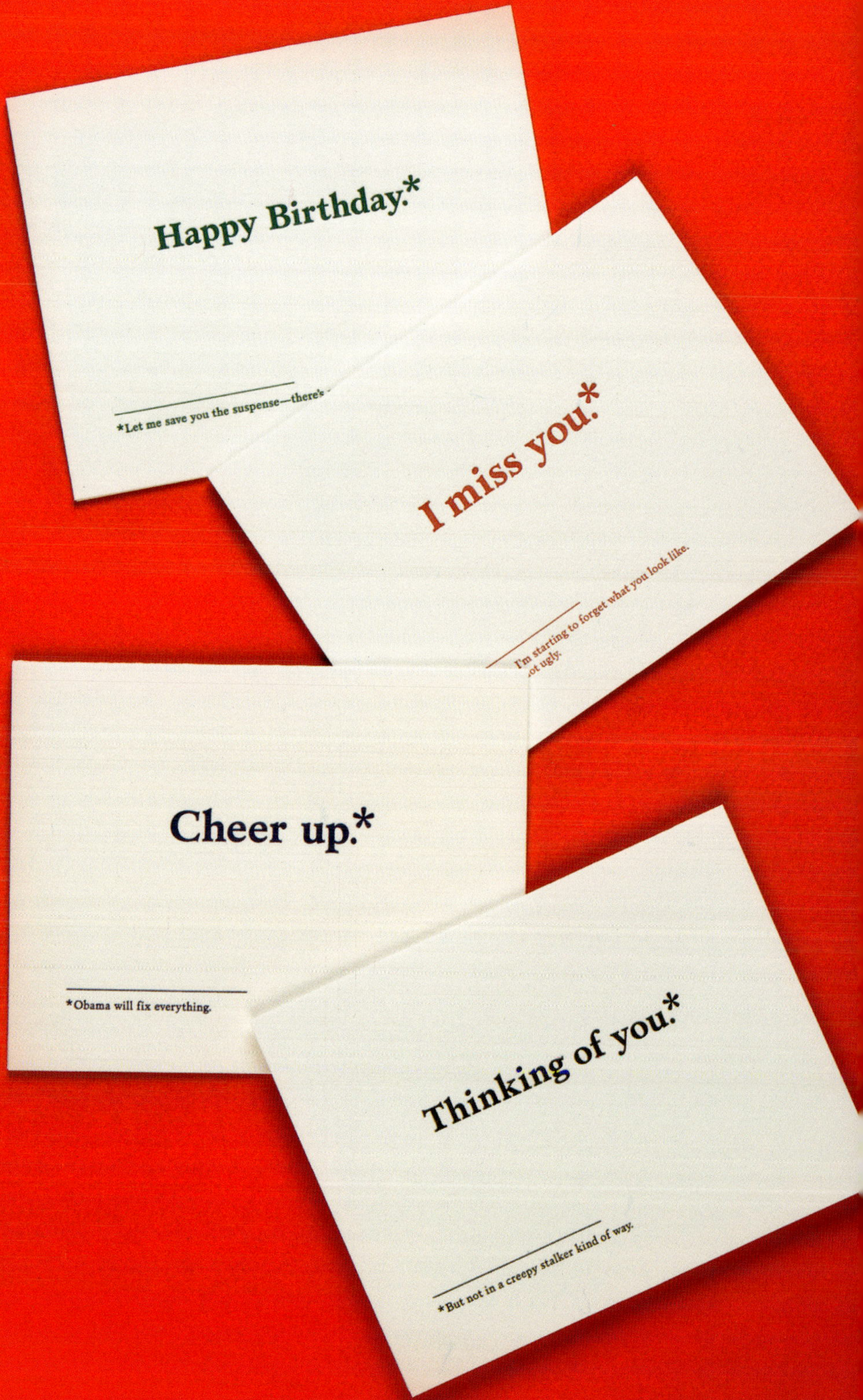

Old Tom Foolery

www.oldtomfoolery.com

Old Tom Foolery is the brainchild of husband and wife team Joel Gryniewski and Lauren Weinblatt. Joel was born in Minneapolis, Minnesota, and Lauren was born in Toledo, Ohio. The two met in graduate school for advertising at Virginia Commonwealth University's Brandcenter. While dating, Joel and Lauren used to buy each other funny greeting cards from a quirky Richmond gift boutique called Mongrel. Thanks to Mongrel's eclectic selection of independent card lines, they began to appreciate greeting cards for their creativity and craftsmanship, and entertained the notion of starting their own line. After a few years of working for ad agencies in Seattle and San Francisco, they decided it was time to strike out on their own. So, in 2007, they bought a vintage letterpress and founded Old Tom Foolery.

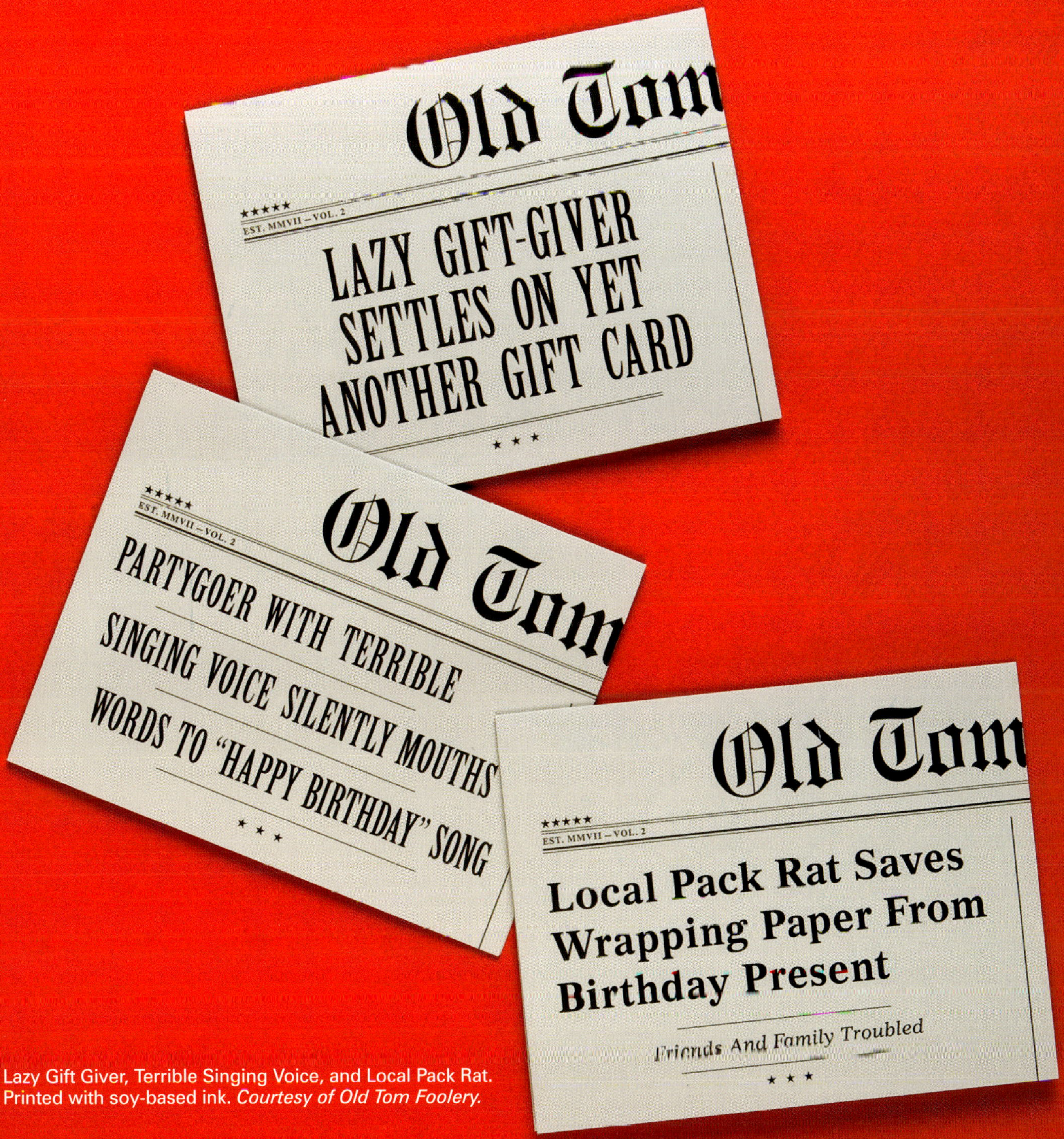

Lazy Gift Giver, Terrible Singing Voice, and Local Pack Rat. Printed with soy-based ink. *Courtesy of Old Tom Foolery.*

Paper Stories
www.paperstories.com

Kelly Maron started Paper Stories as a custom invitation design studio in 2005. She started working on a small line of cards in 2006 and started selling her stationery in the fall of 2006. After spending nearly ten years as a high school photography and design instructor, Kelly wanted to get back to making art on a more full time basis. That eventually led her to her 1200 lb. printing press and she couldn't be happier. She enjoys spending time in her Chicago area studio, designing and printing all sorts of fun paper goods. She tries to make cards that are funny and thought provoking. In January 2010 Kelly started a new venture called "Indie Wed", an alternative to the traditional bridal show, highlighting independent designers and artists.

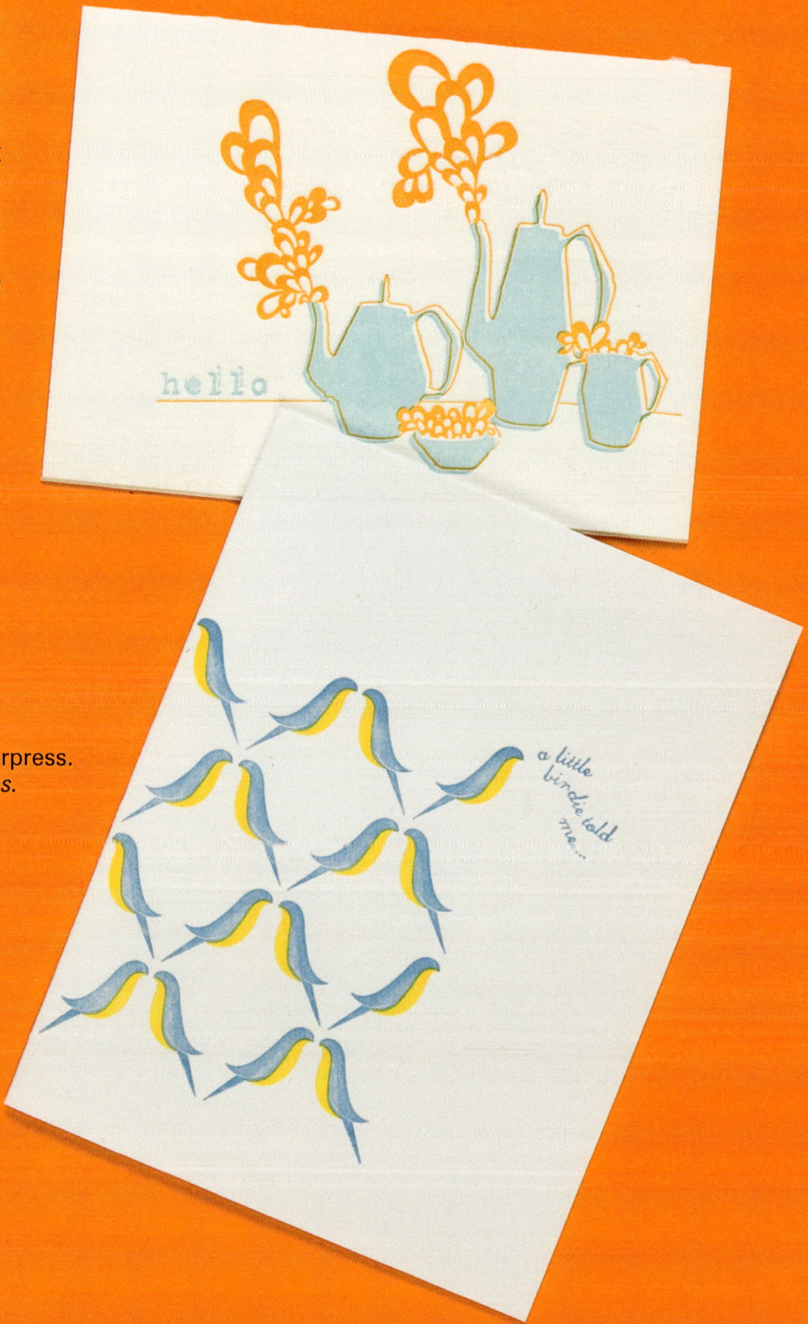

Hello and A Little Birdie Told Me. Letterpress.
Courtesy of Kelly Maron / Paper Stories.

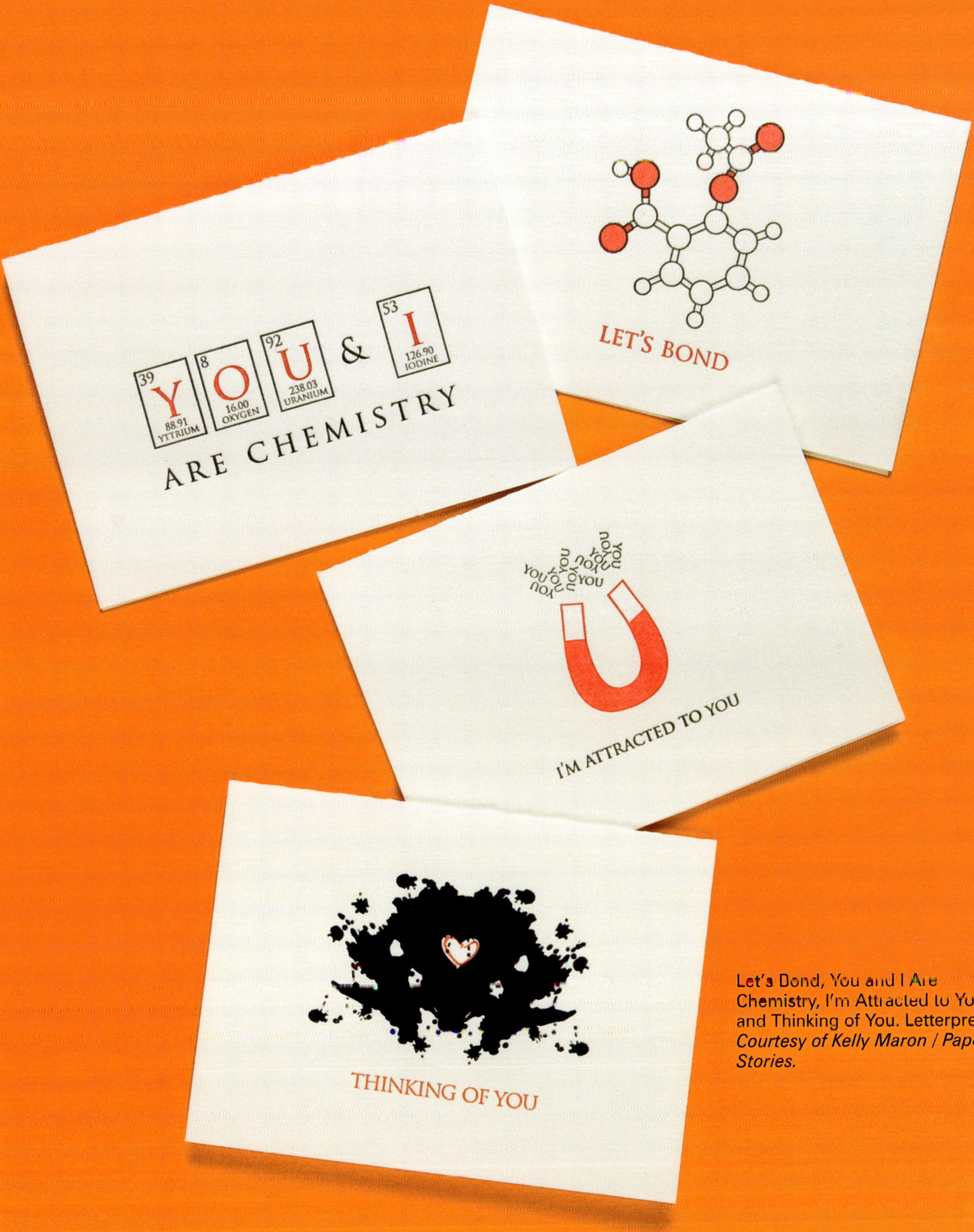

Let's Bond, You and I Are Chemistry, I'm Attracted to You, and Thinking of You. Letterpress. *Courtesy of Kelly Maron / Paper Stories.*

Pearl & Marmalade

www.pearlmarmalade.com

Danielle Jean Nelson and Charlene Lee Dickerson (Dani and Char Lee) became fast friends when they realized they shared a love for striking paper products, thoughtful design, and the endangered art of sending handwritten notes. In an increasingly electronic world where letters and artifacts of one's personal connections are rare, they embrace creating sentimental mementos. Pearl & Marmalade was launched in 2005 and is based in Chicago, a city that is filled with a charming network of independent designers and artists. They have recently designed their own line of sneakers for Keds and in 2010 they won an award from the Poppytalk Design blog for stationery and paper goods design.

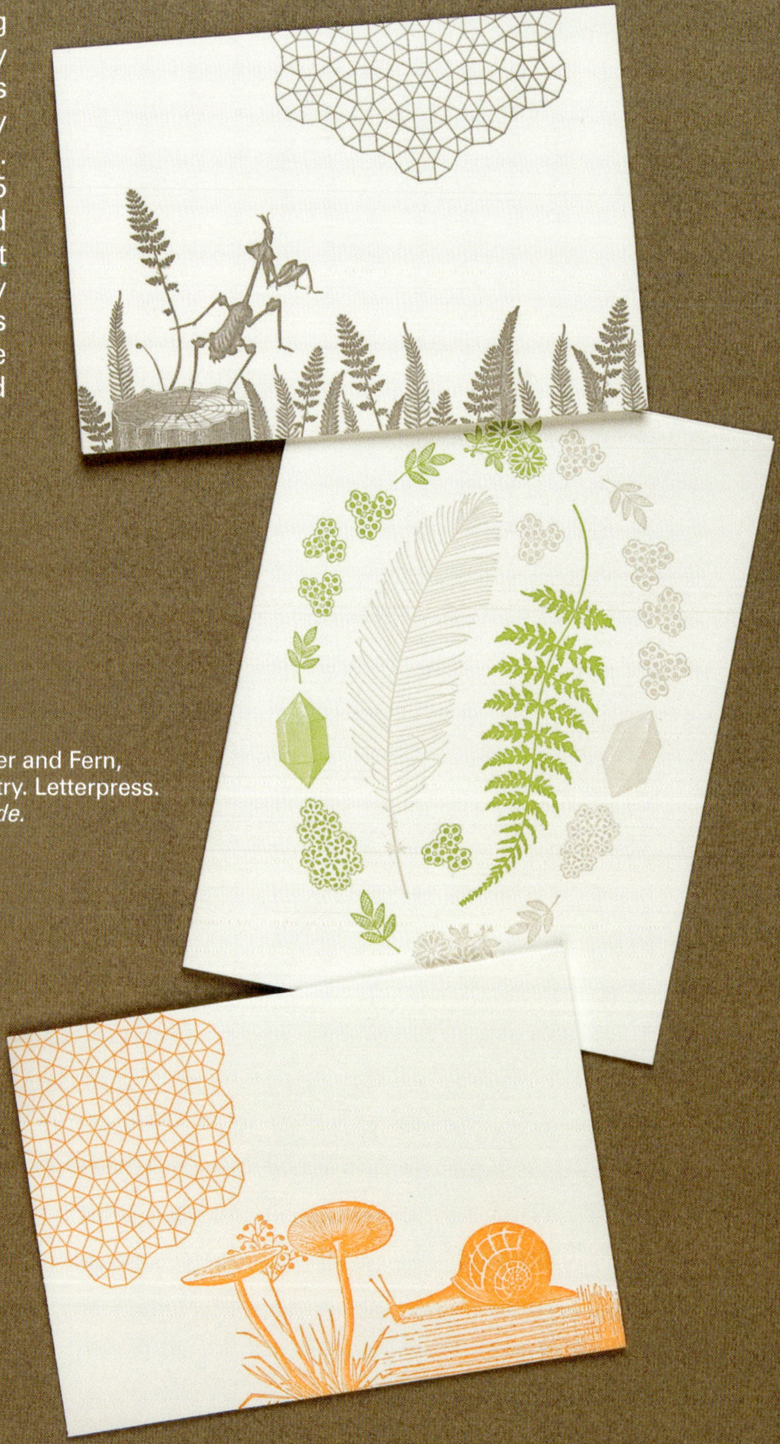

Mantis Fern Geometry, Feather and Fern, and Mushroom Snail Geometry. Letterpress. *Courtesy of Pearl & Marmalade.*

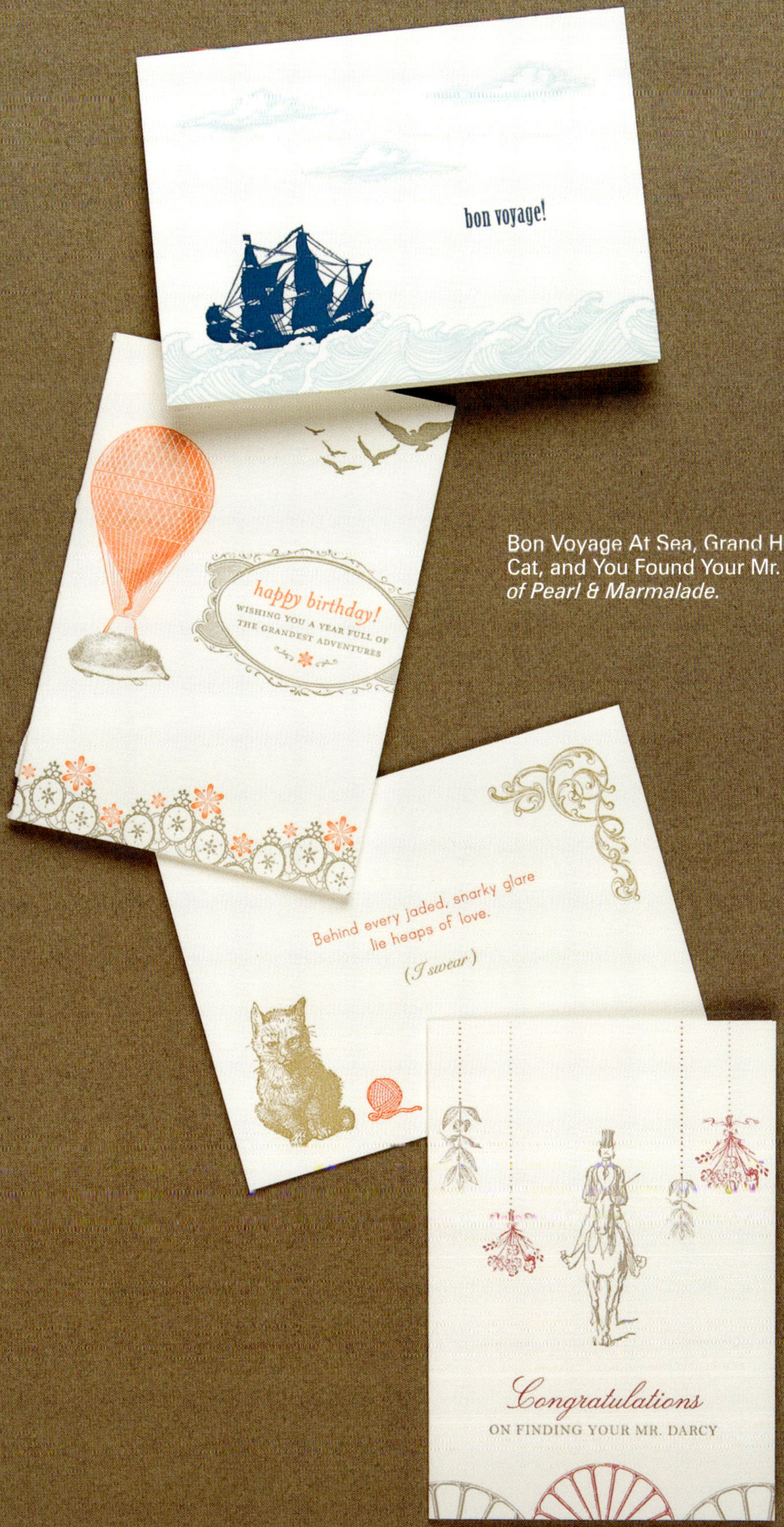

Bon Voyage At Sea, Grand Hedgehog Birthday, Snarky Cat, and You Found Your Mr. Darcy. Letterpress. *Courtesy of Pearl & Marmalade.*

Pinkerton Design

www.pinkertondesign.com

Prior to launching Pinkerton Design in 2004, Penny Richards Eversole worked for several award-winning design studios in Chicago and as a freelance designer. She will always be a Chicago girl, but currently lives in Seattle with her husband John and their young son, Theo. Penny's designs reflect her love for color, illustration, pattern, typography, printing, and paper. Other sources of inspiration include her grandmother's quilts, her parents' old cookbooks, 1950s roadside signage, Ed Emberley's drawing books, and Seattle's strange and beautiful plants. Her cards have been seen in *Lucky, Instyle, Blueprint, The Wall Street Journal, San Francisco Magazine*, and many blogs.

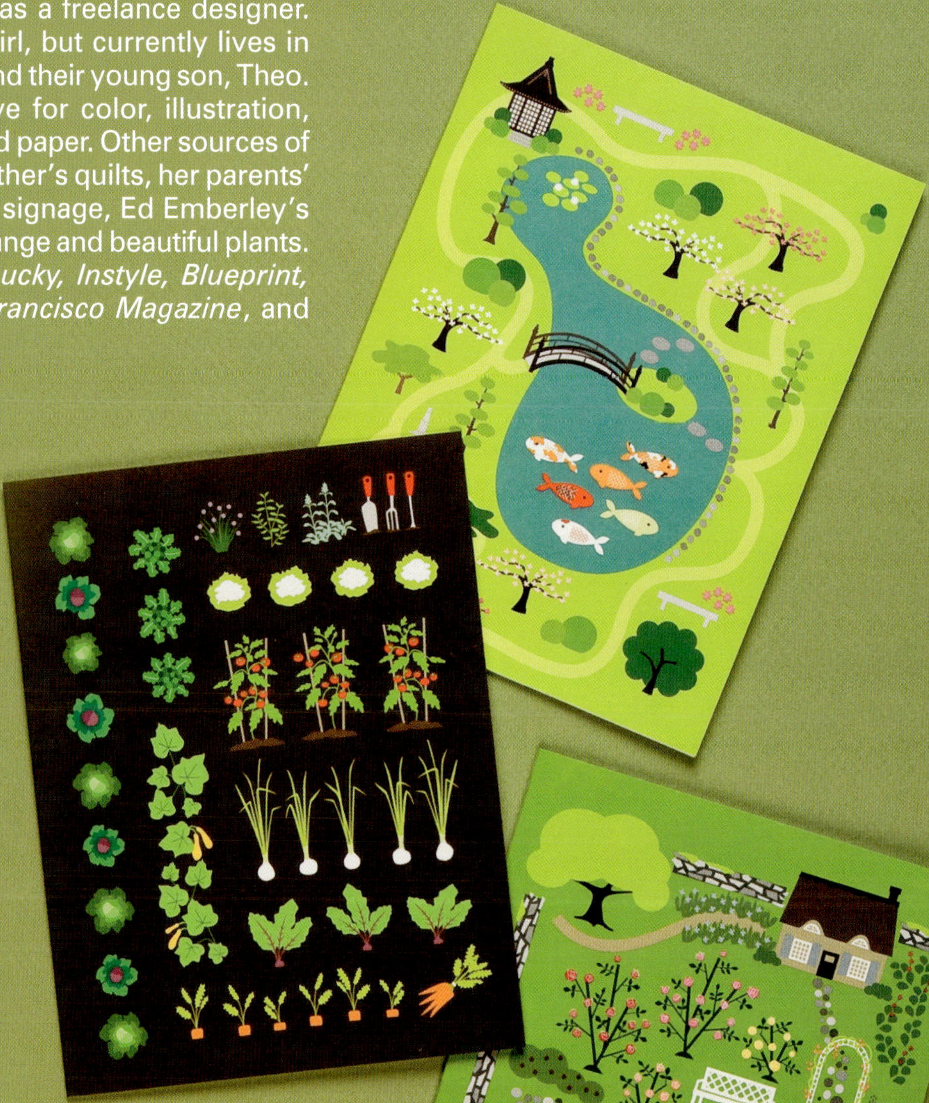

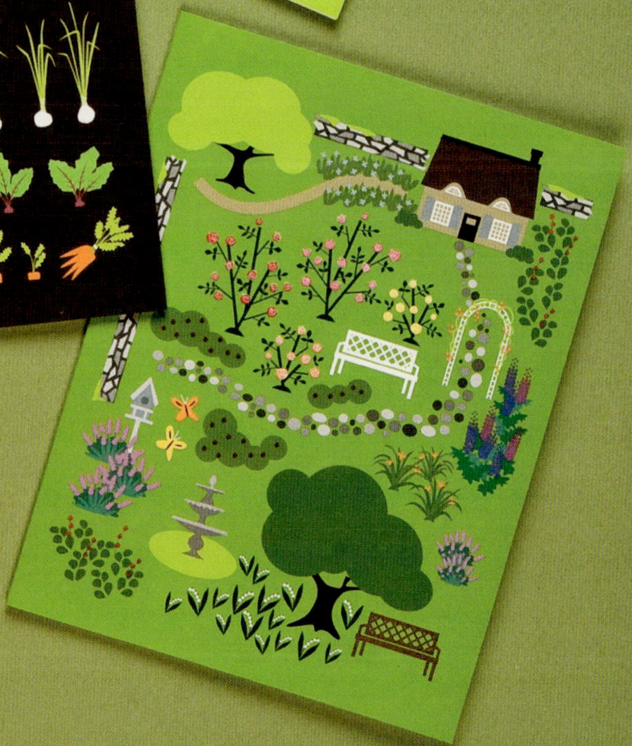

Japanese Garden, Veggie Garden, and English Garden. Printed with vegetable ink on 100% PCW paper. *Courtesy of Penny Eversole / Pinkerton Design.*

Motel Belated Birthday, Motel I Love You More Than, Motel Congrats, and Motel Deluxe Birthday. Printed with vegetable ink on 100% PCW paper. *Courtesy of Penny Eversole / Pinkerton Design.*

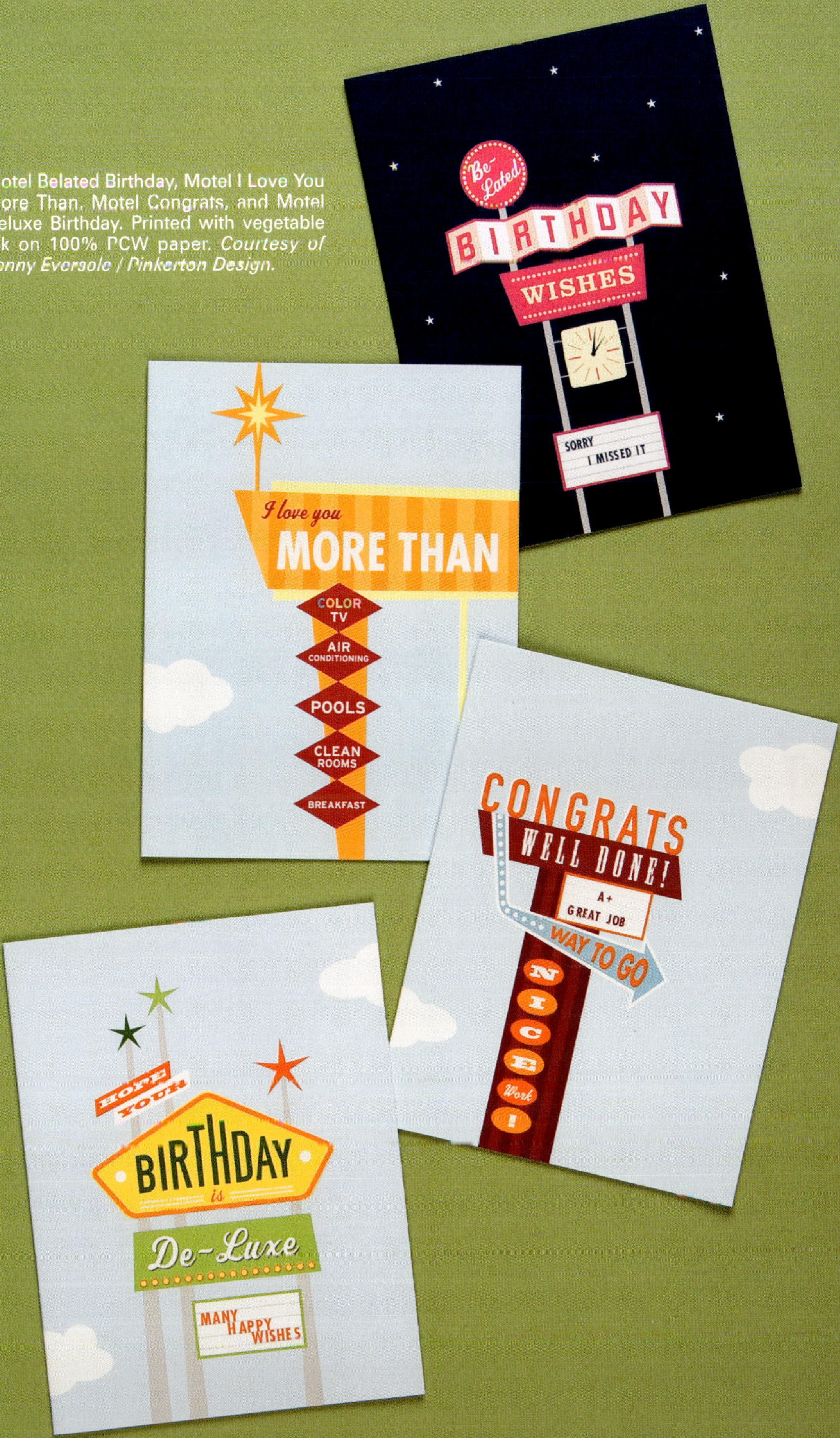

Rifle Paper Co.

www.riflepaperco.com

In 2009, after attending college for graphic design and working as an art director at a magazine, Anna Bond decided to launch Rifle Paper Company by combining her love for illustration, graphic design, and stationery. Now, together with her husband Nathan, they run their business out of their studio in Winter Park, Florida. Within a year of starting their company, they have gone from a home-grown operation to a fully established business with products featured in publications such as *Martha Stewart Weddings, O the Oprah Magazine, Real Simple Weddings*, and more. Brides.com even named one of their wedding invitations as one of the twelve best invitations of 2009.

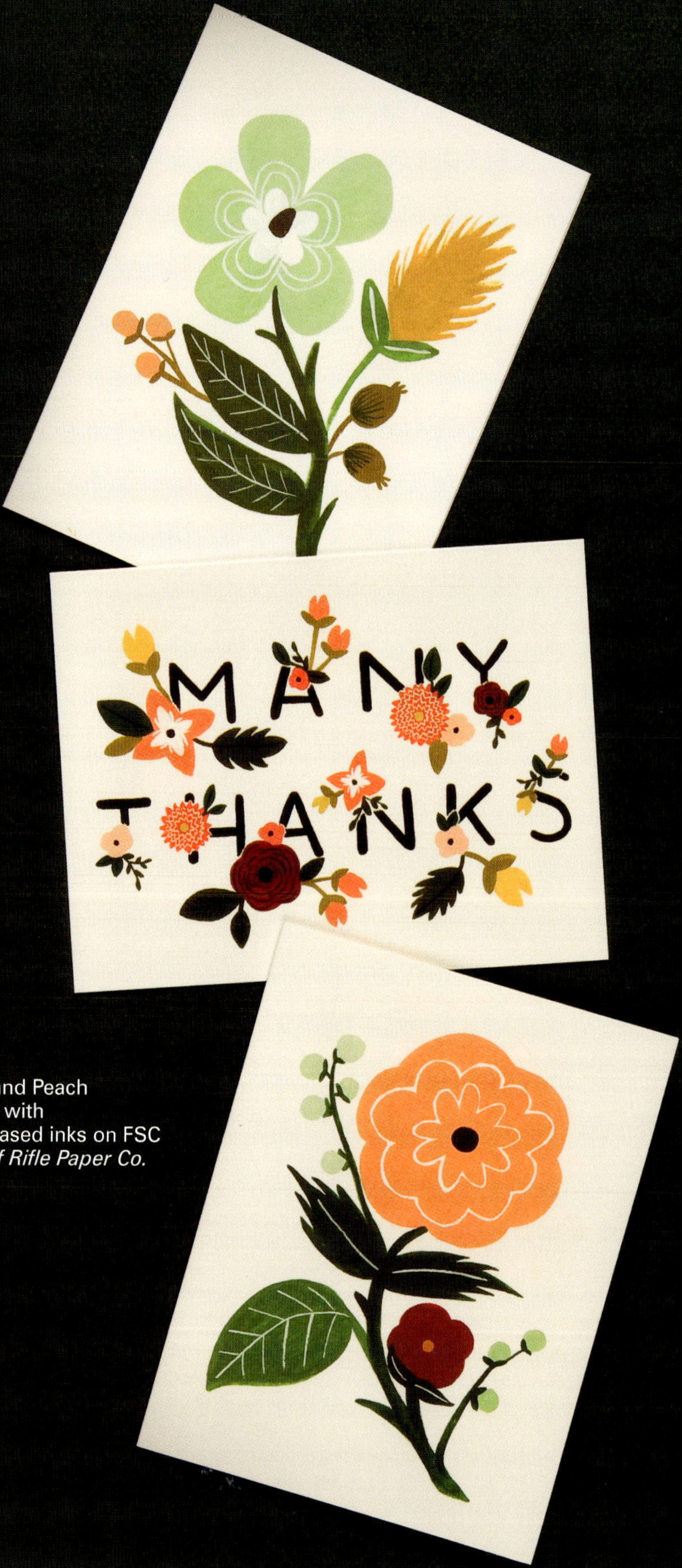

Mint Botanical, Ava Thank You, and Peach Botanical. Offset printed. Printed with environmentally friendly water-based inks on FSC certified paper stock. *Courtesy of Rifle Paper Co.*

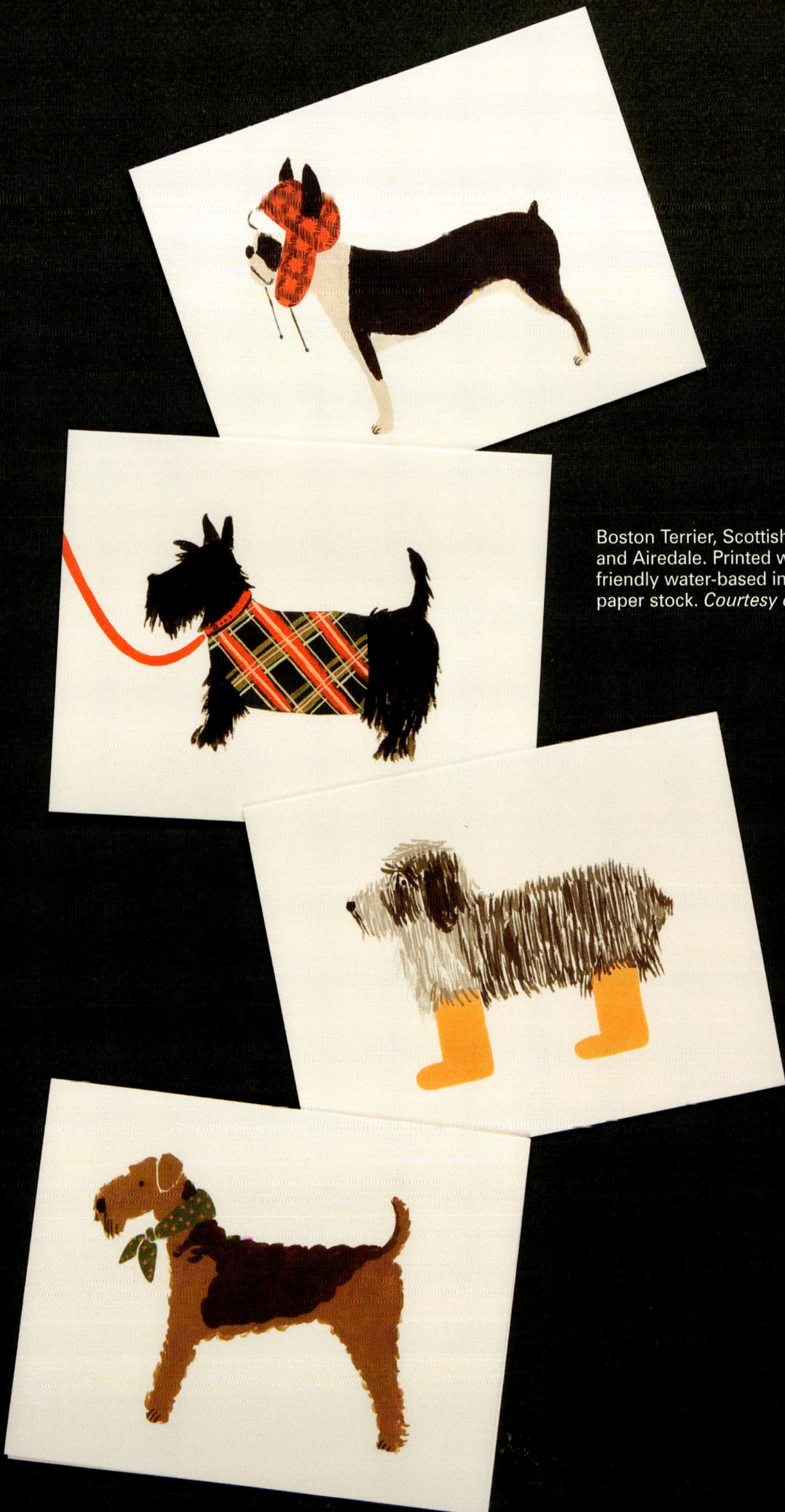

Boston Terrier, Scottish Terrier, Shaggy Dog, and Airedale. Printed with environmentally friendly water-based inks on FSC certified paper stock. *Courtesy of Rifle Paper Co.*

Round Robin Press

www.roundrobinpress.com

Shannon Lowry started Round Robin Press in January of 2007 and runs it out of her backyard studio in Austin, Texas. She tries to stay connected to what she is working on and what is in her future amidst raising two very active little boys. Her main focus with Round Robin Press is running a company that enables her to put her designs on lots of different surfaces while always putting the environment first. She makes letterpress plantable cards, art, and children's books. Her work has been featured in *Texas Monthly, Austin Monthly, Urbis (NZ), Canadian Family, Wondertime, The Today Show, Design*Sponge,* and *Poppytalk*.

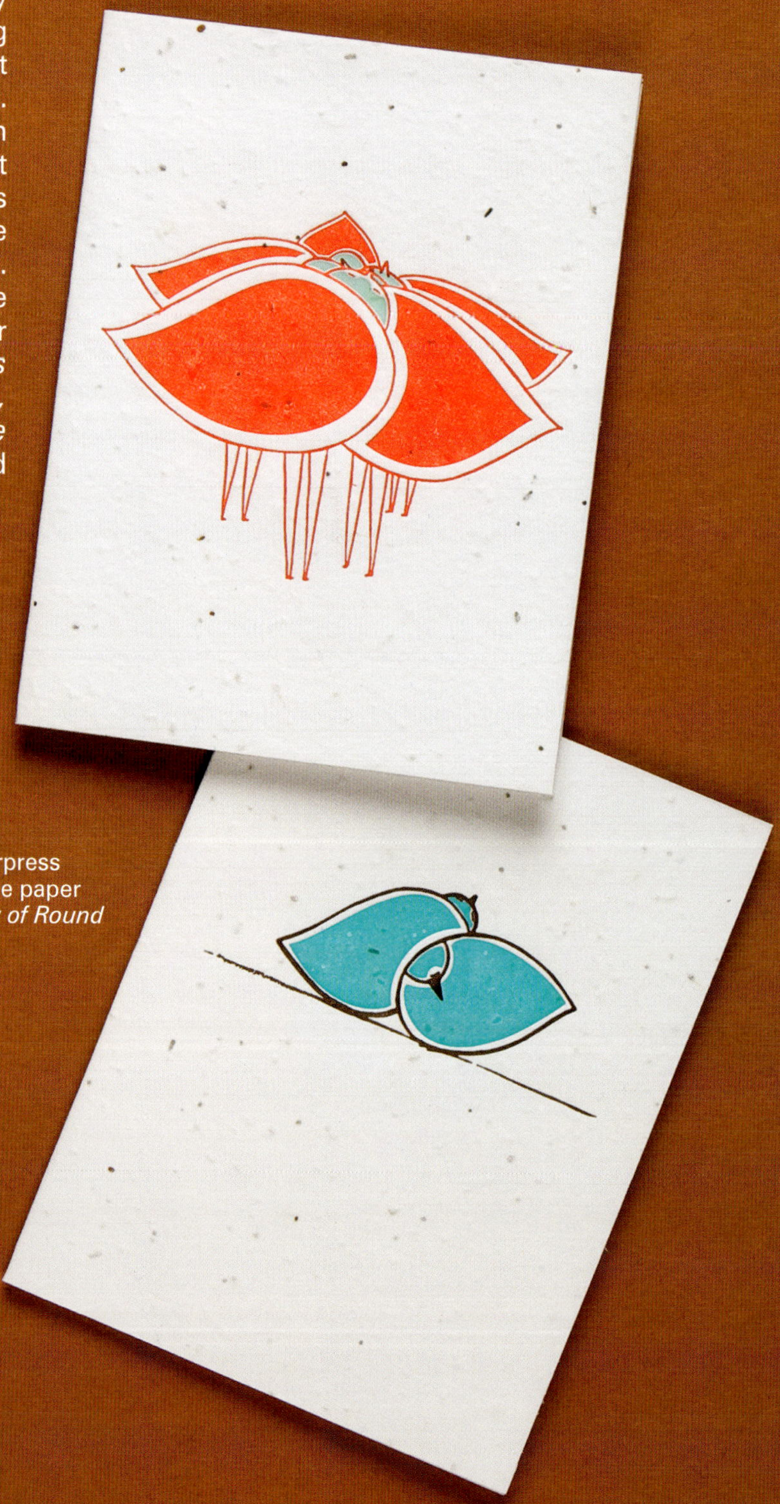

Love Birds and Best Buds. Letterpress printed onto handmade plantable paper embedded with seeds. *Courtesy of Round Robin Press.*

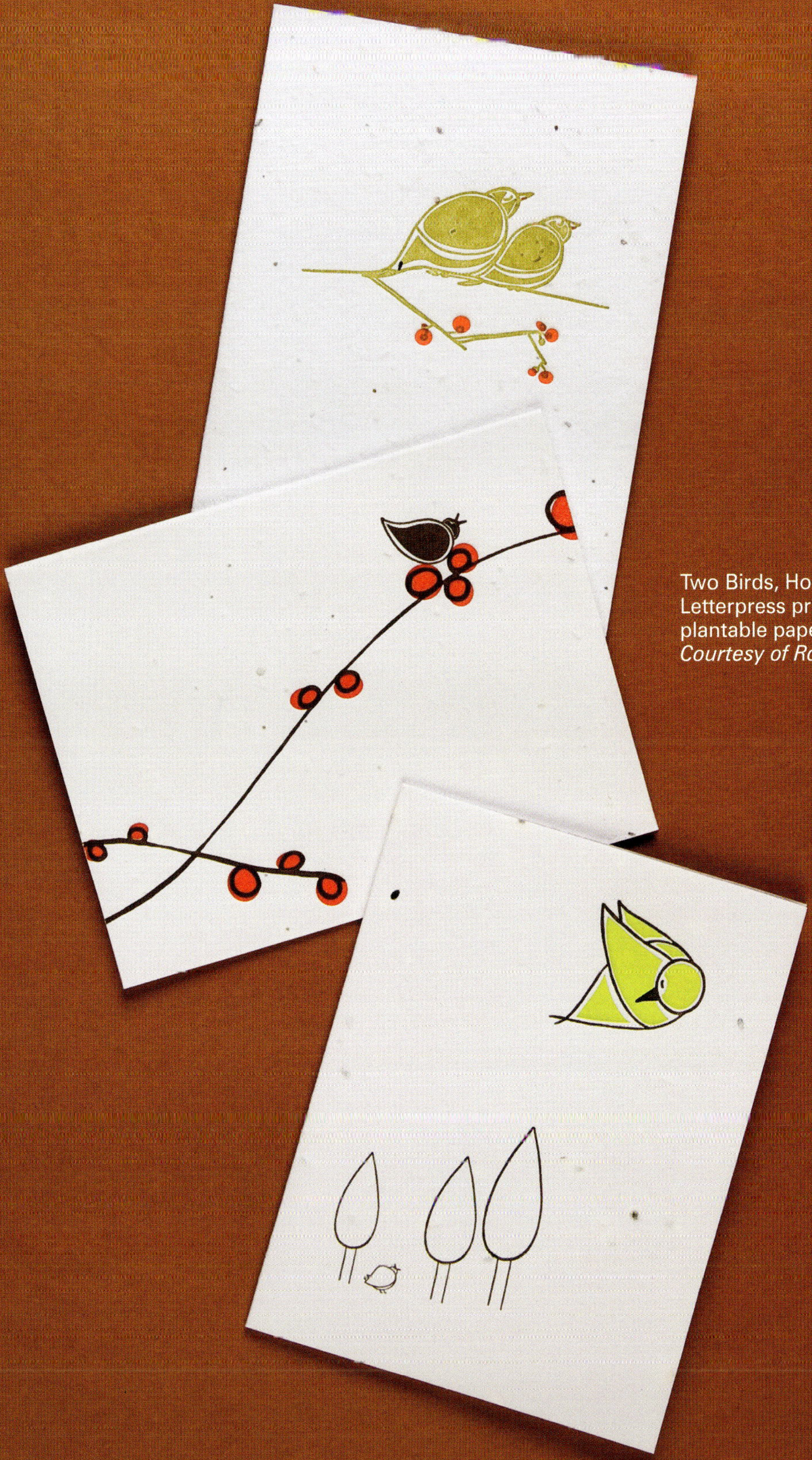

Two Birds, Holly Bird, and Fly Bird. Letterpress printed onto handmade plantable paper embedded with seeds. *Courtesy of Round Robin Press.*

Screech Owl Design

www.screechowldesign.com

Screech Owl Design began in the winter of 2008. Jacqueline and George Schmidt wanted an avenue for their creativity where they would have complete creative control, and an opportunity to share their work with a broad public. They think of their cards as tiny and inexpensive works of art. Their work has been seen in *ReadyMade, Better Homes and Gardens, O at Home, Time Out NY Gift Guide, Cookie, Page Six Magazine, NY Metro, Small Magazine*, and numerous online features. Both Jacqueline and George are continually inspired by their love of nature, particularly birds, and all things associated with the outdoors. They also love modern furniture and design, and try to meld these two areas of inspiration in their line of cards.

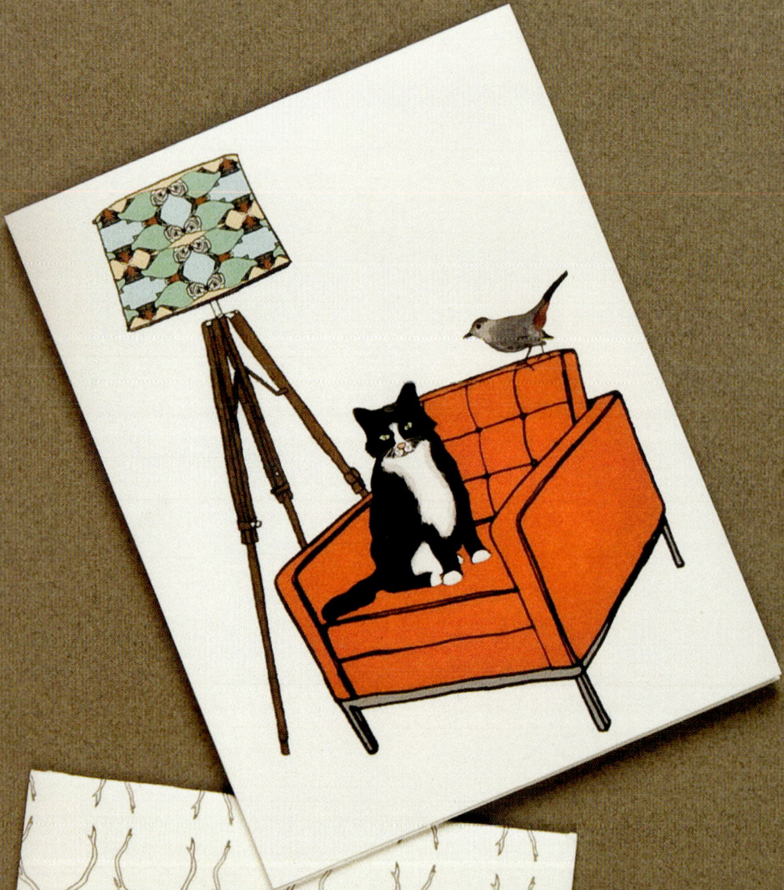

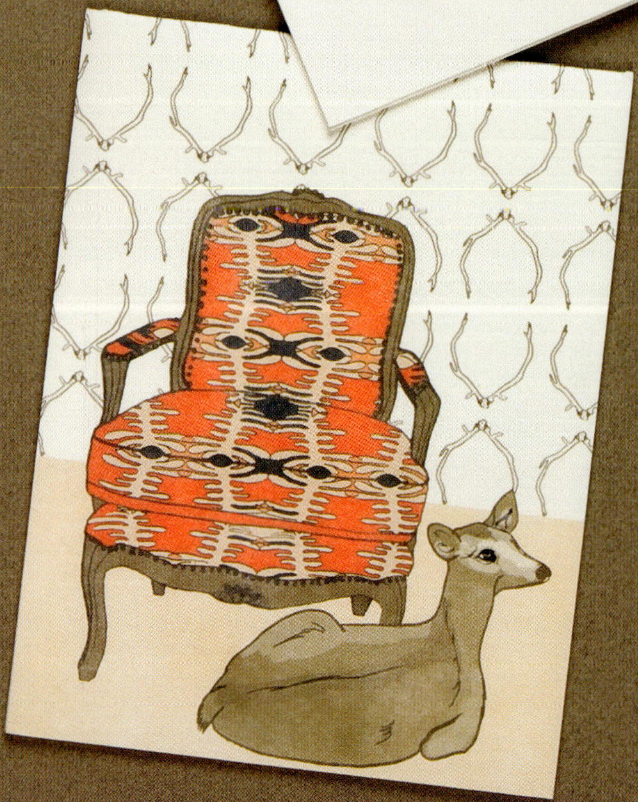

Sitting in the Catbird Seat and Dearest. Offset printed onto 100% tree free cotton. *Courtesy of Jacqueline Schmidt.*

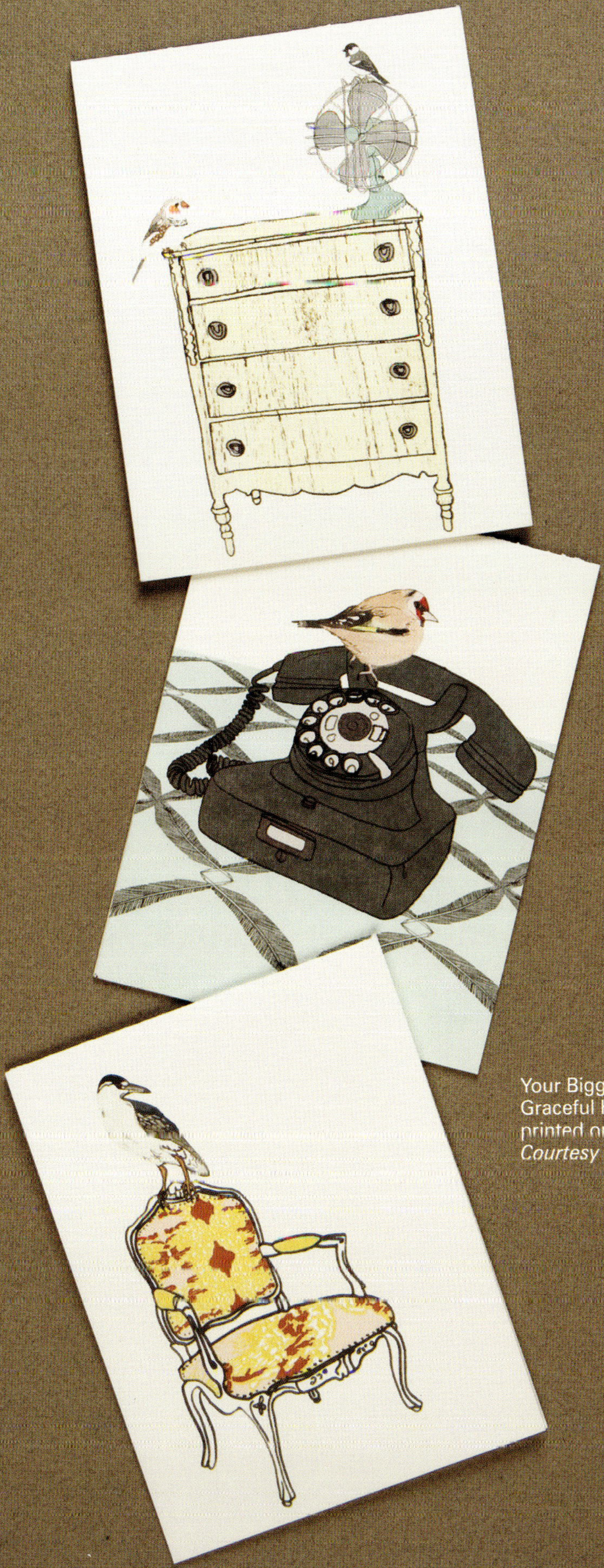

Your Biggest Fans, Give Me a Ring, and Graceful Heron on Elegant Chair. Offset printed onto 100% tree free cotton. *Courtesy of Jacqueline Schmidt.*

Sesame Letterpress & Design

www.sesameletterpress.com

Breck Hostetter had a fine arts background with a primary interest in artists' books and became interested in letterpress printing as a method for publishing limited edition prints and multiples. She acquired her first printing press in 1999, moving it from a retired printer's basement in Massachusetts to a sun filled studio in Brooklyn, New York, under the Brooklyn Bridge. She learned how to print by experimentation through making cards, stationery, and coasters for friends as gifts. She fell in love with the process and started printing full time around 2004, hired employees and launched her wholesale line shortly after. She now has a dozen presses, most of which are nineteenth century platen presses, and spends her days printing greeting cards, coasters, invitations, note cards, and anything else that will fit in the press. She is currently working with West Elm on a line of holiday items.

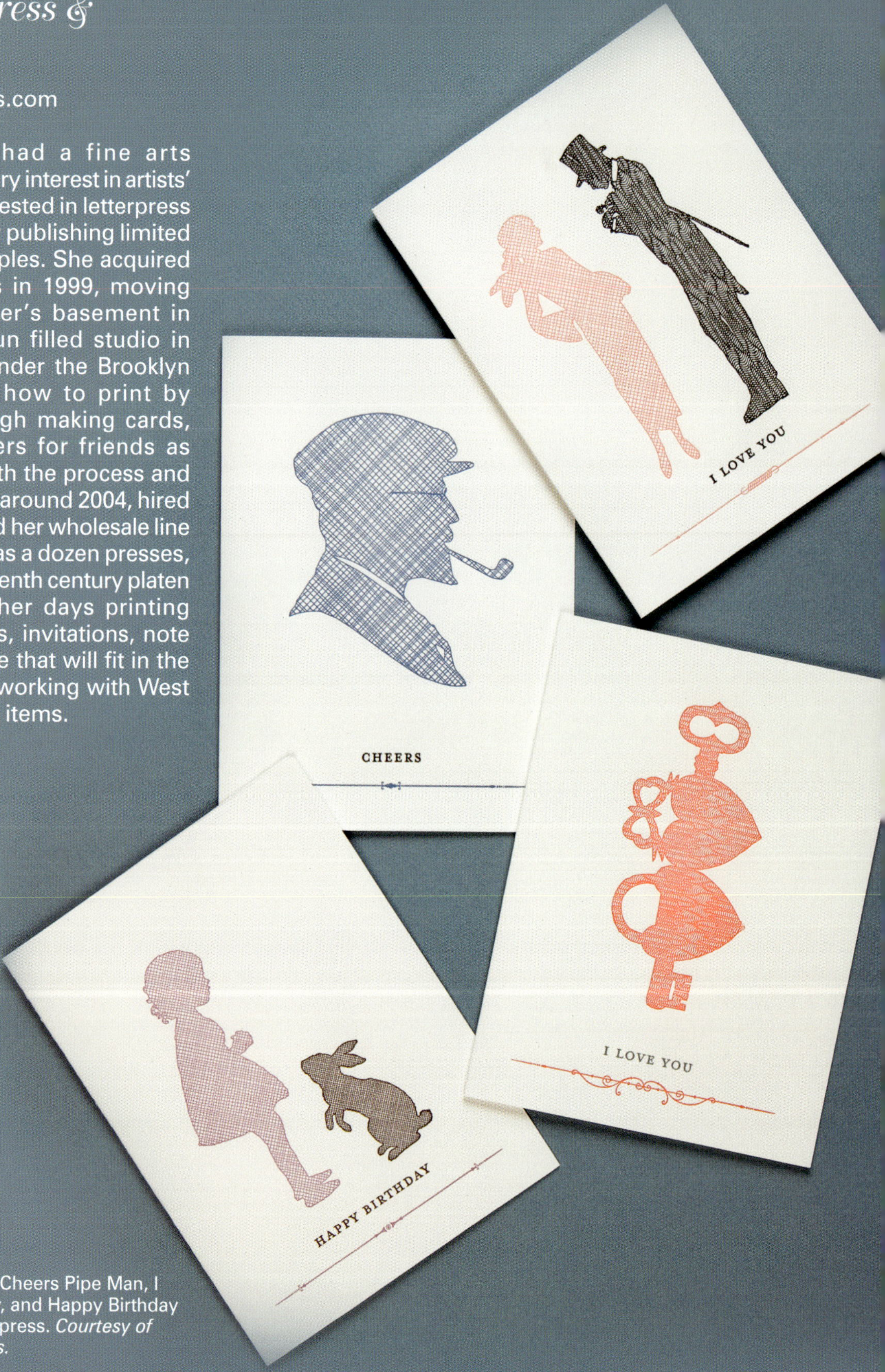

I Love You Couple, Cheers Pipe Man, I Love You Heart Key, and Happy Birthday Girl & Bunny. Letterpress. *Courtesy of Sesame Letterpress.*

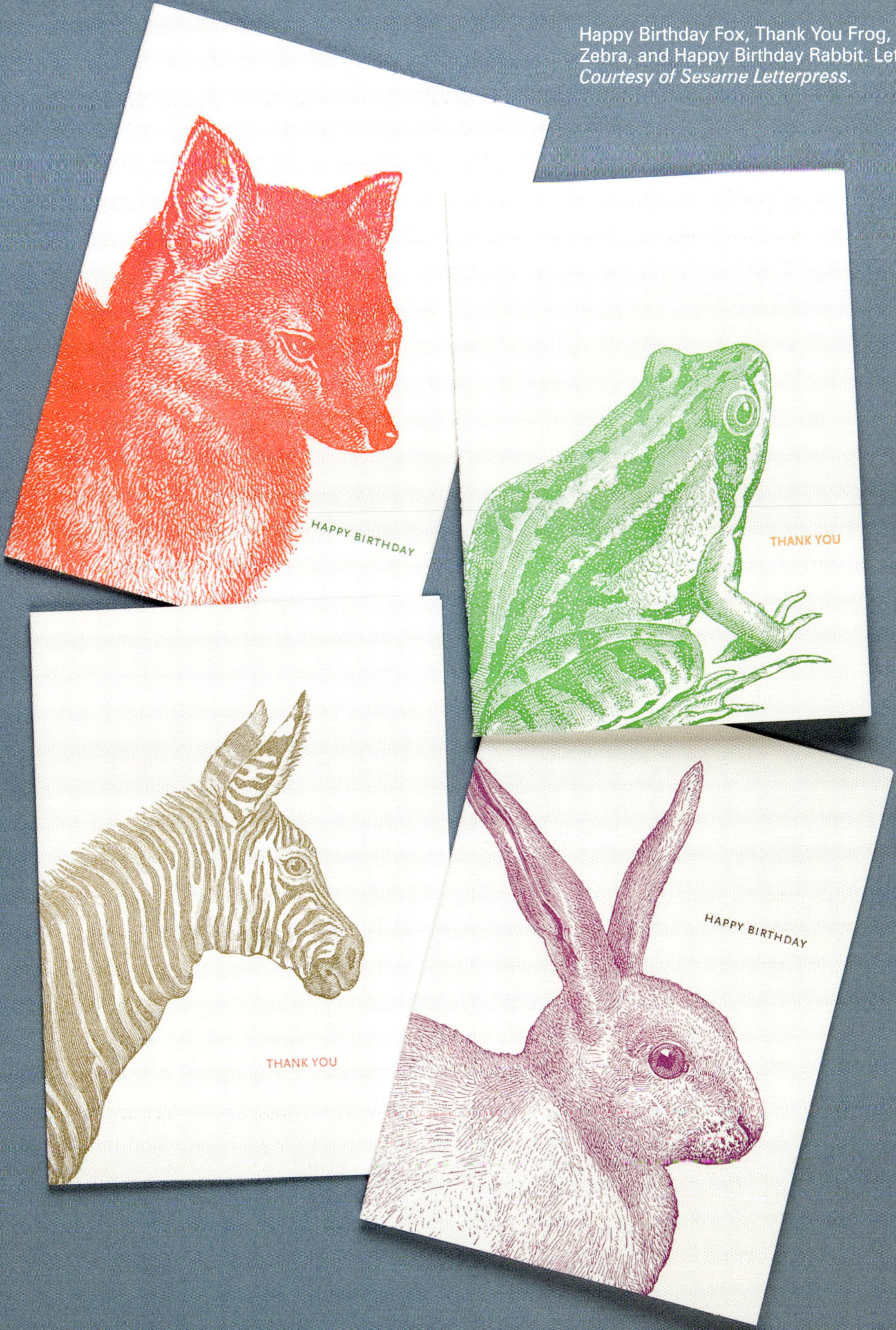

Happy Birthday Fox, Thank You Frog, Thank You Zebra, and Happy Birthday Rabbit. Letterpress. *Courtesy of Sesame Letterpress.*

Smitten ...

www.smittenkitten...

Amy Kwong started her co... Smitten Kitten (a 1950s expressi... describing a young girl in love, which also describes Amy's feeling about good design) in 2005. She holds a Bachelor of Fine Arts degree and for many years worked as an award winning creative director for a large-scale giftware manufacturer. She is often inspired by vintage designs, patterns, and pallet, but also enjoys working with actual vintage materials. Creatively reworking vintage materials into beautiful modern day pieces not only inspires Amy's designs, but also helps her create a more sustainable planet. She fancies herself as the fairy godmother for the unloved and forgotten and takes great joy in transforming them to be the belle of the ball.

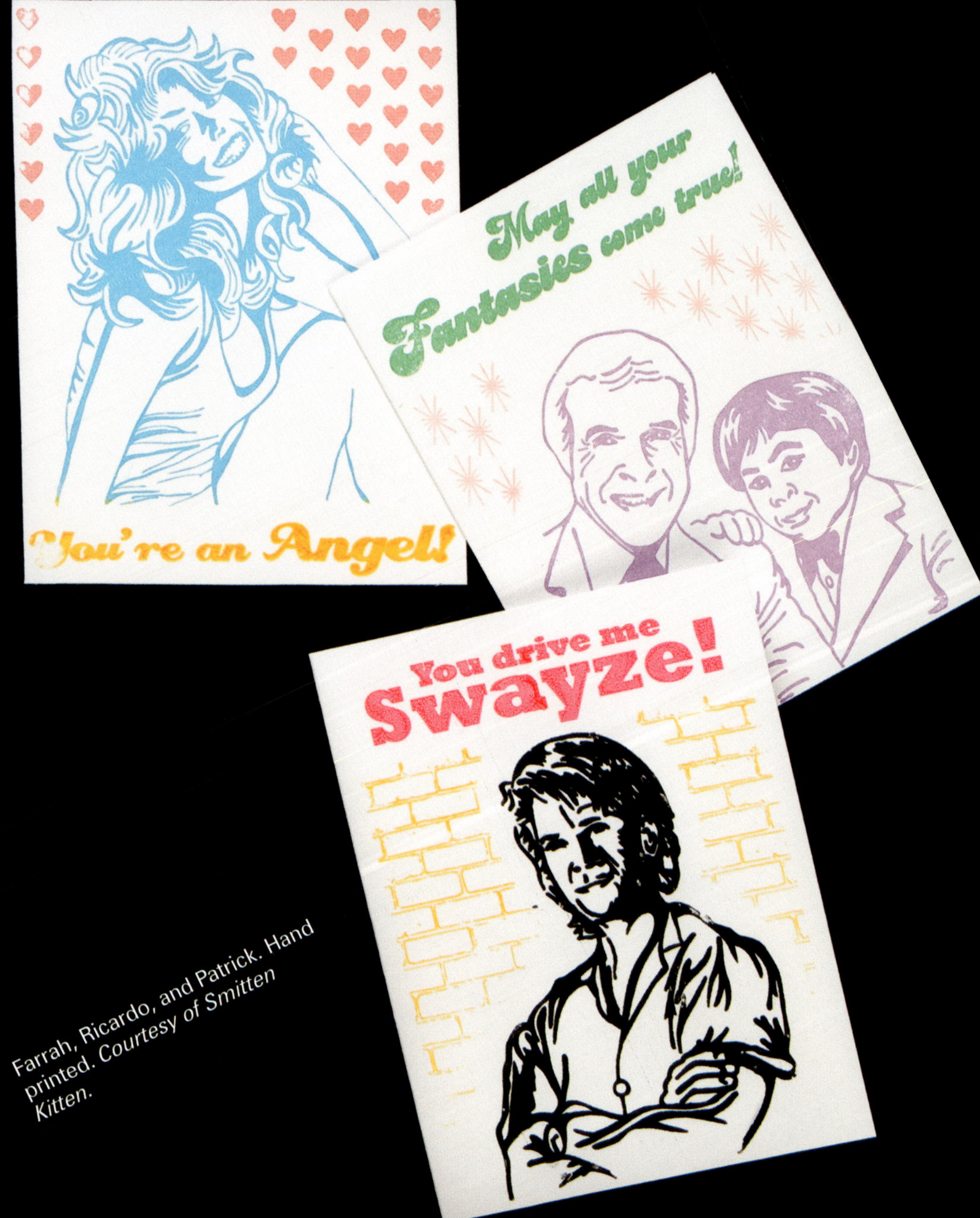

Farrah, Ricardo, and Patrick. Hand printed. *Courtesy of Smitten Kitten.*

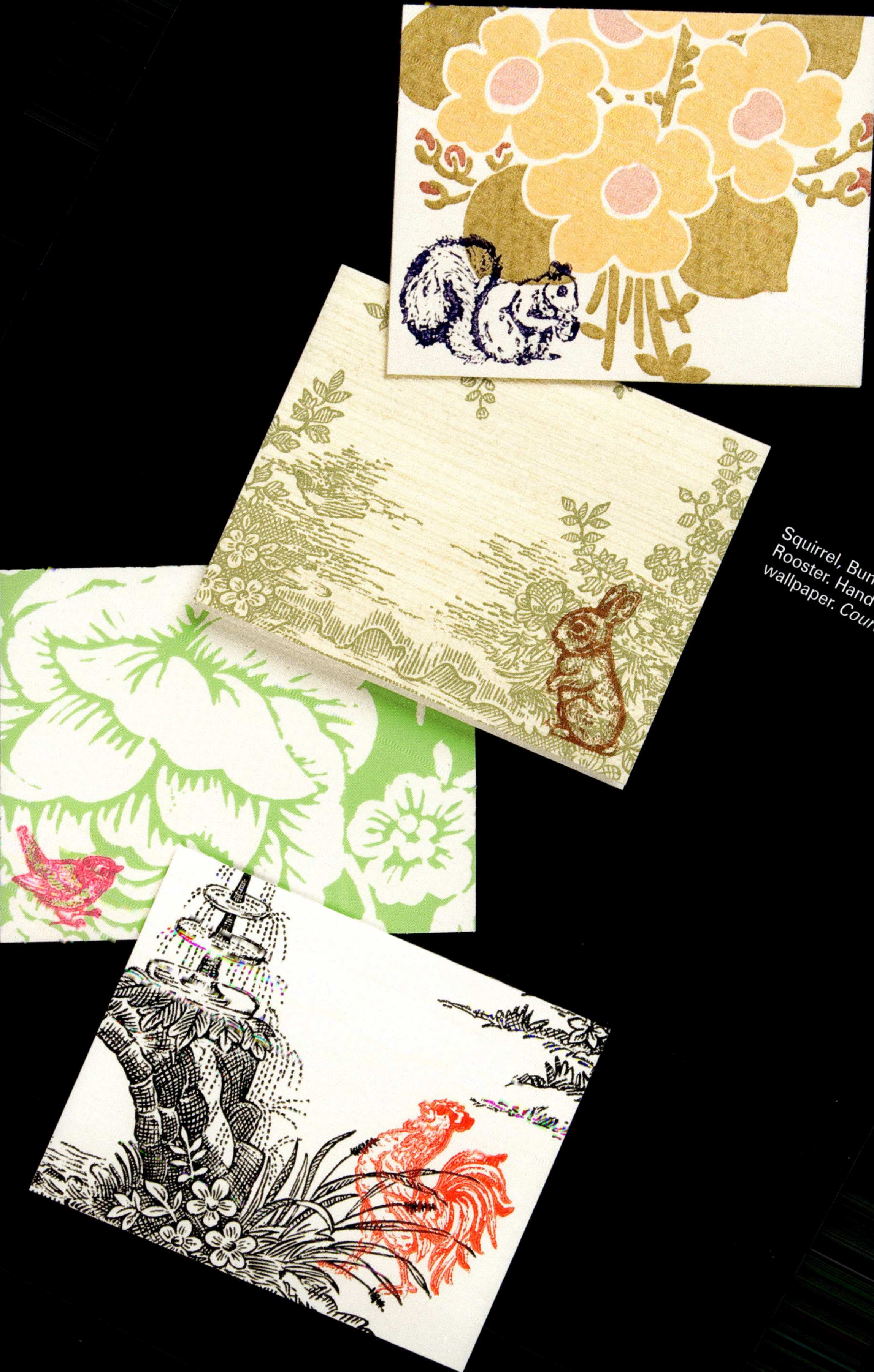

Squirrel, Bunny, Sparrow, and Rooster. Hand printed onto vintage wallpaper. *Courtesy of Smitten Kitten.*

Smock

www.smockpaper.com

Amy Graham Stigler launched her popular card line in May of 2008. After many years in Chicago, Amy and her husband, three children, and dog moved north to a quiet lake town in Wisconsin. Trained as an art historian, Amy's love of books, illustration, and design inspired her profession as a designer. Currently based in Syracuse, New York, Smock is an eco-friendly letterpress stationery line sustainably printed on a luxurious bamboo paper. Amy loves old houses, flea markets, ephemera, attics, word and image, collecting, rearranging, exploring, looking, and making. She draws inspiration from antique embroidered linens, monograms and family crests, the paintings of Milton Avery, farmers' markets, vintage wallpapers, block-printed fabrics, gardening books, hand lettering, design books from the 1940s, '50s, '60s, and kindhearted people.

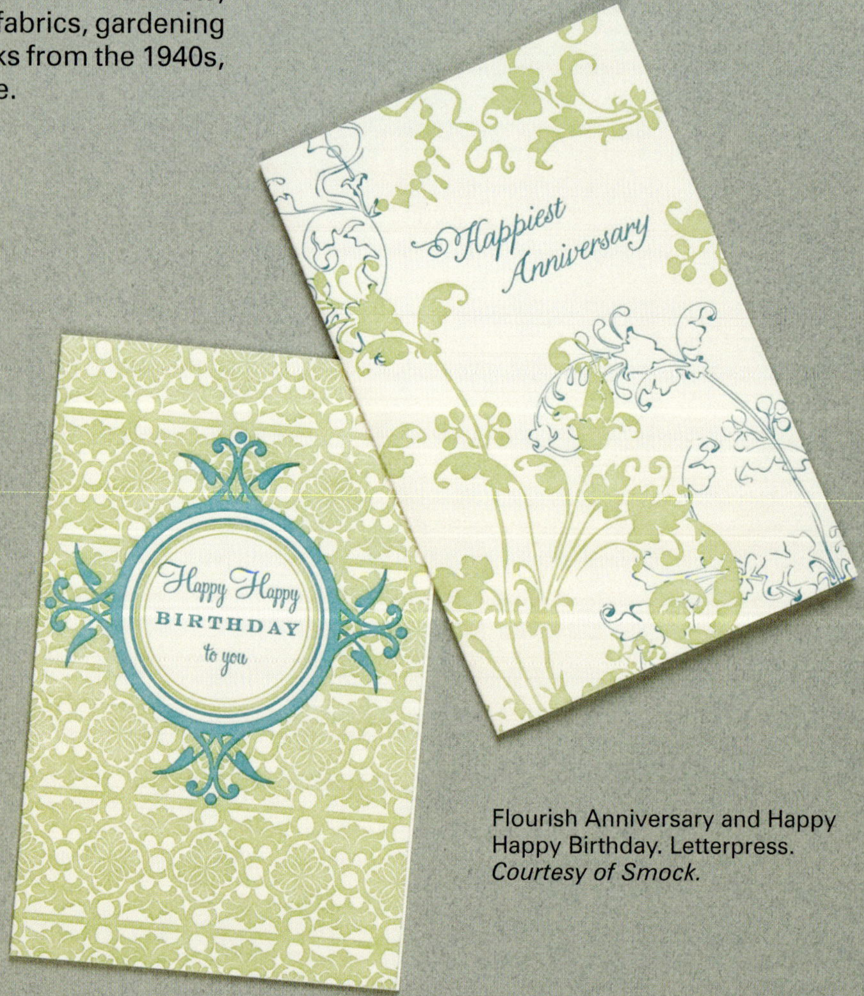

Flourish Anniversary and Happy Happy Birthday. Letterpress. *Courtesy of Smock.*

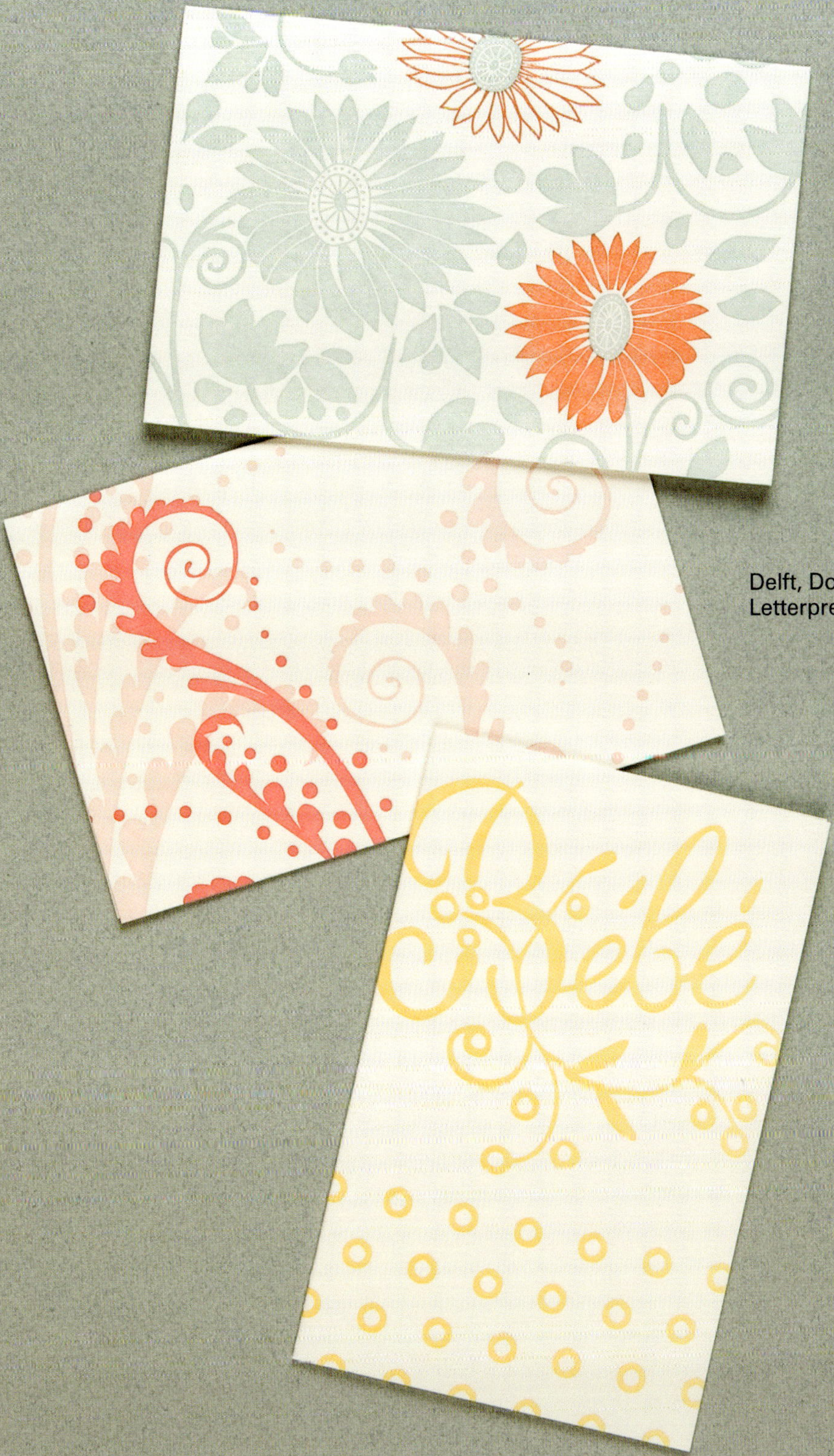

Delft, Dots & Circles, and Bebe. Letterpress. *Courtesy of Smock.*

led to making other notebooks and cards. They started Sukie from their tiny, one bedroom apartment in Notting Hill but quickly ran out of space and decided to move back to Brighton, where they now have their studio and warehouse. They currently sell their wares all over the world in addition to working regularly with Chronicle Books and the card company Nineteen Seventy Three.

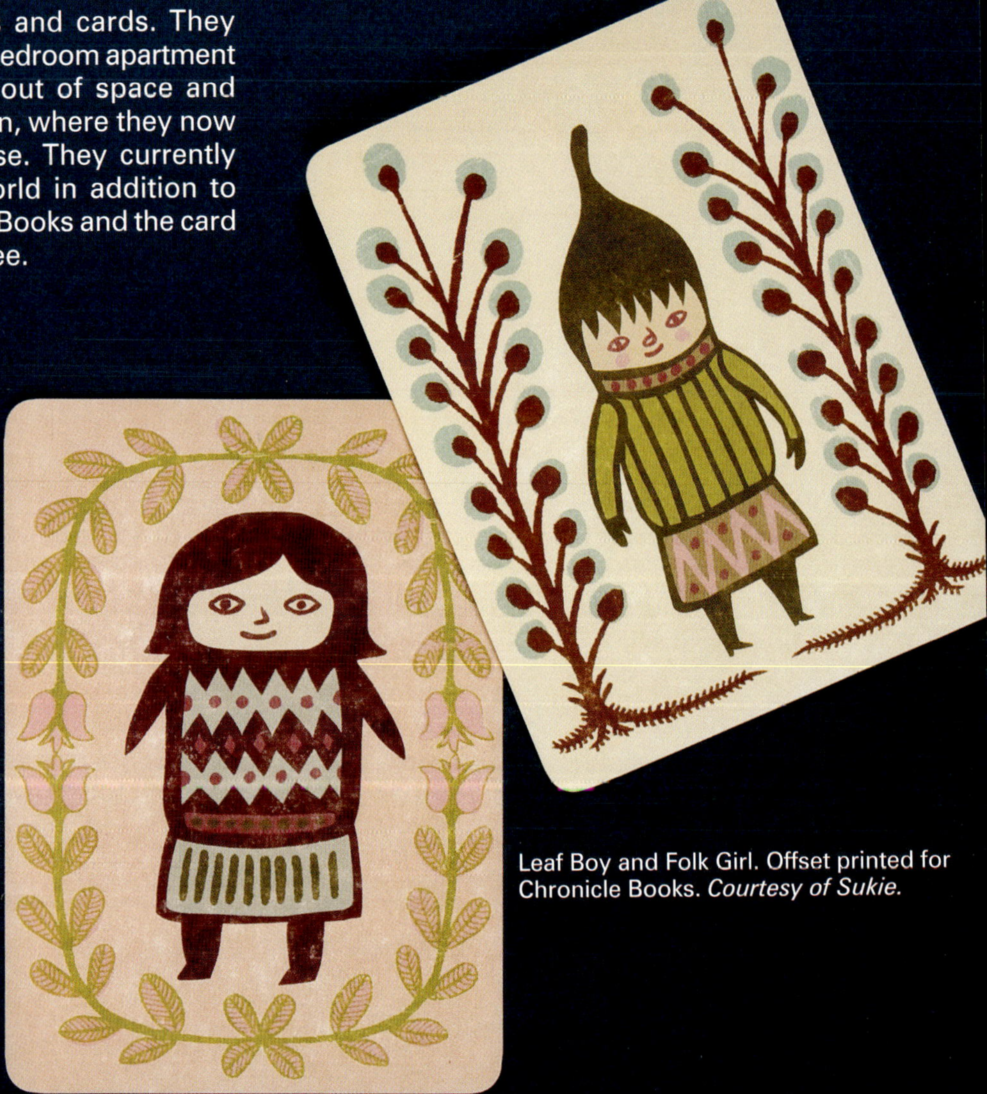

Leaf Boy and Folk Girl. Offset printed for Chronicle Books. *Courtesy of Sukie.*

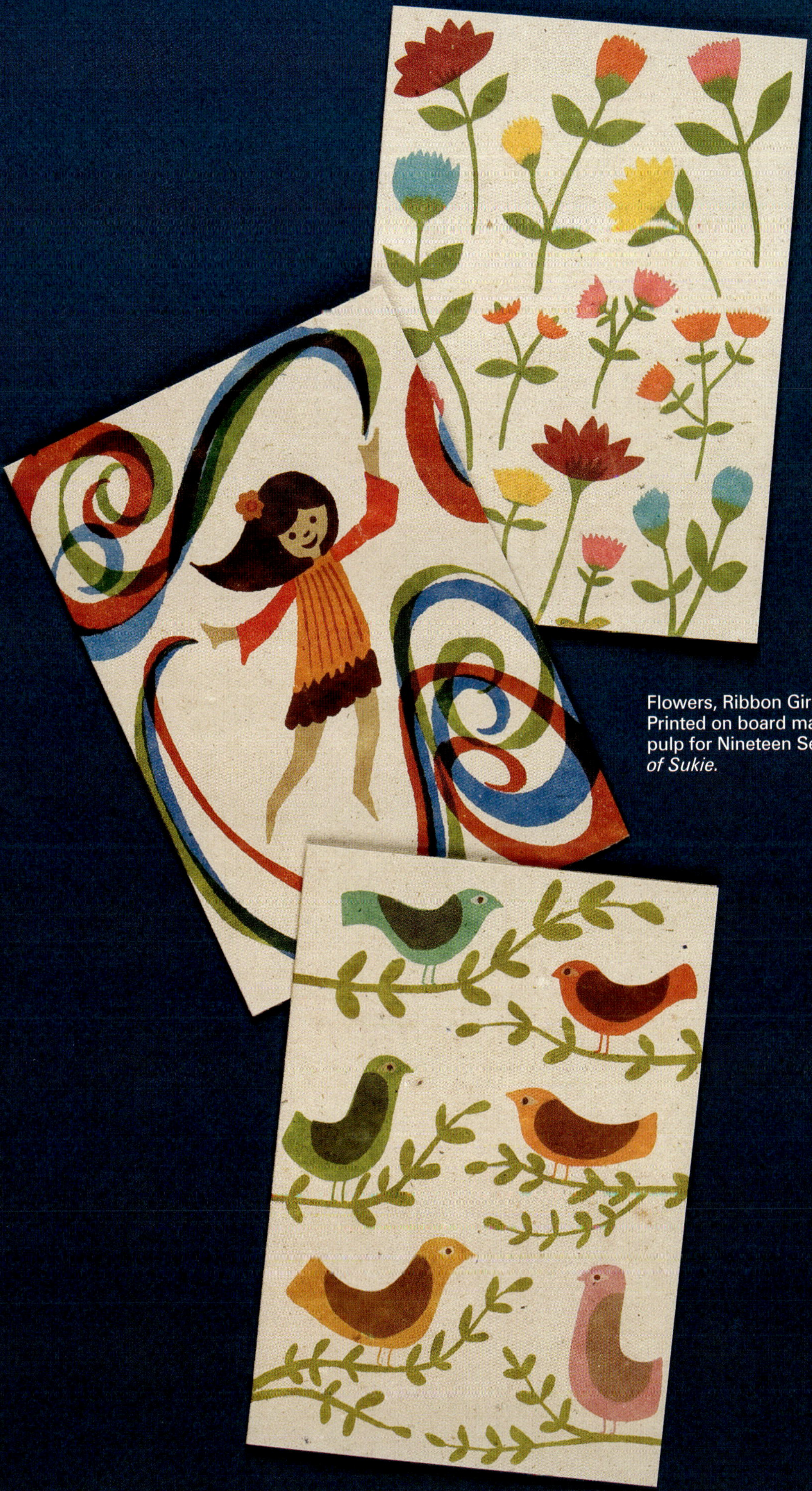

Flowers, Ribbon Girl, and Bird Branch. Printed on board made from 100% recycled pulp for Nineteen Seventy Three. *Courtesy of Sukie.*

Susy Jack Contemporary Paper, LLC

www.susyjack.com

Susan Connor launched her company in April of 2007 after a career in branding and design for boutique and corporate clients. She wanted to create paper that was neither too frilly nor too preppy or predictable, but truly contemporary. This took the shape of an eco-friendly line, printed locally, and made in the USA. Supporting the local economy, keeping the environment in the front of her mind, and creating multipurpose, useful items with a fun, minimalist twist is at the core of her modern take on paper. Susy is inspired by so many things. One day, it might be graffiti; and the next, a gorgeous textile, a can of soup, or a great punk rock album cover. She also writes a daily blog called *Hey Susy* where she chronicles her thoughts on trend, fashion, and style.

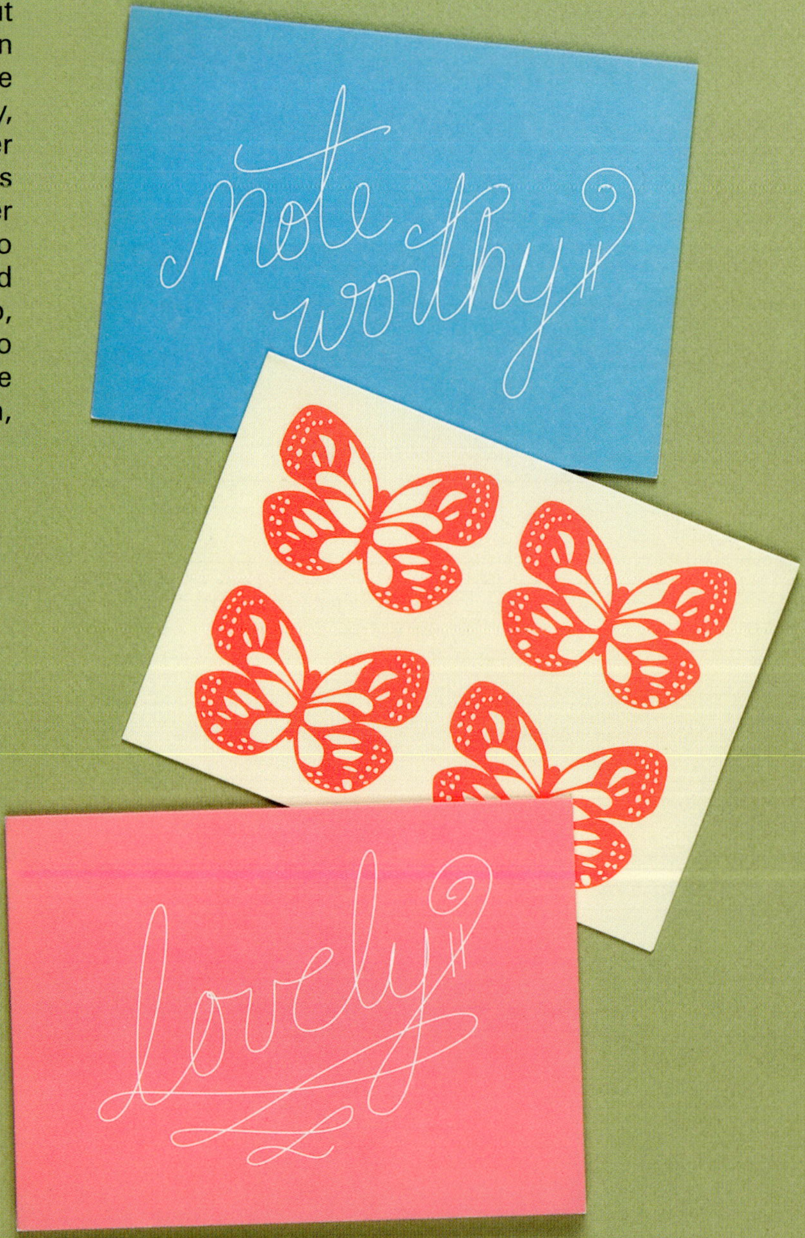

Note Worthy, Flutter, and Lovely. Printed with vegetable inks on 100% p.c.w. recycled paper. *Courtesy of Susy Jack Contemporary Paper, LLC.*

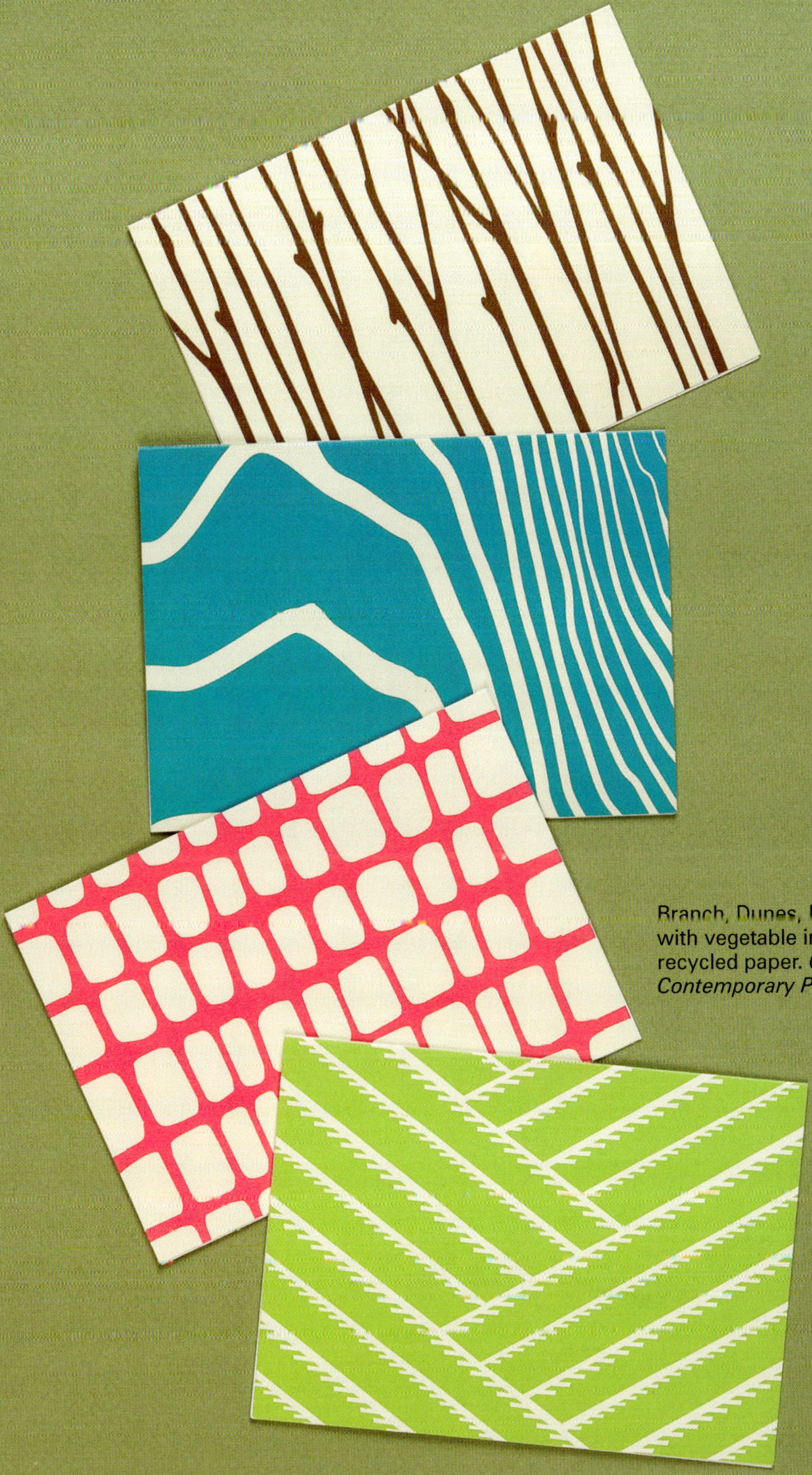

Branch, Dunes, Net, and Fields. Printed with vegetable inks on 100% p.c.w. recycled paper. *Courtesy of Susy Jack Contemporary Paper, LLC.*

Sycamore Street Press

www.sycamorestreetpress.com

In the fall of 2007, Kirk and Eva Jorgensen moved into a charming little place on a brick-paved road called Sycamore Street in Columbus, Ohio. A week later, a 1000 lb. Vandercook #3 letterpress took up residence in their dining room, and Eva began using it to print her quirky little drawings. Since then, Sycamore Street Press has grown into a full time family business for the Jorgensen duo. They no longer print in their dining room, and have relocated from the Midwest to the Mountain West. But they still print everything with care on their beloved hand-cranked letterpress. They collaborate regularly with a few of their good friends such as the very talented Stephanie Ford, Kirstin Mills, and Amy Shaffer, with whom they have created a collection of heirloom-quality letterpress greeting cards, business cards, invitations, posters, and other paper goods.

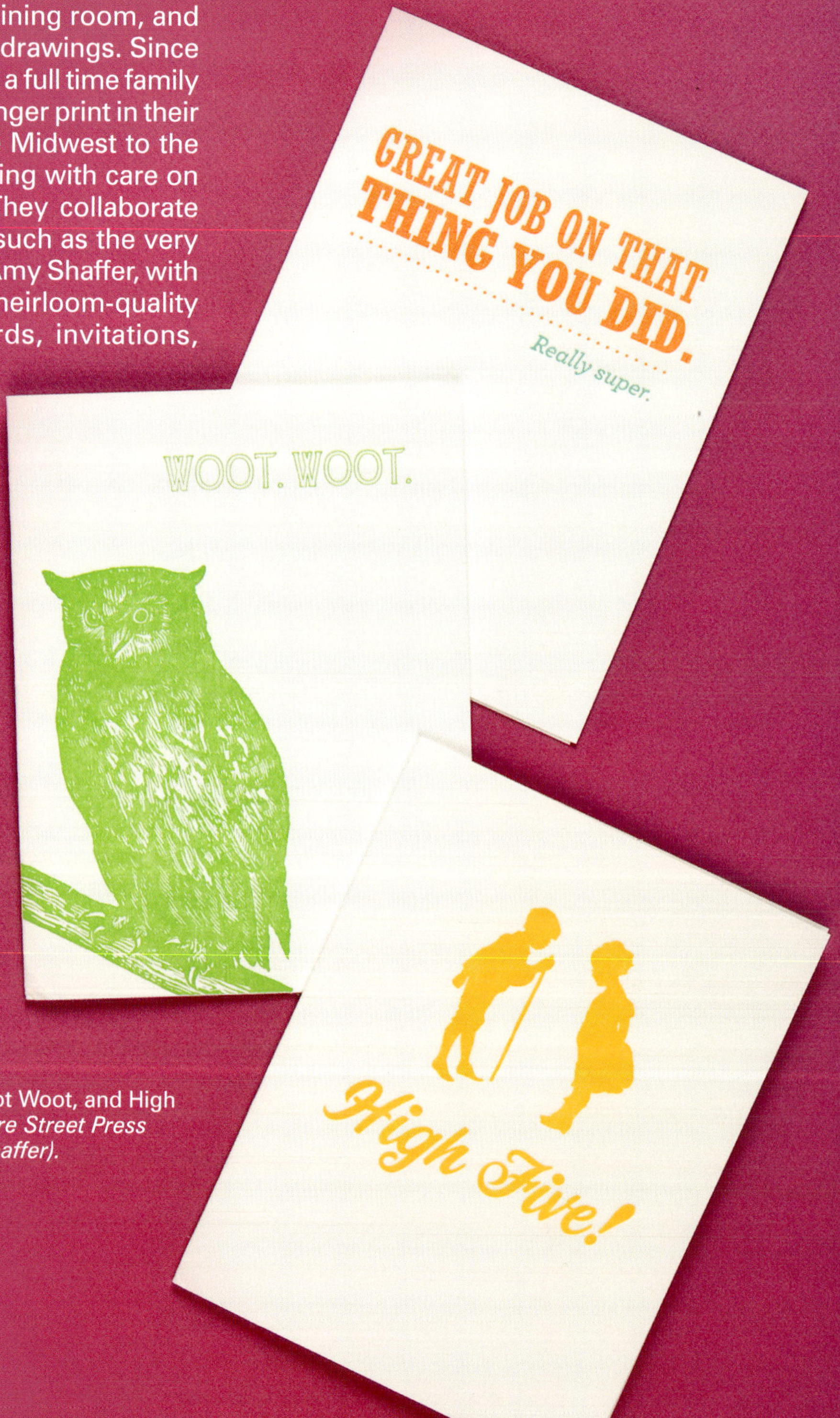

Great Job on That Thing You Did, Woot Woot, and High Five. Letterpress. *Courtesy of Sycamore Street Press (designed by Kristin Mills and Amy Shaffer).*

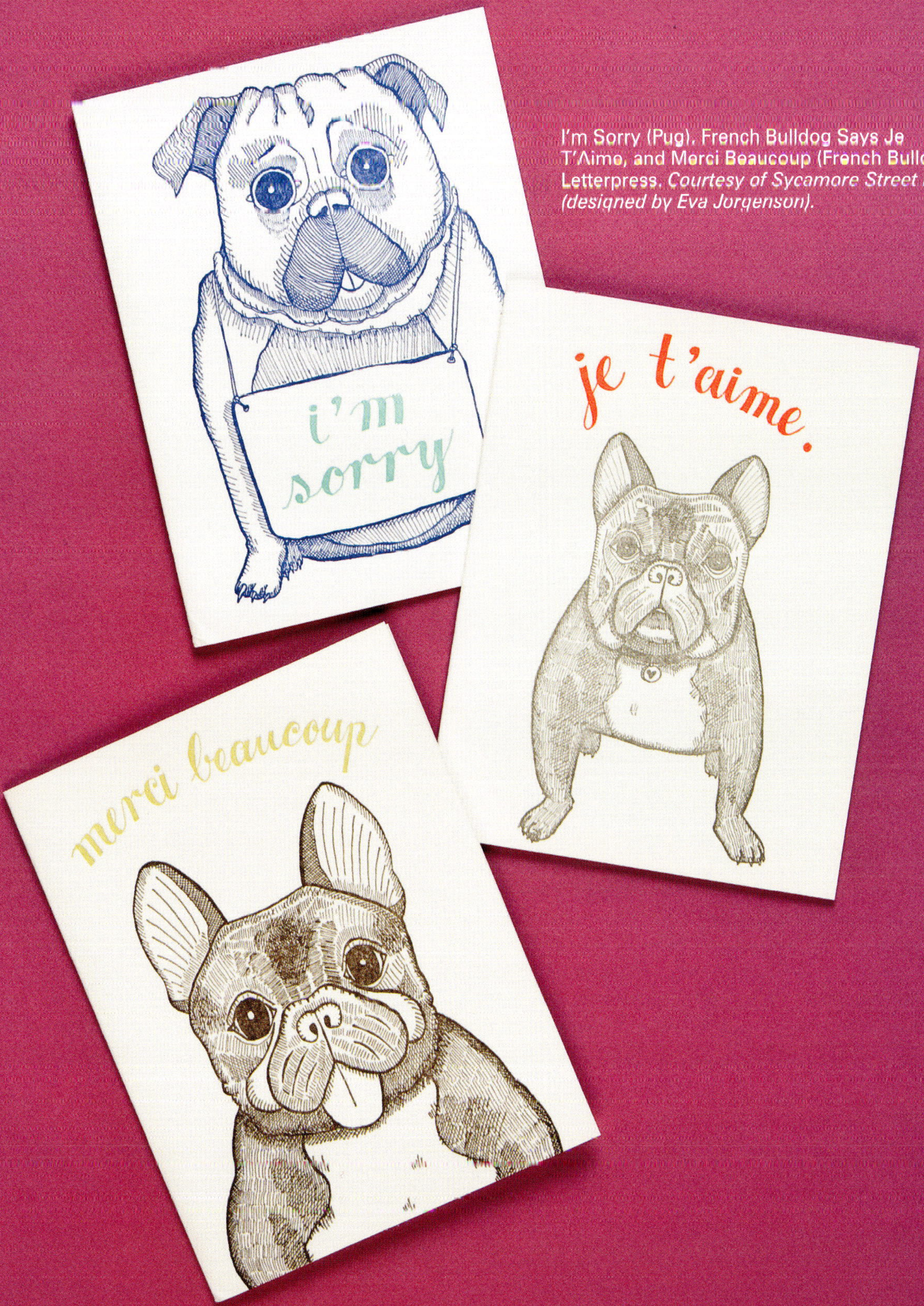

I'm Sorry (Pug), French Bulldog Says Je T'Aime, and Merci Beaucoup (French Bulldog). Letterpress. *Courtesy of Sycamore Street Press (designed by Eva Jorgenson).*

Tallu-lah

www.tallu-lah.com

Before starting Tallu-lah in 2002, Danielle Spinetta refined her keen business sense as manager of both multi-million dollar Gap Inc. stores and store communications for Old Navy. She followed her paper obsession to Union Street Papery in San Francisco as the store's manager, where she polished her retail and wholesale expertise. While she pursues her passion with Tallu-lah, she also works as an event planner in San Francisco, because she found a few extra hours in the day. Danielle also finds time to design for Tinyprints.com and Weddingpaperdivas.com. Her work has been featured in many top magazines and blogs such as *Modern Bride, Wedding Channel, Brides Magazine, Martha Stewart Weddings Blog, Daily Candy, Snipet and Ink, Design*Sponge, Wedding Bee, Classic Bride*, and more.

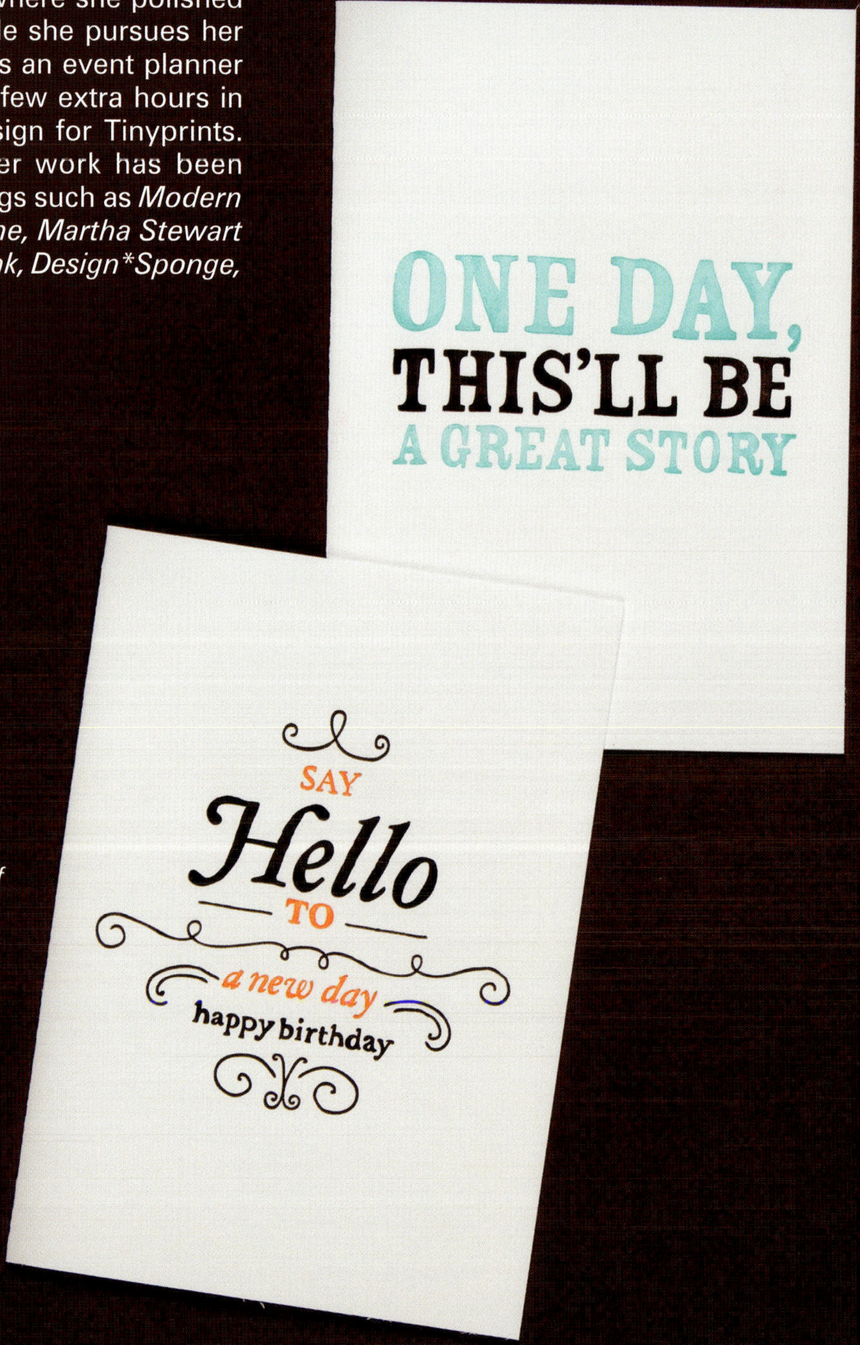

One Day and New Day. Letterpress. *Courtesy of Danielle Spinetta.*

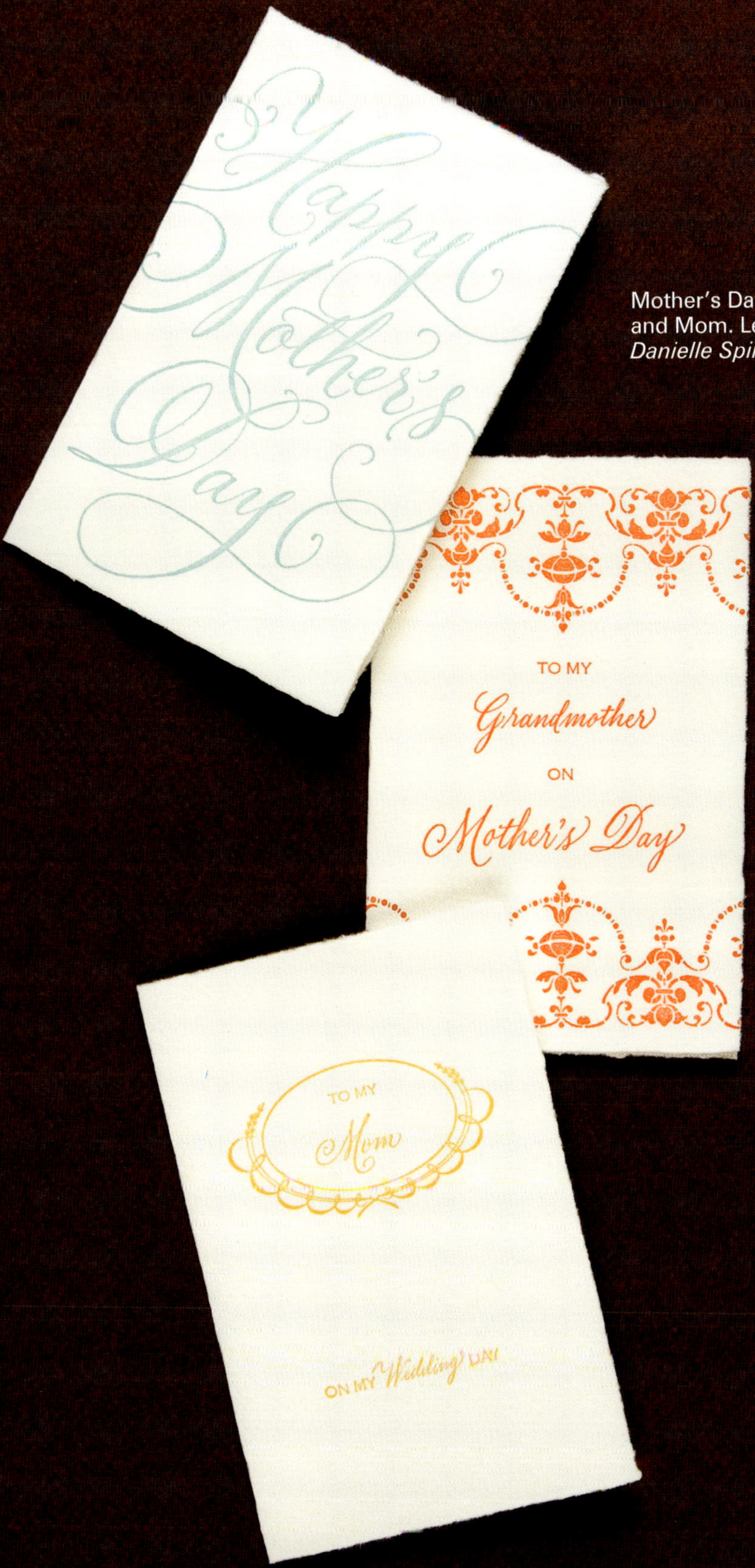

Mother's Day, Mother's Day Grandma, and Mom. Letterpress. *Courtesy of Danielle Spinetta.*

TamTam Design

www.tamtamdesign.com

Tami Rasmussen, the designer behind TamTam Design Studio, opened as a custom design studio in September 2007 and launched their first wholesale lines the following June of 2008. Notably, her very first job after college was designing boxed Christmas cards for Hallmark in Kansas City. Today, Tami resides just outside of Chicago and has recently been named one of the ten designers to watch for in 2010 by *Stationery Trends Magazine*. In addition to her handmade line, she also licenses her illustrations and designs to Cardstore.com for customizable greeting cards and invitations. Tami is inspired by elements of childhood nostalgia mixed together with modern elements. And it's definitely safe to say if she is not at the studio, she is probably at the local thrift store "researching."

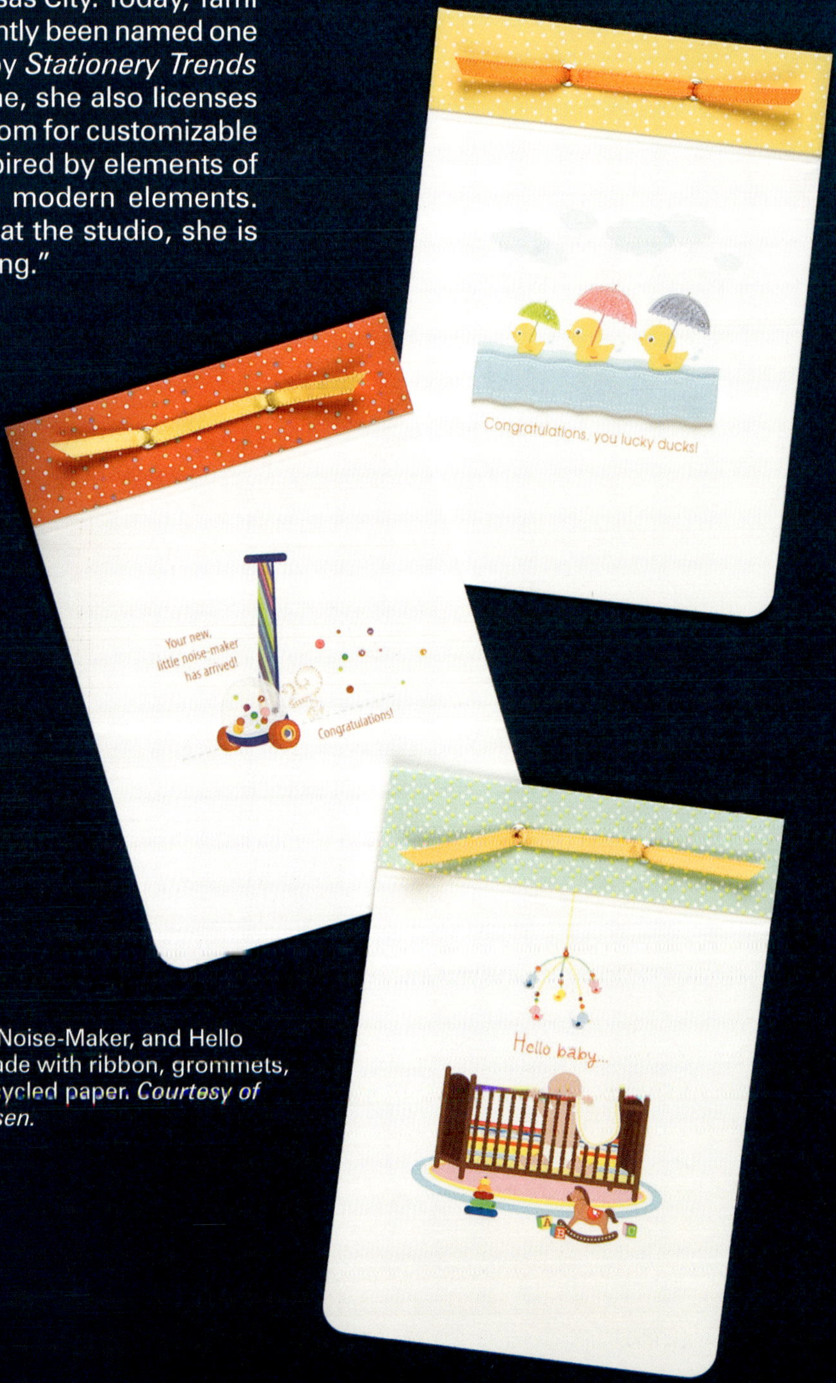

Lucky Ducks, Noise-Maker, and Hello Baby. Handmade with ribbon, grommets, glitter, and recycled paper. *Courtesy of Tami Rasmussen.*

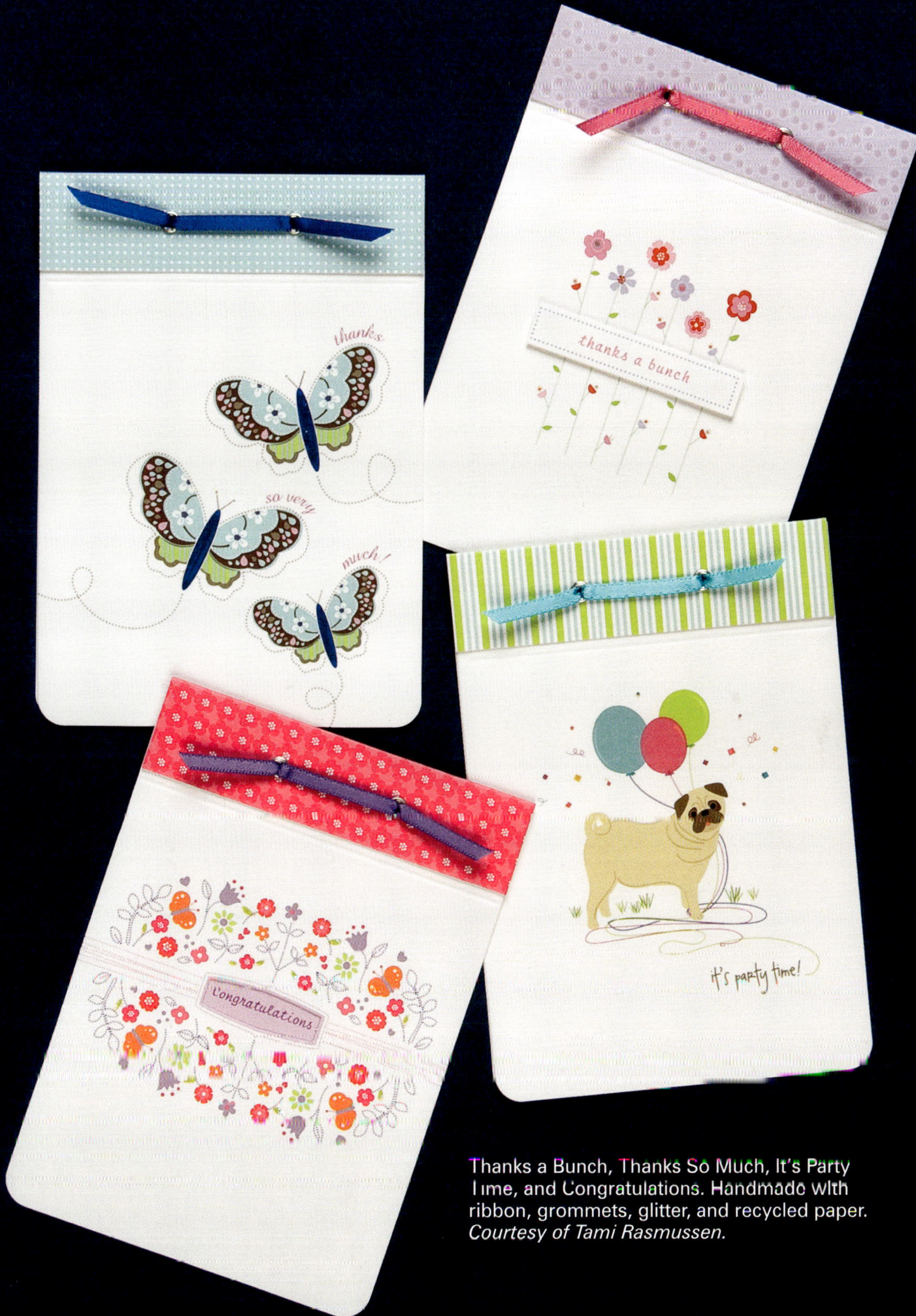

Thanks a Bunch, Thanks So Much, It's Party Time, and Congratulations. Handmade with ribbon, grommets, glitter, and recycled paper. *Courtesy of Tami Rasmussen.*

Two Trick Pony

www.twotrickpony.com

Laurie Mee and Carrie Siegel (aka: "The Ponies") met while working for the same paper retailer in Boston, Massachusetts. They bonded over a shared love of vintage wallpaper and eco-friendly design, and in the summer of 2006 decided the time had come to saddle up and ride towards their paper dreams. Two Trick Pony allows both women to utilize their backgrounds in fine art and graphic design. Screen-printing produces unique results on the page, a rich, vibrant color unmatched by other printing methods. They design in a way that highlights and exploits those characteristics to achieve maximum effect. Their work has been featured in *Country Living, Stationery Trends,* and *Greetings Etc*., and regularly receives coverage on a variety of blogs, including *Design*Sponge, Paper Crave,* and *Oh So Beautiful Paper*. They are also featured in *Handmade Hellos*, a book of paper projects by Chronicle Books, and are currently licensing designs to Cardstore.com.

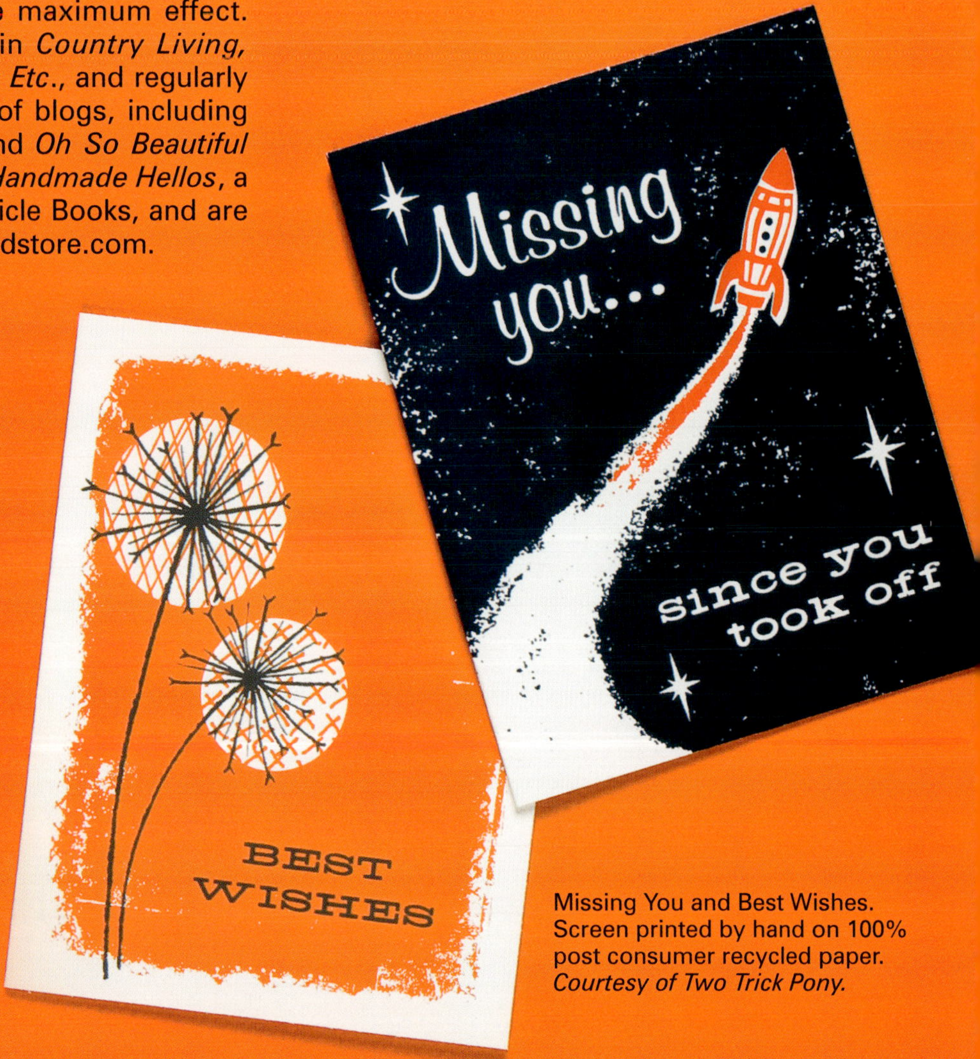

Missing You and Best Wishes. Screen printed by hand on 100% post consumer recycled paper. *Courtesy of Two Trick Pony.*

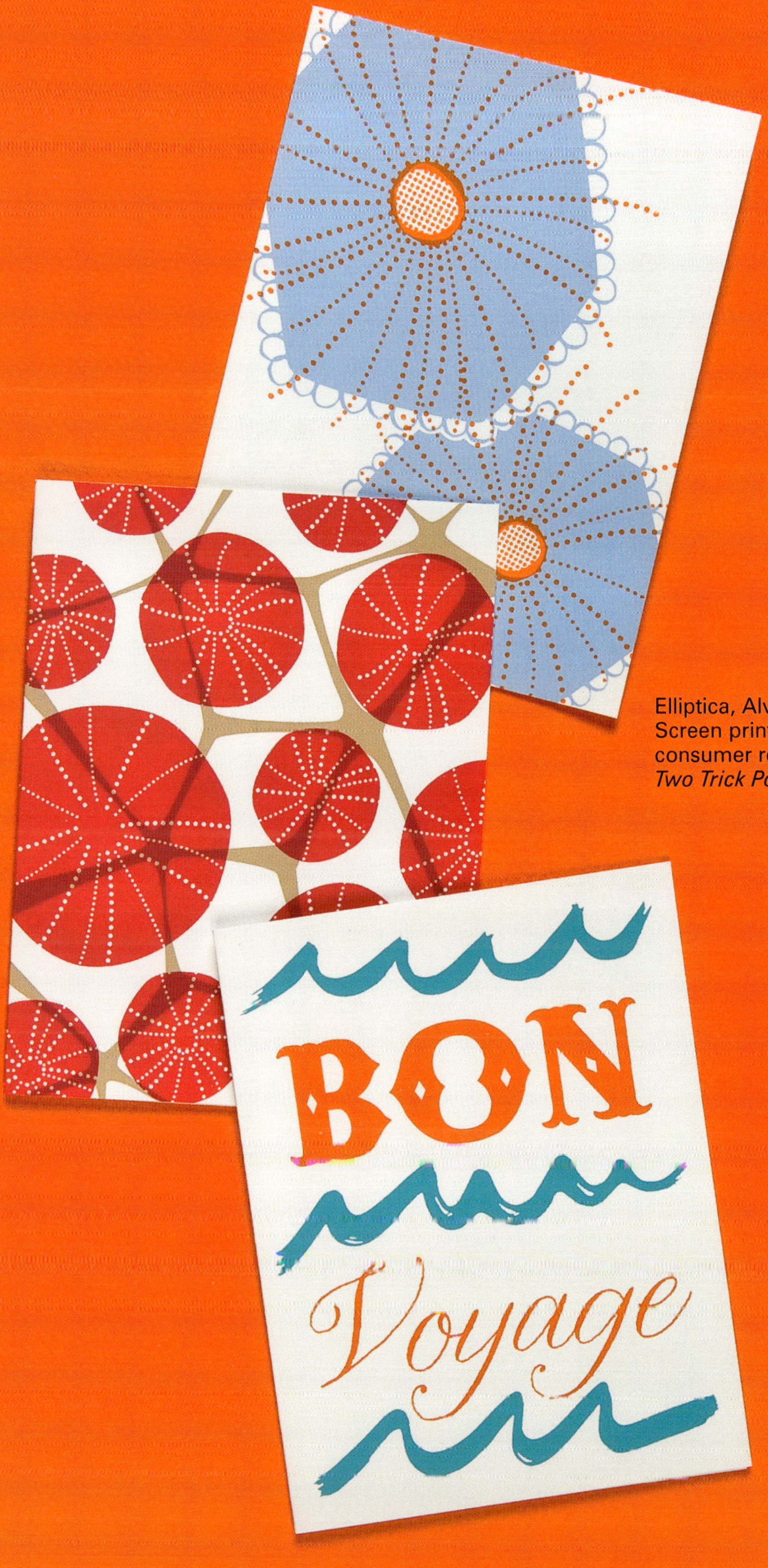

Elliptica, Alveolina. and Bon Voyage. Screen printed by hand on 100% post consumer recycled paper. *Courtesy of Two Trick Pony.*

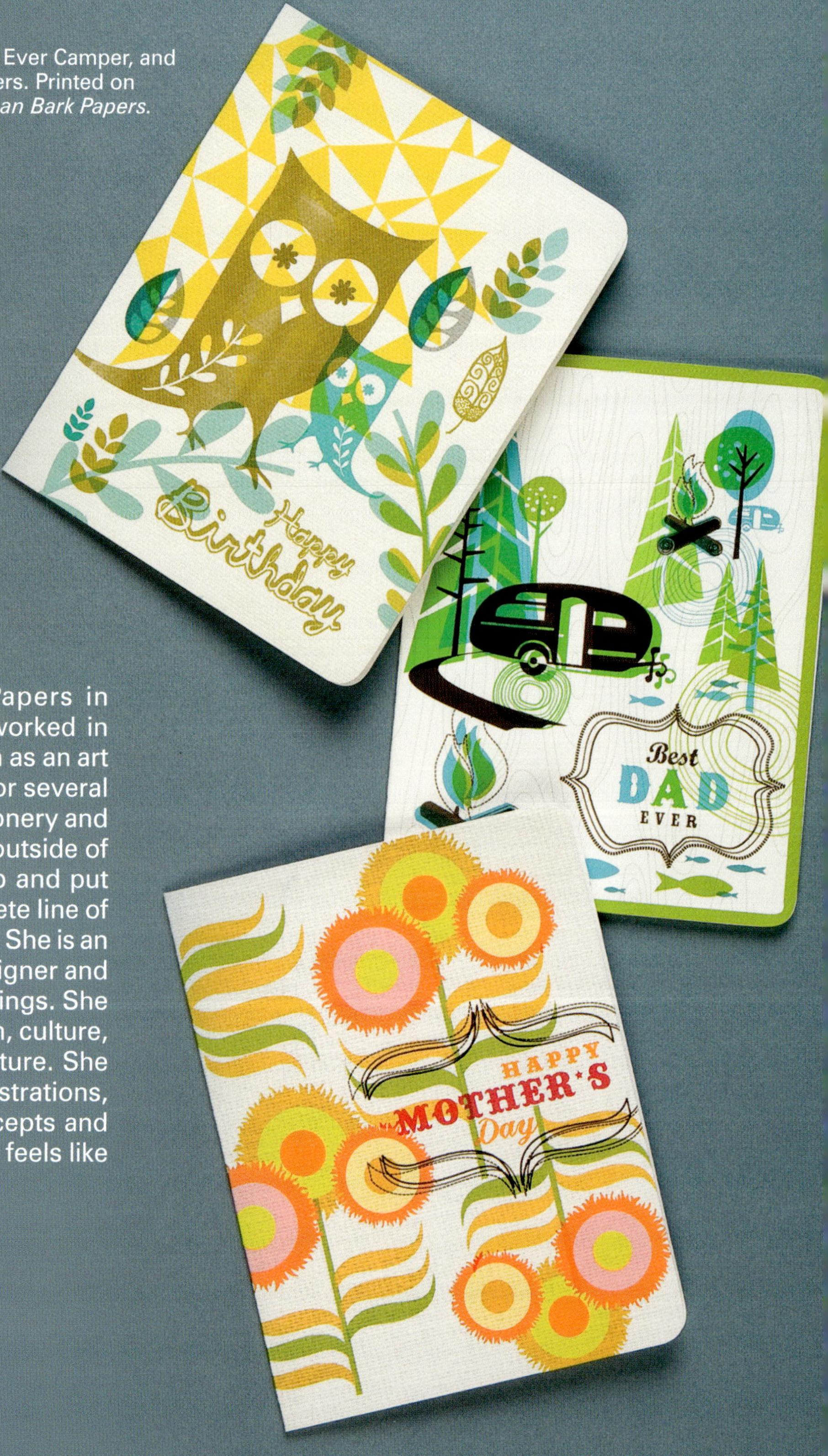

Happy Birthday Owls, Best Dad Ever Camper, and Happy Mother's Day with Flowers. Printed on recycled paper. *Courtesy of Urban Bark Papers.*

Urban Bark Papers

www.urbanbarkpapers.com

Prior to starting Urban Bark Papers in October of 2007, Corrie Lauridsen worked in the corporate world of graphic design as an art director at a boutique design group for several years. She always had a love for stationery and worked to create custom invitations outside of her day job. She finally took the leap and put all of her creative efforts into a complete line of stationery to launch her own business. She is an Orange County, California, based designer and is heavily influenced by her surroundings. She is inspired by modern textiles, fashion, culture, and the organic patterns found in nature. She is passionate about hand-drawn illustrations, vintage fabric, eclectic mixes of concepts and graphics, and creating stationery that feels like custom works of art.

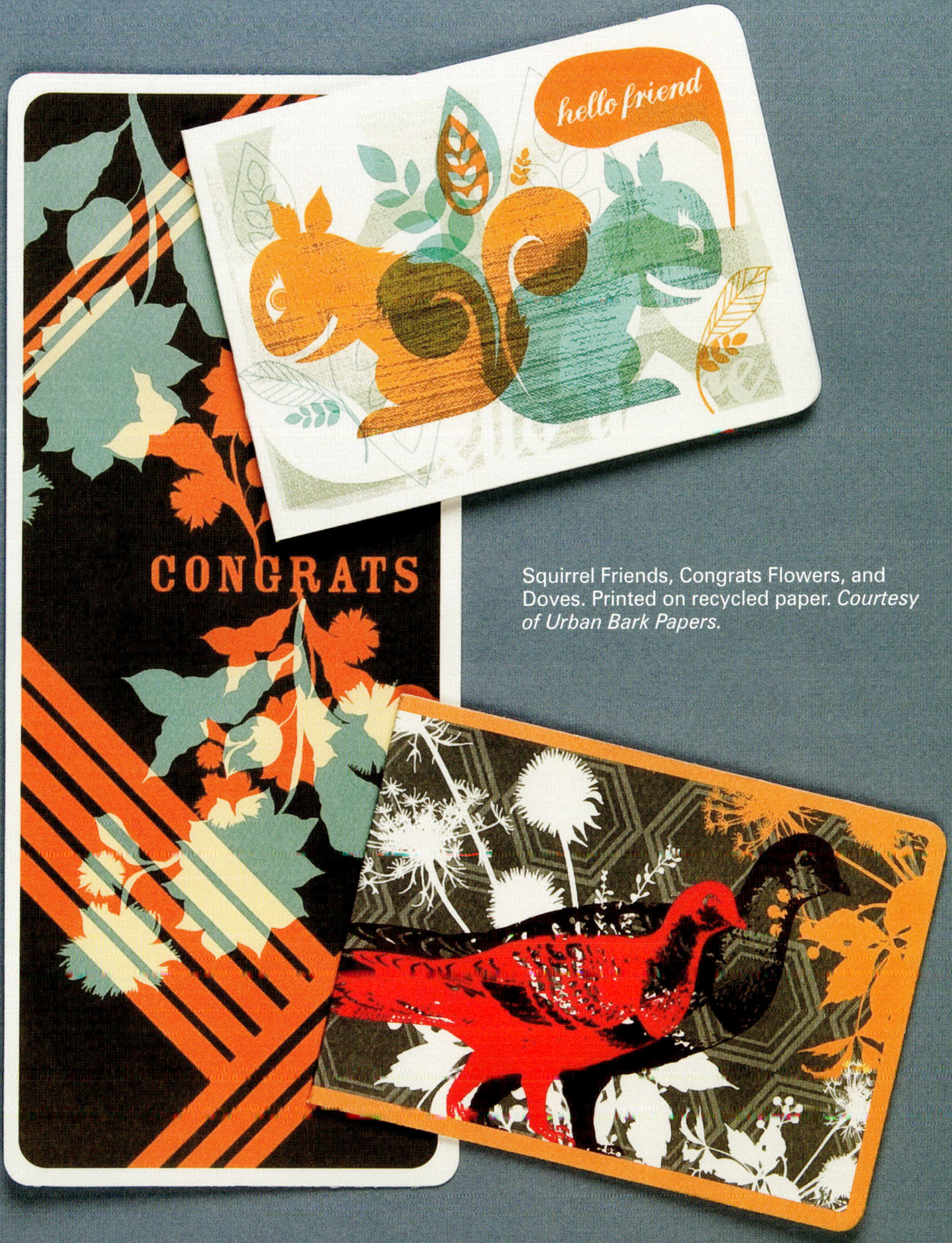

Squirrel Friends, Congrats Flowers, and Doves. Printed on recycled paper. *Courtesy of Urban Bark Papers.*

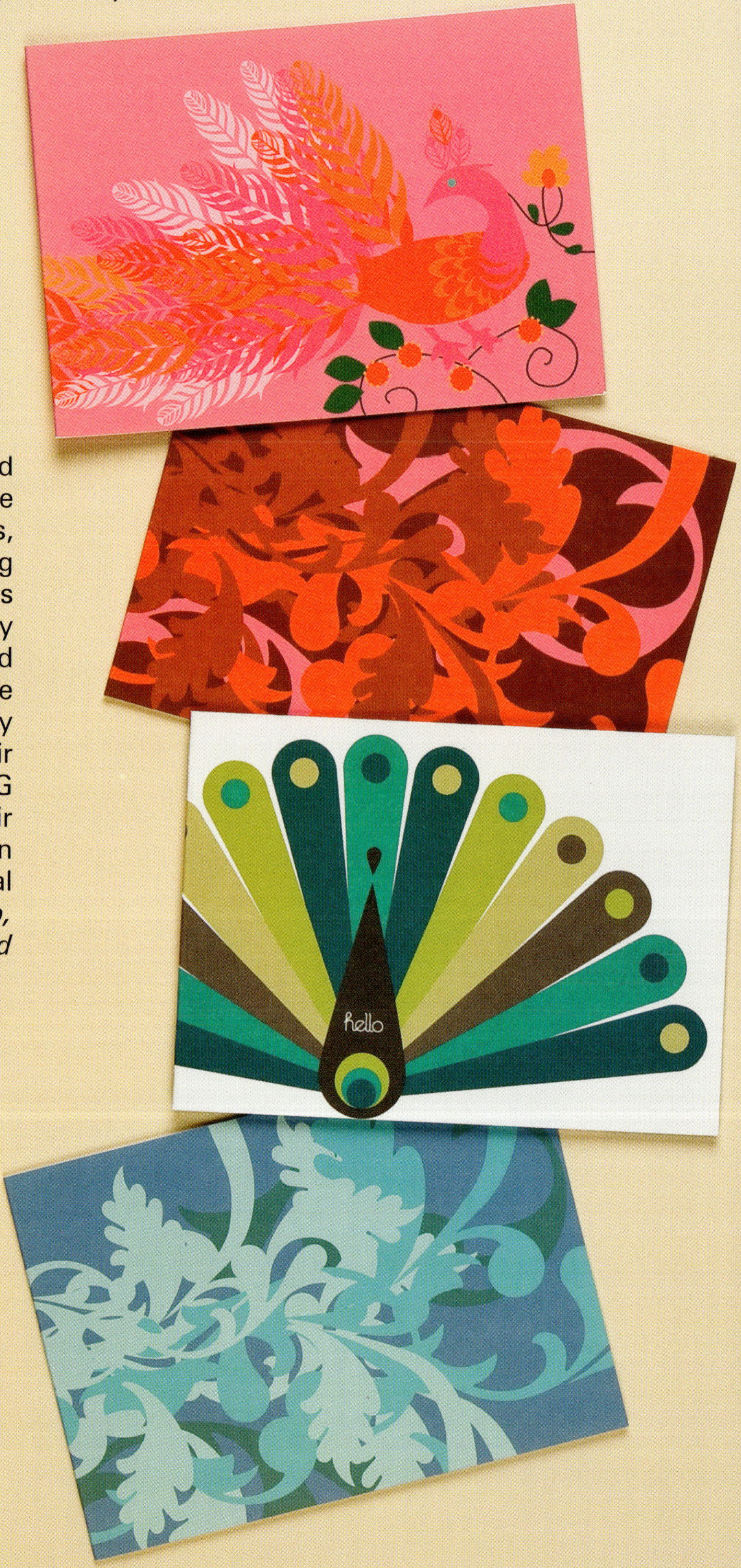

Pink Peacock, Boughs of Whimsy, Hello, and Ivy Envy. Printed on recycled paper. *Courtesy of Whimsy Press.*

Whimsy Press

www.whimsypress.com

In 2006 Whimsy Press sprouted out of an ad agency with strong ties to retail and fashion. While deciding what to give out as client holiday gifts, they agreed on designing their own wrapping paper, which was a huge success with the clients even begging for more. Since then, Whimsy Press has created custom gift-wrap for The Red Cross as well as invitations for the Style Lounge at the Emmy and MTV Movie Awards. They have licensed their designs to Lancôme for their gift with purchase packaging as well as to SIGG for use on their aluminum water bottles. Their cards, gift wrap, and other products have been featured in numerous national and international publications including *InStyle, Lucky, Domino, Southern Accents, Better Homes & Gardens, Good Housekeeping,* and *Everyday with Rachael Ray.*

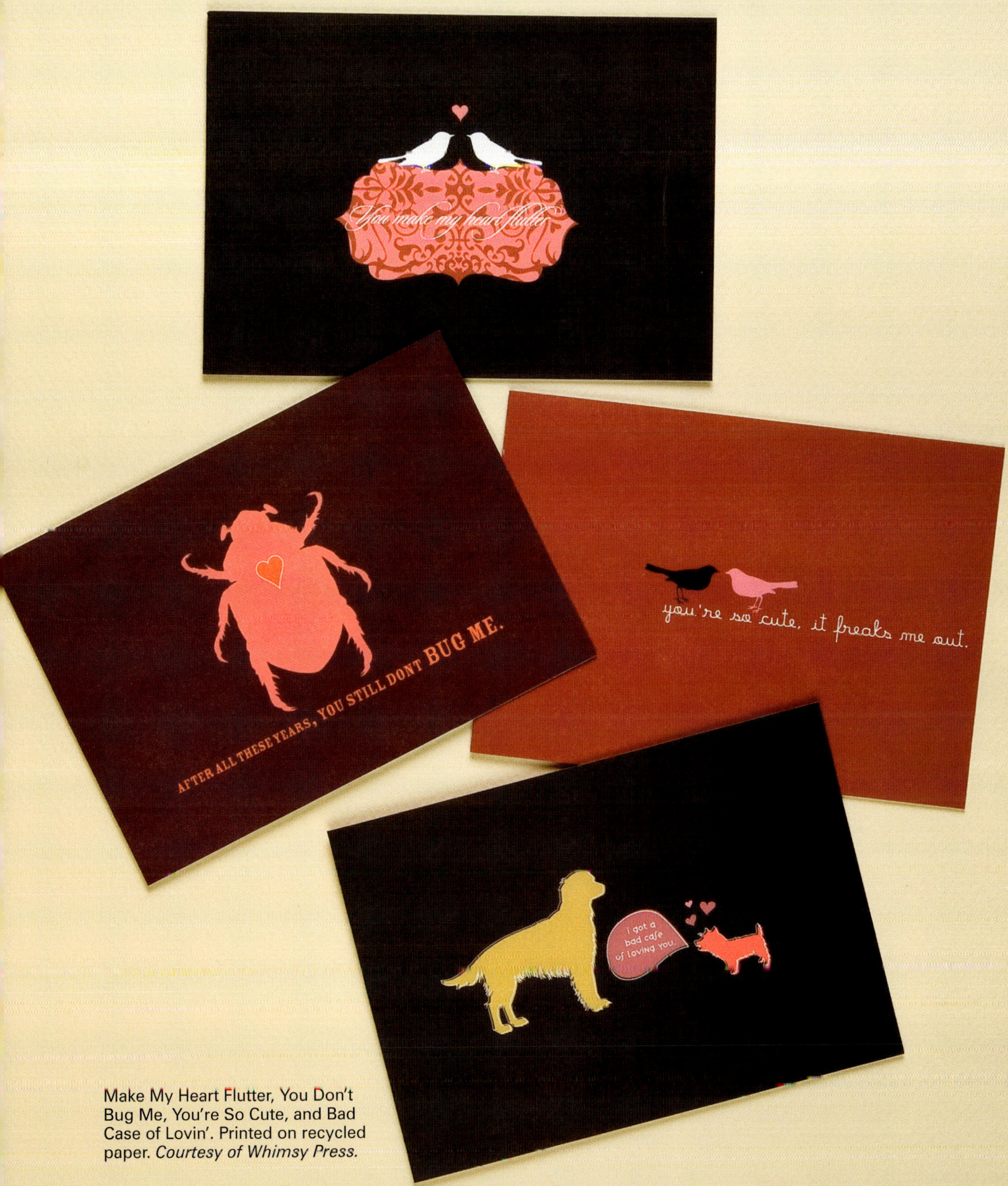

Make My Heart Flutter, You Don't Bug Me, You're So Cute, and Bad Case of Lovin'. Printed on recycled paper. *Courtesy of Whimsy Press.*

Whitney English

www.whitneyenglish.com

Whitney English Kolb officially founded her company in 2002. Since that day, Whitney English, LLC has grown from a back-room business to a warehouse of several thousand square feet chock full of note cards, invitations, enclosure cards, and other paper goods. With more than a dozen employees and close to two thousand accounts later, those humble beginnings are still maintained in the company's reputation for excellent customer service and new classic designs.

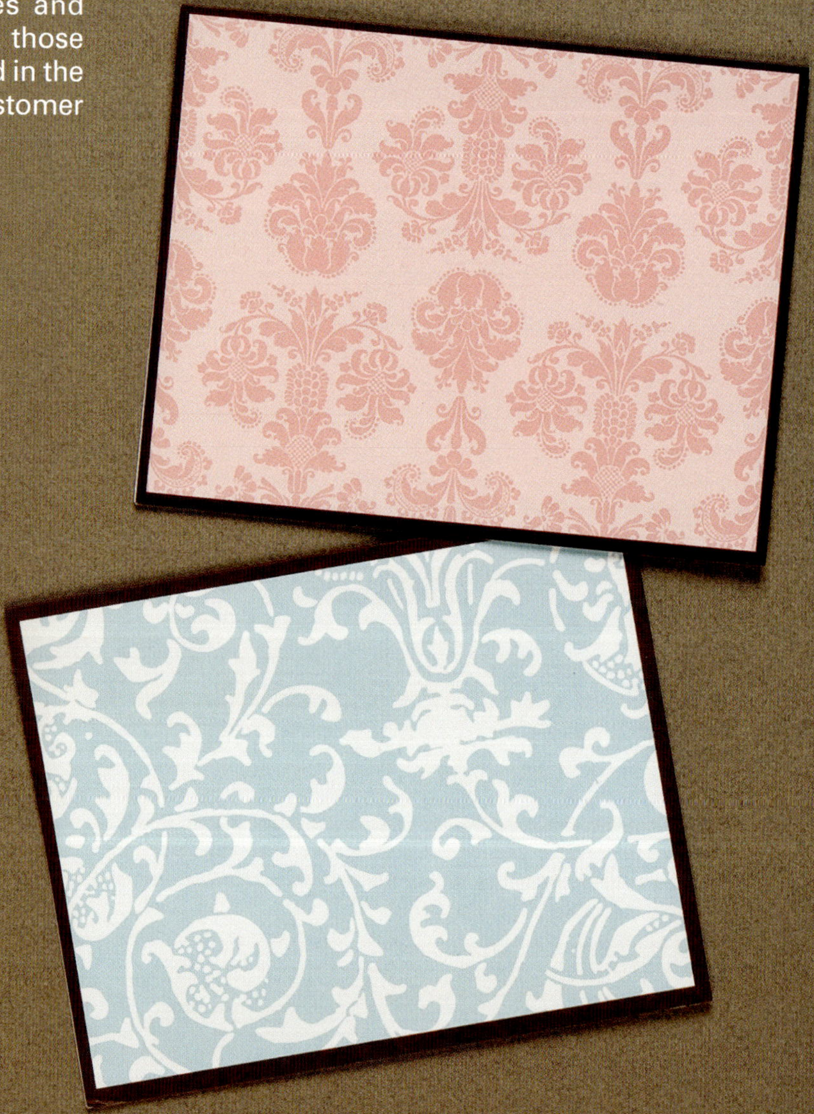

Bella Pink and Emma Aqua. Offset printed. *Courtesy of Whitney English Kolb.*

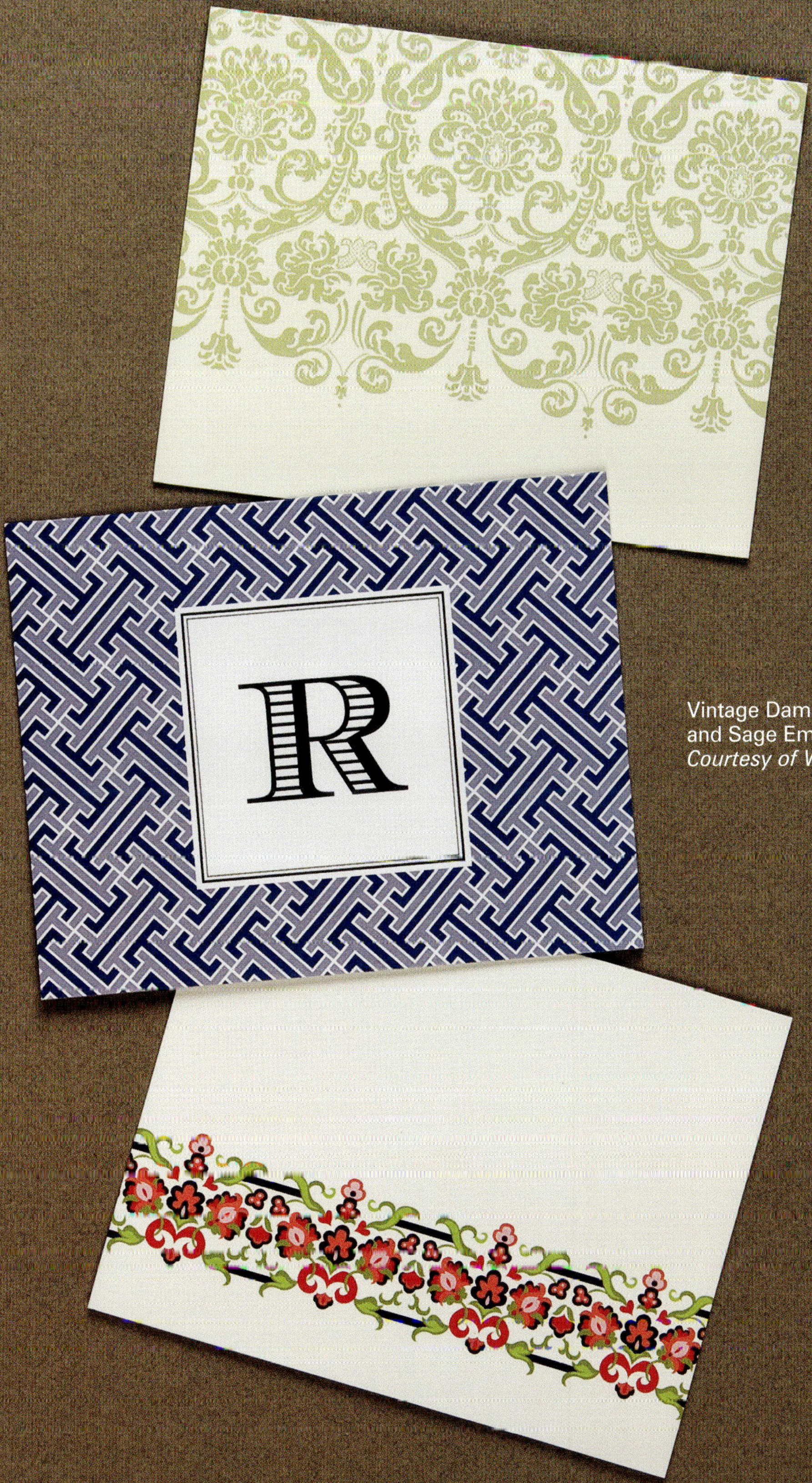

Vintage Damask, Classic Initial R, and Sage Emily. Offset printed. *Courtesy of Whitney English Kolb.*

Wiley Valentine

www.wileyvalentine.com

Emily Owen and Rachelle Schwartz met while working at a small graphic design firm. They quickly found that they shared the same passion for paper delights and invitations and seeing a lack in the market for an eco-conscious line that had their personal aesthetic, they decided to start Wiley Valentine in 2001. Since then, their work has been featured in many publications such as *Lucky, In Style Weddings, Modern Bride, Brides, Victoria, The Knot* as well as high profile blogs such as *Brooklyn Bride, Ritzy Bee, Style Me Pretty, Once Wed, 100 Layer Cake,* and *Amy Atlas*.

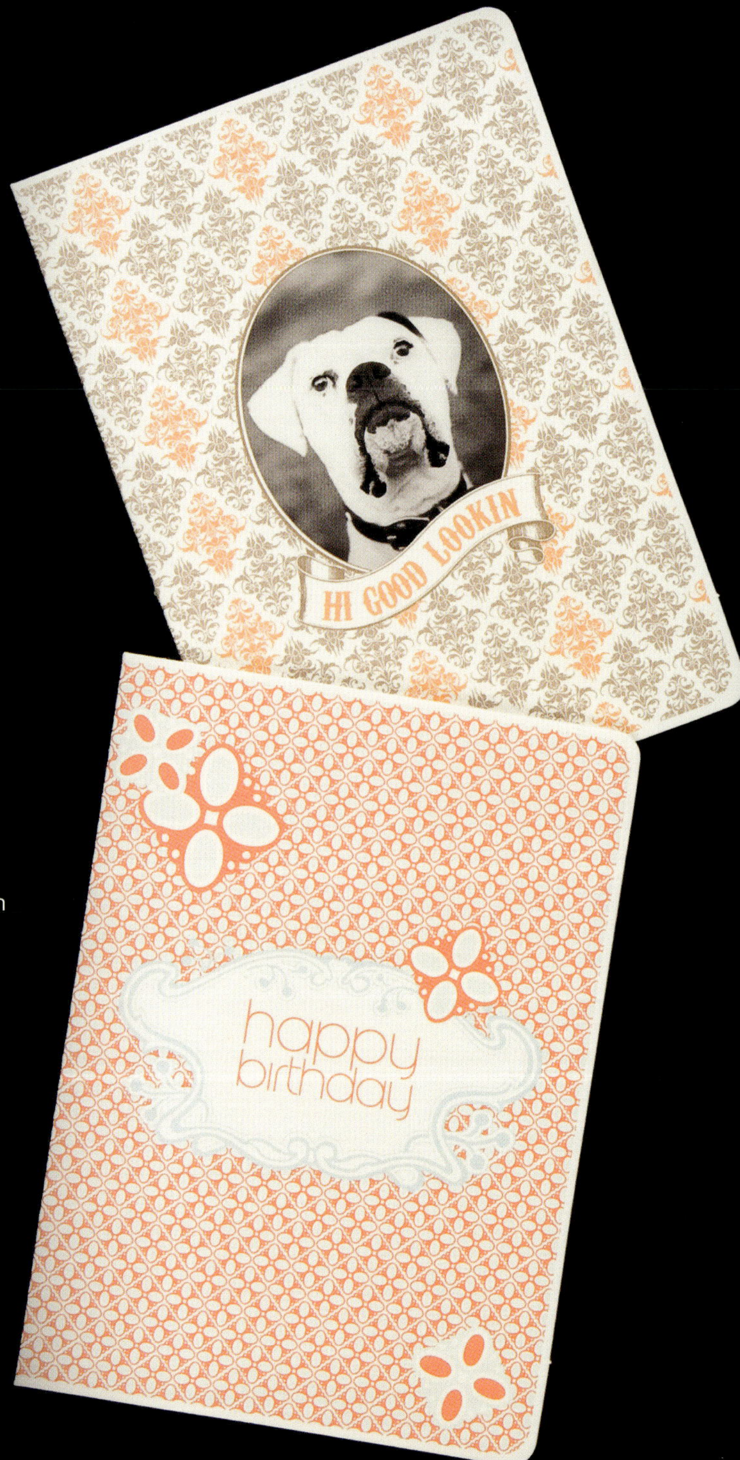

Hi Good Lookin and Happy Birthday. Printed on cotton and recycled paper. *Courtesy of Wiley Valentine.*

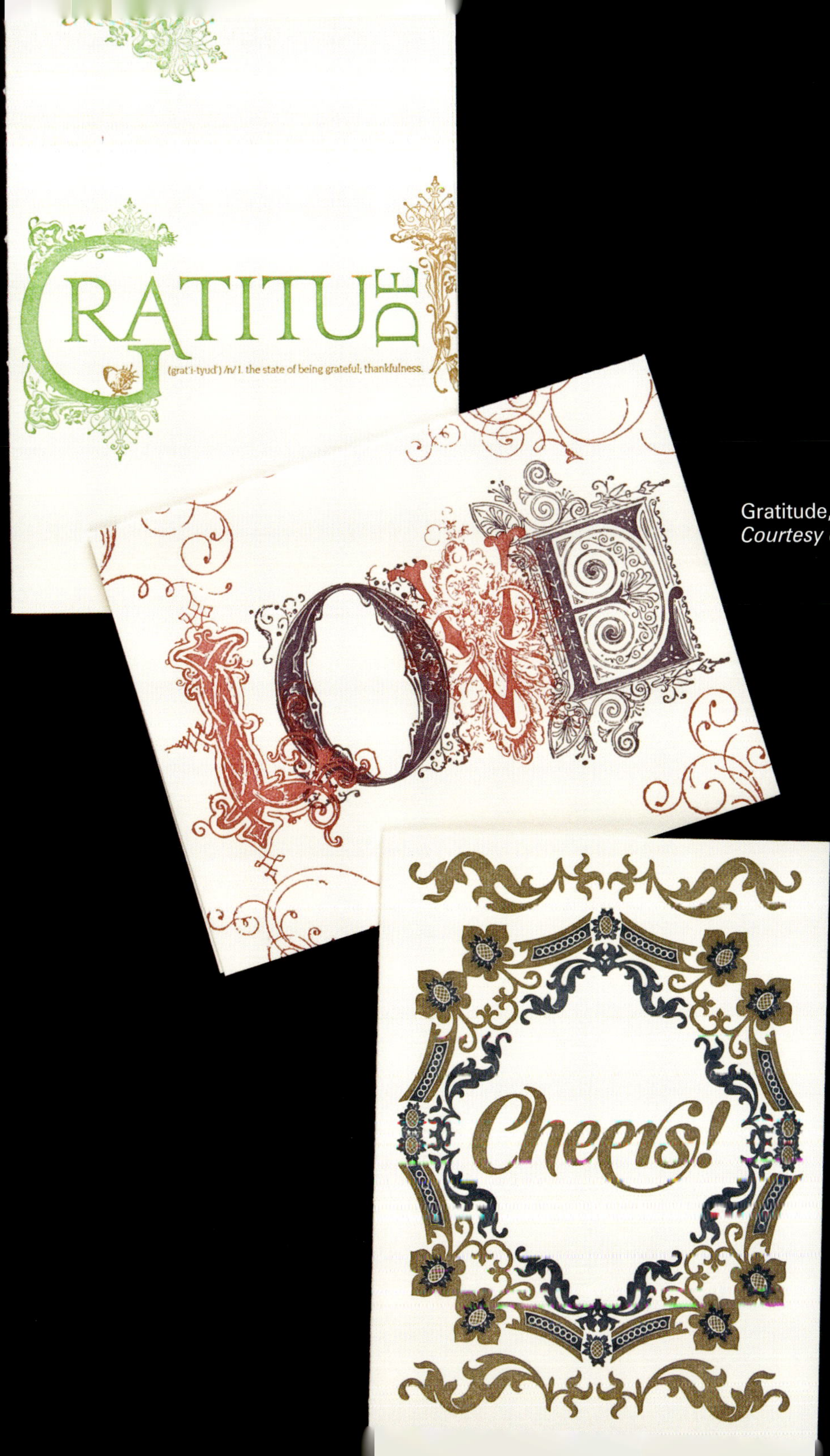

Gratitude, Love, and Cheers. Letterpress.
Courtesy of Wiley Valentine.

Yellow Bird Paper Greetings

www.yellowbirdgreetings.com

Charmaine Carlson earned a degree in fashion design and marketing and spent ten years working in the business as a fashion buyer before the corporate culture began to make her yearn for freer pastures. Her infatuation with paper lead to the creation of Yellow Bird Paper Greetings in 2002. Charmaine finds inspiration everywhere: the colors of the spring flowers, an ad in a magazine for face cream, her beloved yellow Lab's hot-pink jeweled and studded collar, and travel. She has three young boys who inspire her and finds that with living in a male dominated household her designs tend to be very girly-girl. One might notice that pink is a predominant color in her designs. Perhaps "pink and all things girly" are her inspiration ... for this week anyway.

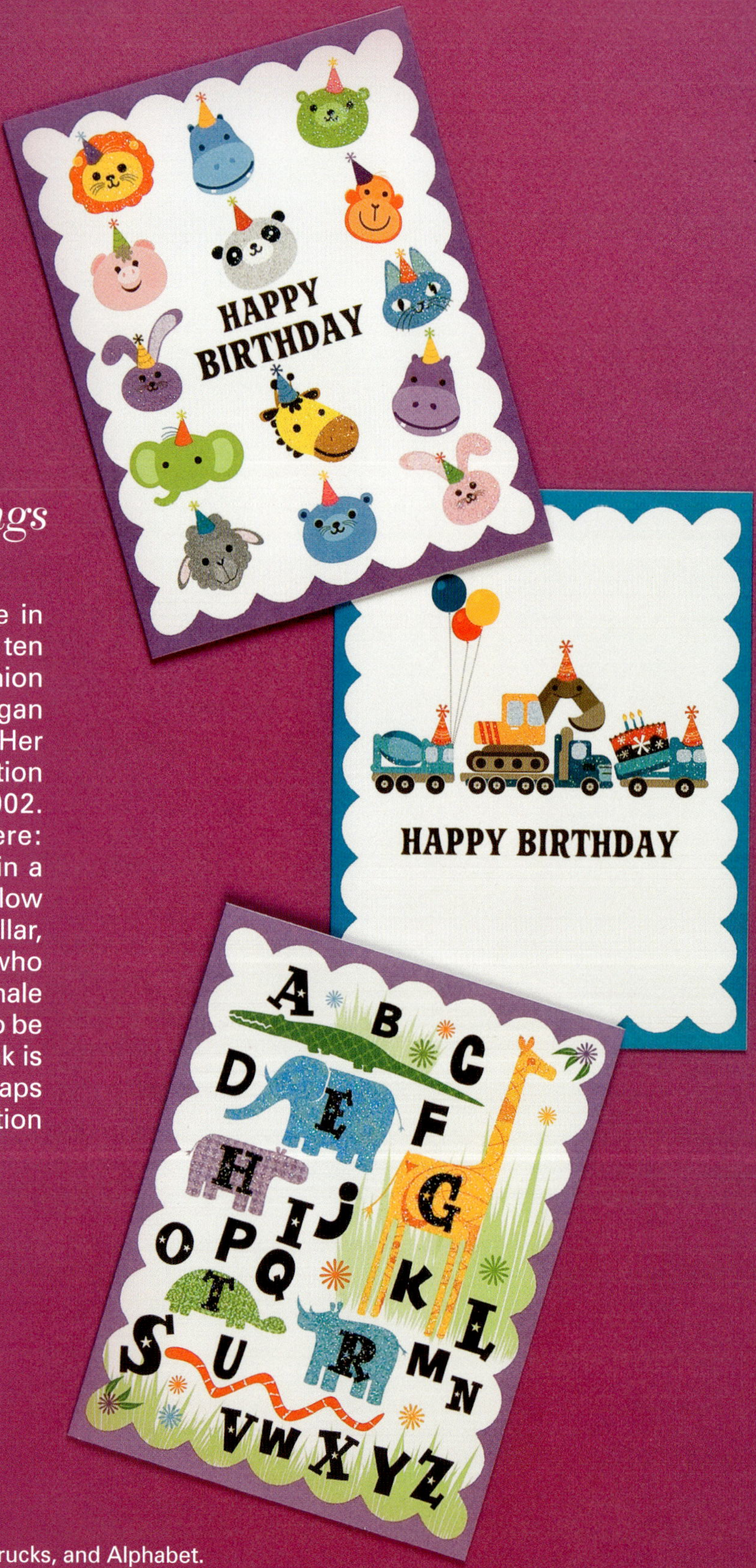

Birthday Animals, Birthday Trucks, and Alphabet. Printed on recycled paper and hand embellished with glitter. *Courtesy of Yellow Bird Paper Greetings.*

Congratulations, Kiss Me, Bridal Shower, and Love Birds. Printed on recycled paper and hand embellished with rhinestones. *Courtesy of Yellow Bird Paper Greetings.*

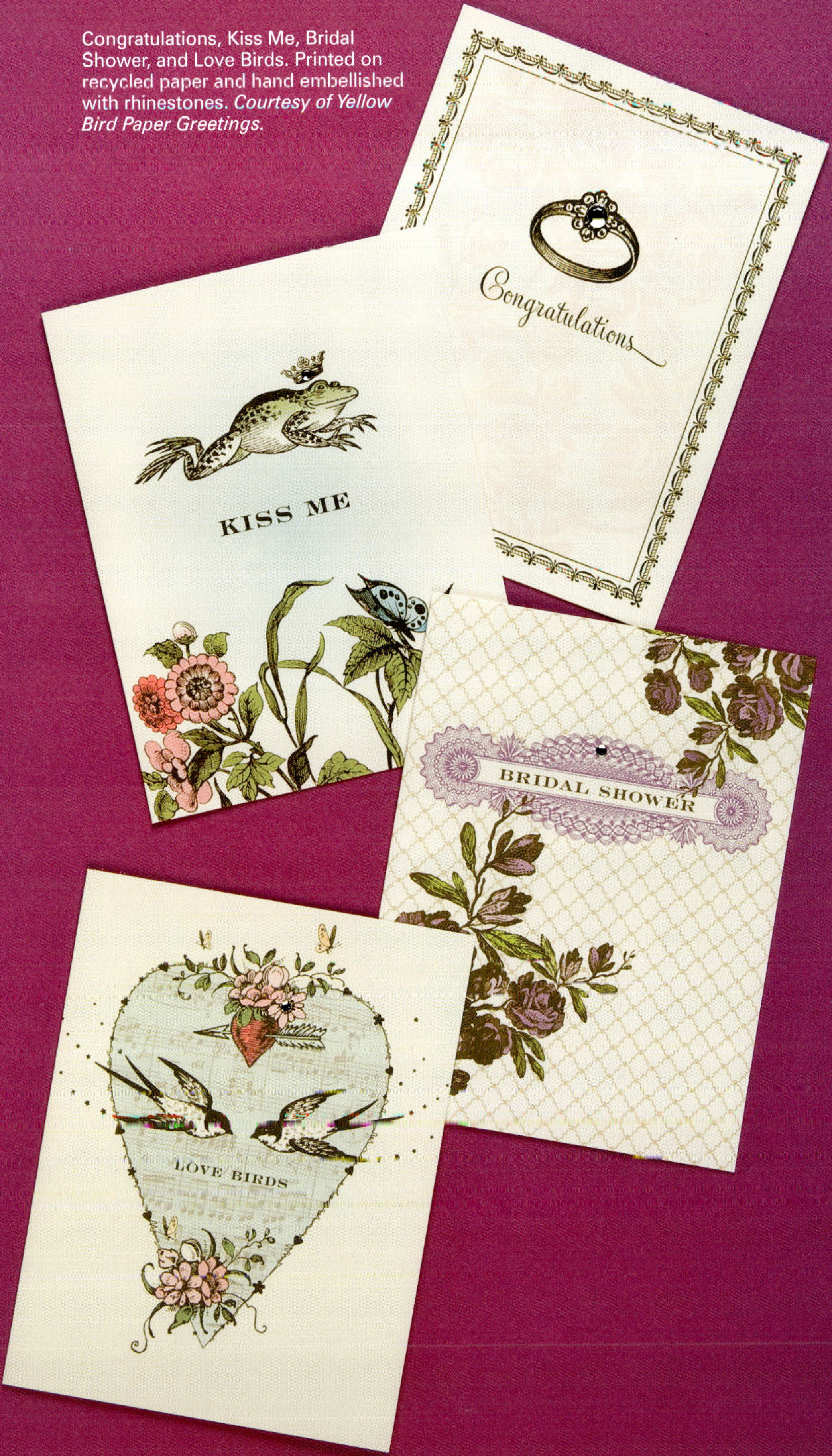

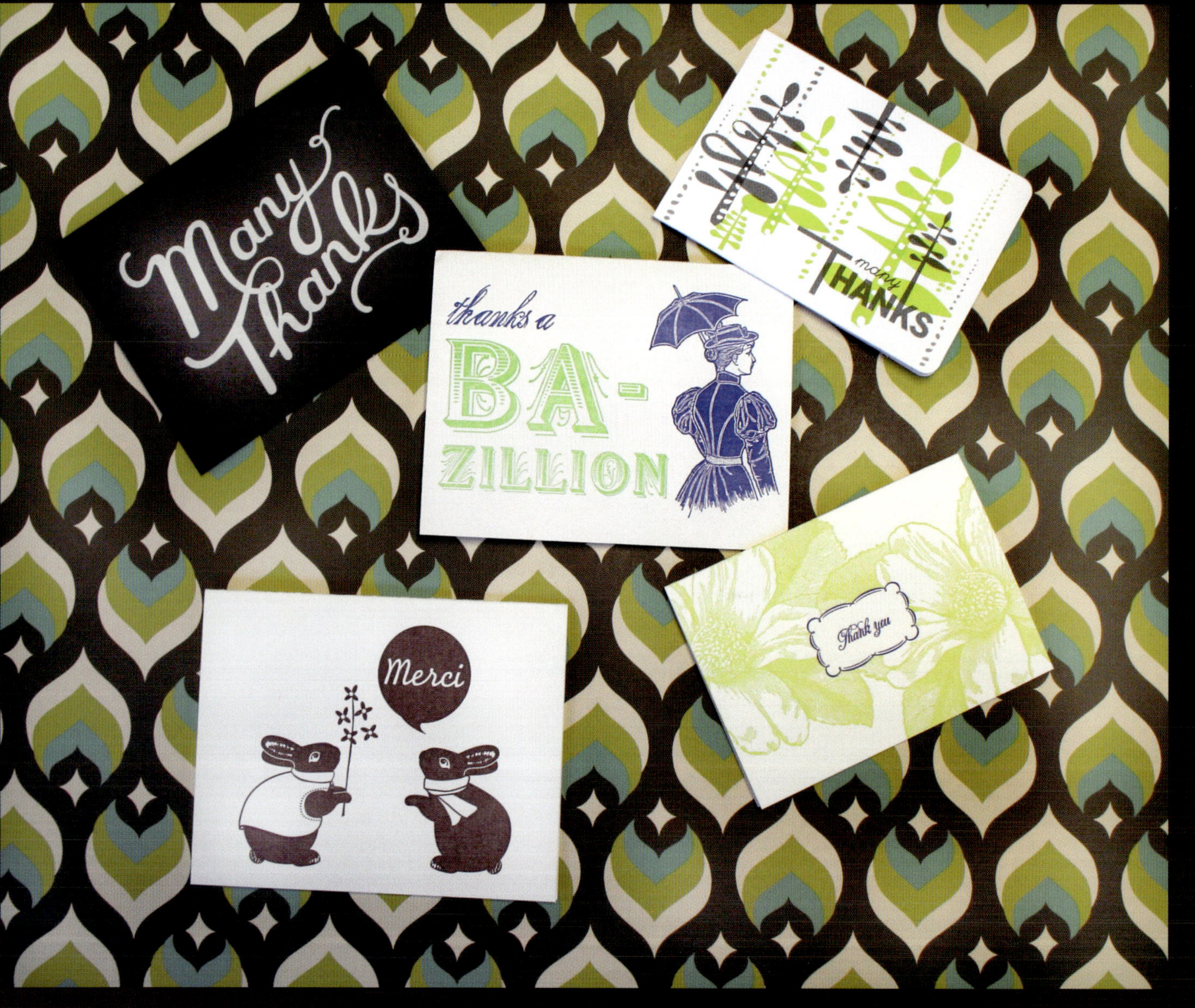

Greeting cards by (clockwise) Rifle Paper Co., Sycamore Street Press, Urban Bark Papers, Blue Ribbon Design, and Motormouthpress, LLC. Wrapping paper by Whimsy Press. *Photograph by Wendy Hicks.*

Acknowledgments

I would like to give a big thanks to all of the talented artists who have contributed to *Today's Top Stationery Artists 2*. It means so much to me to have so many of my personal favorites be a part of this project. Not only are they all great to work with, but they are leaders in the industry and I am truly honored to have them be a part of this book.

I would like to extend another big thanks to Katy Greenspan of Cardstore.com for her insight, input, and encouragement. Her genuine excitement and love for all things stationery truly left me inspired and motivated to take on such a large project.

A very special thank you to my dear friend, Wendy Hicks, for lending her photography skills.

Thank you to all of my close friends for their confidence in me, even when I didn't seem to have it in myself.

A very heartfelt thanks to my family (particularly my parents and in-laws) for being such a support and encouragement in all of my creative endeavors.

Thank you to my editor, Jeff Snyder, for all of his guidance and support.

And lastly, I would like to offer a huge thanks to my husband, Branden, for his unending support, which came in the form of encouraging words, proofreading, listening to my ideas, reviewing cards when I needed a second opinion, and even taking our two year old son out of town on a "guy's weekend" so that I could meet my deadline.

Index